CLAIRE CLAIRMONT
AND THE SHELLEYS
1798–1879

Claire Clairmont and the Shelleys 1798–1879

ROBERT GITTINGS
and
JO MANTON

Oxford New York
OXFORD UNIVERSITY PRESS
1992

Oxford University Press, Walton Street, Oxford OX2 6DP
Oxford New York Toronto
Delhi Bombay Calcutta Madras Karachi
Petaling Jaya Singapore Hong Kong Tokyo
Nairobi Dar es Salaam Cape Town
Melbourne Auckland
and associated companies in
Berlin Ibadan

Oxford is a trade mark of Oxford University Press

Published in the United States
by Oxford University Press, New York

British Library Cataloging in Publication Data
Data available

Library of Congress Cataloging in Publication Data
Gittings, Robert.
Claire Clairmont and the Shelleys 1798–1879/Robert Gittings and Jo Manton.
Includes bibliographical references and index.
1. Shelley, Mary Wollstonecraft, 1797–1851—Biography—Family.
2. Shelley, Percy Bysshe, 1792–1822—Biography—Family.
3. Clairmont, Clara Mary Jane, 1798–1879—Family. 4. Authors, English—19th century—Biography—Family. 5. Adventure and adventurers—Great Britain—Biography 6. Sisters—Great Britain—Biography. 7. Romanticism—Great Britain. I. Manton, Jo, 1919– II. Title.
PR5398.G58 1991 823'.7—dc20 [B] 91–2517
ISBN 0–19–818594–4

Typeset by Latimer Trend
Printed and bound in Great Britain by Biddles Ltd
Guildford and King's Lynn

For

Christina Gee

Curator of Keats House Hampstead

and

Friend of Researchers

Acknowledgements

In old age, Claire Clairmont admitted one regret and one hope. 'I would willingly think that my memory may not be lost in oblivion as my life has been.' To disentangle the threads of her love and anger, high ideals and worldly wisdom, independence and family feeling through the scenes of eighty years demands more than individual skill. We are grateful to all those who have generously helped our attempt to fulfil Claire's last wish.

Our first thanks should go to the pioneer of Clairmont studies, the late R. Glynn Grylls, and to Marion Kingston Stocking, editor, with her late husband, of the *Journals of Claire Clairmont*. Her forthcoming edition of the Clairmont *Letters* should make many manuscript pages now darkened by damp accessible to the reader. Meanwhile, she has answered our continual questions with patience and care. *The Letters of Mary Wollstonecraft Shelley*, edited by Betty T. Bennett, adds to our detailed knowledge of the shared background of the stepsisters and their changing relationship. *The Journals of Mary Shelley, 1814–1844*, edited by Paula Feldman and Diana Scott-Kilvert, record the facts of Claire's earlier life as seen through Mary's eyes. Joan Rees, author of *Shelley's Jane Williams*, lent us her own manuscript notes of Jane's unpublished letters in the Pforzheimer Library. Dr Timothy Webb, Professor of English Literature, University of Bristol and editor of the *Keats–Shelley Review*, kept us informed of current Shelley studies. We also owe personal thanks to Kenneth and Dagmar Prichard Jones, owners of Field Place, for the use of their photograph and for permission to explore their land.

We are indebted to the Bodleian Library for access to letters in the Abinger MSS, and to the sympathetic staff of the West Sussex Reference Library for their help with the microfilm. We also thank the British Library for access both to MSS and printed books, the Public Record Office for providing their copies of dissenting marriages and baptisms, and the Bristol Record Office for making their parochial transcripts available. We are grateful to the New York Public Library Astor, Lenox and Tilden Foundations for permission to reproduce materials from the Carl H. Pforzheimer Shelley and his Circle Collection. Acknowledgement for Claire Clairmont's letter of 31 December 1862 is due to the Harry Ransom Humanities Research

Center, University of Texas at Austin. We thank the Curator, Keats House, Hampstead, for access to rare items in the collection, scholarly advice, and long-valued friendship. We thank Margaret Mullen and Amanda Howard for preparing the manuscript.

Finally, it is a pleasure to thank the Society of Authors for making our work possible by a generous grant from the Author's Foundation.

ROBERT GITTINGS *and*
JO MANTON

Chichester

Contents

List of Plates

We acknowledge permission to reproduce plates as follows: 1: City of Nottingham Museums Newstead Abbey. 2: John Murray, London. 3: Victoria and Albert Museum Library. 4, 5, 6, and 9: British Library. 7: Bodleian Library. 8: K. V. Prichard Jones, Esq.

PART I

Claire and the Shelleys (1798–1822)

1 *Jane among the Godwins (1798–1814)*

Jane Clairmont, known to history as Claire Clairmont, makes her first appearance at the age of 3, apparently from nowhere. She believed that she was born on 27 April 1798. This, at any rate, is the birthday and age she set down several times in her voluminous journals. There is, however, no record of any church or Nonconformist baptism. She was almost certainly illegitimate, and colour is given to this idea by her own championship of illegitimacy. As to her place of birth, there is no evidence.[1] She seems to have thought she had some connection with Switzerland, wrote to Byron of 'Switzerland: the land of my ancestors', though what she meant is not clear; equally vaguely, she thought she might have 'Relations at Geneva'.[2] Her brother Charles's middle name was 'Gaulis', a Swiss family name, but this does not prove she was Swiss, though she used on one occasion the name 'Trefusis', a member of the Gaulis family.

Jane's childhood was, in general, happy. When she was just 3, her mother, who went by the name of Mrs Clairmont, moved with Jane and her brother Charles to the Polygon, Somers Town, a circular set of balconied houses on the edge of open fields stretching to Camden. Mrs Clairmont's next-door neighbour was the well-known political philosopher and novelist William Godwin, famous for his *Political Justice*, published in 1793, exactly at the time of Louis XVI's execution in the French Revolution. Though believing in pure reason rather than political revolution, Godwin became a byword with both political thinkers and the general public. According to a popular story, Mrs Clairmont, seeing him on his Somers Town balcony, exclaimed loudly from her own, 'Is it possible that I behold the immortal Godwin?'[3] In his diary on 5 May 1801, he wrote 'Meet Mrs Clairmont', but made no further comment.

Charles Lamb, a recent friend of Godwin, whom he nicknamed 'The Professor' because of his pedantic manner, soon reported satirically, 'the *Professor* is *Courting*', comparing his behaviour with Shakespeare's Malvolio and adding, 'with more affectation than a canary bird'. On 21 December 1801, the neighbours were married by banns at St Leonard's, Shoreditch, the bride using her assumed name of 'Mary Clairmont, widow'. Apparently worried that the validity of this entry might be questioned, they married again an hour later at St Mary's, Whitechapel, by licence, when the bride gave her name as 'Mary Vial, of the parish of St. Mary le-bone, Middlesex, spinster'. This entry would seem to confirm that Mary's daughter Jane was illegitimate, as her niece later said. Henry Crabbe Robinson also reported a story that the so-called Mrs Clairmont had previously been left destitute by the death of 'her keeper'. It may also explain Lamb's description of the 'widow' as 'a very disgusting woman', which in the language of the day implied moral disapproval.

By her mother's marriage to Godwin, Jane became part of an oddly assorted family. Godwin was a widower. His deceased wife had been Mary Wollstonecraft, author of *A Vindication of the Rights of Woman* and other works. She brought to him her own illegitimate daughter, Fanny Imlay, gave birth to Mary Godwin in 1797, but died when the latter was an infant. The need to provide a mother for his daughter and stepdaughter probably hastened Godwin's precipitate marriage, though by it he added Jane and her elder brother Charles to his family. Since Charles was almost certainly illegitimate himself, though not by the same father as Jane, the Godwin household now contained four children, all by different fathers. It says a great deal for Godwin that he was an impartial father-figure to these children of disparate stock. Jane always stressed that the household had an exceptionally happy and united atmosphere, in spite of personal differences of temperament.

This family soon included a fifth child, Godwin's namesake William, born in 1803. All were taught, at least in part, by Godwin himself, according to his principle that 'the object of education is the future man or woman'. He believed that children should learn at their own pace and according to their natural aptitudes. He taught the girls Roman, Greek, and English history, and they learnt French probably from Mrs Godwin, who was fluent in the language. Mary and Fanny drew well, but as Jane showed talent for singing, she learned music instead. Charles knew Latin, Greek, French, and mathematics, while even small William at quite an early age lectured from a home-made pulpit to his admiring sisters on a theme which Mary had composed.

The serpent in this apparent Eden was lack of money. In only half a dozen years, Godwin had changed from a bachelor author maintaining himself by the sale of his books to a man with a wife and five children to support. He set this out quite clearly in a fragment of autobiography:

As long as I remained alone, I neither asked nor would accept aid from any man—I lived entirely as I listed.

Since I have been a married man, the case has been otherwise. I never repented the connections of that sort I have formed, but the maintenance of a family and an establishment has been a heavy expense, and I have never been able, with all my industry, which has been very persevering, entirely to accomplish this object.[4]

Nevertheless, the world of Jane's childhood, and her recollections of life at the Polygon, contained a number of happy incidents. For example, one evening Coleridge came to read *The Ancient Mariner* to the adults, and the children, hidden behind the sofa, listened to his broad Devonshire speech. A few years later, Jane remembered that homely voice reciting magically:

Beyond the shadow of the ship
I watched the water-snakes.

The children also enjoyed numerous family excursions. Even the smallest of them was included when the Godwins went out to dinner. In 1802 when the temporary peace of Amiens in the war with France was proclaimed, Godwin organized a special family party to see the illuminations. From 1803 onwards, Jane joined in evening parties to the theatre; the English stage at an inspiring peak fired her ambition to be an actress.

Although some of Godwin's friends, notably Charles Lamb, disliked Jane's mother, she showed good sense. She saw that her translations from the French and Godwin's novels would not bring in steady money for the miscellaneous family. She had recently edited for the publisher Tabart a three-volume *Collection of Popular Stories for the Nursery*, and realized that there was a profitable market in books for children. It occurred to her that she and Godwin could set up a children's publishing firm which might bring in a reasonable income. Having borrowed £100 from one of the Wedgwood family who was interested in educational experiments, Godwin rented in summer 1805 a small house in Hanway Street, between Oxford Street and Tottenham Court Road, to serve as a shop for their Juvenile Library venture. It stocked not only school books but all school materials such as copy-books, pens, and pencils.

Godwin put aside his works on political philosophy and his novels to write children's educational books for his own new series. These and other products of this Juvenile Library were first tried out on his family. He was willing to share his reading and even his correspondence with them. Because of his radical reputation, Godwin did not write under his own name. As he told a friend, 'the tabbies who superintend schools either for boys or girls would have been horrified to receive a book under the name of Godwin'.[5] Under the pseudonym of Edward Baldwin, he published on 21 October 1805 *Fables, Ancient and Modern*, based on Aesop, Perrault, and La Fontaine. Exceptionally well received, it went through ten editions in twenty years, and Mrs Godwin made a successful translation into French. Godwin's pseudonym, however, was soon penetrated. When, the next year, he brought out *The Pantheon*, an equally popular account of the gods and goddesses of Greece and Rome, one reviewer said that the author should also have taught young readers the foolishness and absurdity of 'much heathen mythology'.

Godwin's teaching of religion was of course by no means orthodox Christianity. Jane remembered that, about this time, she was 'invited when very young to spend an evening with three very devout old maids'.[6] They had, she thought, suspected she was 'very ignorant' in religious matters, and had attempted to bring this home to her by a display of their own sinfulness. Jane described this with gusto.

> Wo[e]ful days we are fallen upon indeed said one! Worse than those of Sodom and Gomorrah says another!
>
> Sin cries from every corner of the earth said the third, and we may shortly expect that the anger of the Lord will be stirred to destroy us . . . The horrid account these three thin women gave of themselves, of their origin and present life of their future destination . . . plotting mischief every hour of the day and sinning in thought every minute who for heaven's sake can they be . . . but the image of the wierd sisters in Macbeth dancing about the cauldron and reciting their horrid exploits, and with a childish instinctive horror of evil I fled out of the room back to my home.

She adds that when she reached 29 The Polygon she was soon reassured by the calm and rational atmosphere in which she had been brought up. Incidentally, the vivid physical description suggests Jane might have seen the famous performance of Lady Macbeth by Mrs Siddons.

In spite of occasional carping at its lack of religious teaching, the Juvenile Library did so well in its first two years that it proved necessary to extend. In summer 1807, the Godwins gave up the Polygon as a dwelling-place and the Hanway Street premises as a shop and rented a five-storey building to house both. This was 41 Skinner Street, on the corner of Snow Hill, Holborn, where the family lived above the shop. The change after the open fields of Somers Town was a shock. Snow Hill had been for years an area of all trades, from cheesemongers to leather manufacturers. Skinner Street, newly but poorly built, added hosiers, linen-drapers, and a blacking-ball manufacturer; there were also orange and oyster warehouses. The Fleet Prison and the Old Bailey, barely a hundred yards from No. 41, attracted violent and riotous crowds to attend public executions, though the New Drop was probably just out of sight of Godwin's windows. Nearby, Smithfield Market contributed the noise and dung of cattle, and the Fleet Ditch sewer, though covered up, made the air noisome.[7]

On the other hand, the rounded front of Godwin's premises was perfect for the display of books, with windows low enough for children to look in. A stone carving, probably put up by Godwin, showed Aesop reading his fables to an audience of children. The business, managed solely by Mrs Godwin, certainly flowered there, and Charles Lamb, in spite of his dislike of her, had already produced one undoubted best-selling classic for the Juvenile Library, *Tales from Shakespeare*, by Charles and Mary Lamb with illustrations by Mulready, published in 1807.

Though the children were happy enough to be living above the shop, its surroundings were a distinct threat to their health. Jane's mother commented on her daughter's unhealthy looks, and in 1808 the 10-year-old girl spent three months, 3 August to 13 November, at Margate.[8] This, too short a stay for schooling, was almost certainly for health. In 1792 the Royal Sea Bathing Hospital had established Margate as the ordinary Londoners' health resort. Such was the success of Margate as a resort that there were 'passage boats . . . every day to and from London'; and such was 'the rage of *the Londoners* of spending their summer months at these watering places situated upon the coast' that speculative builders ran up a veritable new town of lodging houses at Margate. The 'bathing machine' was a Margate invention: horses dragged carts into the sea, from the back of which there was 'a door through which the bathers descend[ed] into the water, and an umbrella of canvas dropping over concealed them from the public view'. The north wind could be sharp, and the children, who all visited milder Ramsgate, not far away, preferred it to Margate. Yet both were undoubtedly healthy. Not only all the young people but Mrs Godwin too visited Ramsgate, 'a place where you are in search of repose', her husband wrote in 1811.[9] In spring 1811 Mary was sent there under doctor's orders. (Just over five years later, in 1816, John Keats, then a medical student, also spent time at Margate, after an unhealthy and hard-working year in London.)

The family atmosphere at Skinner Street was happy, as it had been at the Polygon. Jane summed it up when in her 70s; though affectionate memory may have coloured the picture, for her description is idyllic.

> All the family worked hard, learning and studying: we all took the liveliest interest in the great questions of the day—common topics, gossiping, scandal, found no entrance in our circle, for we had been brought up by Mr. Godwin to think it was the greatest misfortune to be fond of the world, or worldly pleasures or of luxury or money; and that there was no greater happiness than to think well of those around us, and to delight in being useful or pleasing to them.[10]

This may sound over-solemn for Jane, well known in the family for jokes and fun. When her mother went to Ramsgate with Mary, Jane sent a message via Godwin punning on the family name: 'Jane says she hopes you stuck on the Goodwin Sands.'[11] When Jane herself received a joking message from Godwin, her mother's description of her reaction was 'Jane capered.'[12] She also described Jane as looking unwell but added, 'her spirits are good'. Her lively nature was a contrast with that of Fanny, who was said by Godwin to be 'of a quiet modest unshowy disposition'. Poor Fanny, in fact, had inherited from her mother, Mary Wollstonecraft, the depressive temperament which also burdened her half-sister, Mary Godwin. Jane, outwardly at least, was notably cheerful.

The chief witness to the cheerfulness of the Skinner Street family, and especially the girls, was Aaron Burr, former vice-president of the United States. He became friendly with Godwin, whose radical views he admired, and, unlike some people, was also an admirer of Mrs Godwin, describing her as 'a sensible, amiable woman', and 'a charming lady'.[13] He did not differentiate between the three girls, took tea with all three at their usual time of nine o'clock in the evening, and presented them equally with presents of silk stockings, which he was at first too shy to offer.[14] He called them generally and flatteringly '*les* goddesses'.

Mary Godwin felt it was 'Clairmont style' to be, as she described it, rather wild. Yet both Jane and Charles had a capacity for clear thinking, probably inherited from their mother. Charles showed his ability by six years of hard study as a day boy at severely classical Charterhouse. He then spent a few months with a mathematics tutor and was finally accepted as a bookseller's apprentice by Archibald Constable[15] in Edinburgh, having been recommended by Godwin for his ability and his 'diligent and accommodating temper'. For all her vagaries, this description could also be applied to Jane. Mary's friend, Christie Baxter, remembered Jane as 'lively and quick-witted', although she added, 'and probably rather unmanageable'.[16]

April 1812 saw Jane's fourteenth birthday; by this time, she was considered old enough in looks and manners to join her parents at evening parties. In September of the same year she left home for boarding school in Walham Green,[17] not a serious separation since coaches left every half hour from eight in the morning until nine at night. The village of Walham Green lay around the triangular common at a bend in the road from Hyde Park Corner to Fulham. The greensward was fenced and surrounded by elm trees; the large houses and gardens of the village were famous for exotic trees and for the first moss roses grown in Britain. By Jane's schooldays, the gardens had been converted to smallholdings, from which in summer women carried forty-pound baskets of strawberries on their heads to Covent Garden. Coaching inns such as the Red Lion, the White Hart, and the White Swan offered shelter for mail and passengers and stabling for horses.

The dignified old houses became the 'several excellent boarding academies for ladies and gentlemen', recommended in Daniel Lysons's *Environs of London* for 1811. One of these, overlooking the common, was 'the ladies boarding academy, proprietor Miss Cunliffe of Walham Green', where Jane followed the usual finishing-school course of music and French. Jane's French teacher may have been a French refugee, of whom there were many in Britain at this time. Mme Geneviève du Parc, widow of a French surgeon, was certainly recorded as being at Walham Green during 1811. In any case, Jane showed a real gift for the language, and her fluent and accurate French would decide the future course of her life.

Jane attended this school as a boarder for about fifteen months altogether, leaving it at Christmas 1813. However, since the school was only a few miles away she came home for frequent weekends. With the long summer holiday of two months in 1813, it can hardly have broken her home life. She was an attractive girl, with dark hair and eyes, bright complexion, and lively, impulsive nature, though she could explode into sudden and sometimes wilful rages, and she continued to keep the numerous social engagements which she enjoyed so much. One of these would have a decisive effect on her future, though she did not realize this at the time: one weekend in October 1812, she was home from school when Godwin received a visit from an admiring young disciple, Percy Bysshe Shelley.

Godwin had first heard of Shelley from a letter he received from him on 6 January 1812. Shelley was at that time less than 20 years old, but his life had already run through several personal dramas. He also had the gift of transfusing excitement into the lives of all around him. When people met Shelley, strange events followed. Not many years later, John Keats, realizing this, refused to stay with Shelley, 'that I might have my own unfettered scope'. Without any such prescience, Godwin began a long and warm correspondence with the young man who had read and precociously delighted in his *Political Justice* while still at Eton. Shelley had accepted Godwin's principles, and even attempted to live by them in his own life. At Oxford in 1811, he had been sent down for his pamphlet *The Necessity of Atheism*; the son of a wealthy Sussex baronet, he combined aristocratic and careless charm with a flair for finding ideas to revolutionize the private lives of his circle. Although theoretically opposed to marriage, he soon eloped with and married a very pretty schoolgirl, Harriet Westbrook. He was always specially fascinating to women. As to his looks, Jane later wrote: 'The beholder saw he was beautiful, but could not discover in what it consisted.' Godwin resented the aristocratic style, yet agreed, 'Shelley was so beautiful'. This good-looking young man was to revolutionize the lives of every member of the family at Skinner Street.

By the time Shelley met Godwin and his family for the first time in October 1812, Jane and Mary already knew of the unusual and daring ideas in his letters and keenly awaited more: directly his 'well-known hand was seen, all the females were on tip-toe to know'.[18]

Shelley and his wife were in London at this time for only about a month. They met the 14-year-old Jane on two separate weekends when she was home from school.[19] According to her mother, Jane and Shelley had a 'brother and sister friendship'.[20] It seems unlikely that Shelley met Mary then.

During Jane's school years, Mary was often away in Scotland. William Baxter of Dundee had sought out Godwin during the years after the publication of *Political Justice*. In the dissenting tradition of political and religious liberty, he shared Godwin's views, though in personal morals he was more strait-laced. He seems to have been of good social and economic standing, since Godwin boasted to him later of Mary's 'status' when she married into the Shelley family. During her girlhood, Mary knew the two Baxter daughters, Christy and Isabel, always described as 'her friends'. Christy must have visited the Godwin household, since she remembered Jane. Mary certainly spent 'several long visits' with the Baxters. Godwin had talked at her mother's death bed of educating their infant daughter, but found himself short of cash when the time came to turn talk to reality. No schooling is mentioned for Mary, who read and wrote so remarkably well. She may perhaps have shared the solid Scottish education of the Baxter girls. Shelley and Mary Godwin do not seem to have met for another eighteen months, until late in March 1814, when Mary left her friends in Scotland for good.

When they did, the effect was electrifying for both. Shelley was growing bored with his wife. Mary was still a schoolgirl, as Harriet had been when Shelley married her, but she was infinitely richer and more mature in ideas, inherited from her mother, Mary Wollstonecraft, and learnt from Godwin. Not yet 17, she was also extremely beautiful, with dazzling white skin, golden hair, and brilliant hazel eyes. She had a passionate nature and a determination to succeed. As her father had earlier written, 'She is singularly bold, somewhat imperious, and active of mind. Her desire of knowledge is great, and her perseverance in everything she undertakes almost invincible.'[21]

The dark-haired Jane, herself attractive, formed a perfect foil. She records their meetings at this time thus:

> We both used to walk with him in the Wilderness of the Charterhouse also to Mary Wollstonecraft's tomb—they always sent me to walk some distance from them—alleging that they wished to talk on philosophical subjects . . . I did not know what they talked about.

She did not hear when on 26 June 1814, at her mother's tomb, Mary finally declared her love for Shelley.

The effect on Shelley, who had already written a passionate poem to Mary Wollstonecraft Godwin, was overwhelming. As he afterwards described it, 'The sublime and rapturous moment when she confessed herself mine . . . cannot be painted to mortal imaginations.'[22]

On the following day, he told Godwin. The latter was horrified. Shelley, his beloved disciple, now appeared in the guise of a married man declaring passionate love for his daughter. The situation was complicated by the fact that Shelley was engaged in raising a loan of money for Godwin. The crisis was felt by everyone at Skinner Street. Mrs Godwin, albeit not always the most reliable of sources, described Shelley, looking 'extremely wild', offering Mary a bottle of laudanum, producing a pistol for himself, and proposing a suicide pact, at which Jane, who was also present, 'filled the room with her shrieks'. Godwin tried to confine both Mary and Jane to the house, but the situation was out of his control. They walked each day in the Charterhouse Gardens, where they met Shelley and made plans, observed only by the gardener's wife.[23]

At four o'clock on the morning of 28 July, they put their plans into action. Mary and Jane left a note for Godwin and took a coach with Shelley for Dover, where they arrived just before four o'clock in the afternoon. They arranged with sailors to take them across the Channel in an open boat. The weather, calm and fine when they started, worsened during the night, and they had a perilous crossing to Calais, arriving at sunrise. Shelley exclaimed, 'Mary, look, the sun rises over France,' and they all walked over the sands to an inn. Mary always remembered the date of their elopement, 28 July, with special affection. Ten years later she recalled how young, heedless, and happy they had been.[24] By the evening of 29 July an unwelcome visitor from Skinner Street arrived, Jane's mother, who had taken the packet-boat and pursued them to Calais. Jane spent the night with her mother and promised to return to England, but in the morning she consulted Shelley and announced she would go on with Shelley and Mary. Mrs Godwin left disconsolate, though comforted by the thought that Jane was too immature to attract Shelley, who was, anyway, totally occupied by Mary.

Shelley and Mary had taken Jane with them to France from necessity; they understood surprisingly little French, and needed her for the most simple translations. Later in their travels, a friendly English-speaking Swiss noted Mary and Shelley speaking French so imperfectly that they could scarcely make themselves understood. He concluded that they must have run away, on impulse, for love; but when he asked Jane if she had also run away for love, she answered cheerfully, 'Oh! dear No—I came to speak french.'[25] Then, too, she had been close companion and witness of Mary's whole courtship. She saw herself as company and reassurance for Mary in the adventure of her elopement. She herself was excited by the whole romantic situation and believed she was leaving England for ever.[26] Clearly she also shared, with the others, the sense of release that had flowed over everyone since Napoleon's abdication in April 1814 and the end of the long war years; as Dorothy Wordsworth had exclaimed, 'It is like a dream—peace peace—all in a moment.'

The three young people were thus full of the exhilaration of a new-found freedom in the general sense, as well as of their own escape. Mary later described their feelings in France: 'it was acting a novel, being an incarnate romance'. Jane had escaped from lessons, from the dingy purlieus of Skinner Street and the sharp eye of her possessive mother, into the world of her favourite reading. The landscape was 'most divine', time was meaningless (they had no watch), and, as Mary wrote, even the little boys and girls spoke French. At each new stop Jane exclaimed, 'Oh! this is beautiful enough; let us live here.' The charm of foreign travel blended with the magic of a poet in love. In this heady atmosphere, the girl who had left school only seven months earlier grew up fast. Yet she still swung to and fro at the mercy of her youthful feelings. On one day she wrote, 'How much is lost by those who live in cities—They are never visited by those sweet feelings which to recollect alone is heaven—' On another morning her verdict was a flat 'Disappointed.' They left Calais by cabriolet, and, travelling by Boulogne and Abbeville, arrived on 2 August at Paris. Here they engaged rooms cheaply at the Hôtel de Vienne.

Their chief need was money, though Mary later remembered poverty as part of the excitement at that time. Shelley had been given the address of a banker in Paris named Tavernier, whom he invited to a meal on 4 August, his own twenty-second birthday. Tavernier seems to have induced in Shelley the utmost contempt; this may have been mutual, for money was not immediately forthcoming, and Shelley sold his watch and chain to raise money for running expenses.

By 7 August, however, Tavernier, perhaps won over by the French-speaking Jane, brought the equivalent of sixty pounds, and they were able to make plans.

Their plans were of a strange nature. They determined to walk to Switzerland, though the girls still wore the black silk dresses in which they had left London, and Madame at the inn warned them of danger from Napoleon's disbanded soldiers. On 8 August, Jane helped Shelley to bargain for an ass, they set off south-east. At the end of the first day they had reached as far as Charenton, the ass having proved practically useless. They slept overnight in Charenton, and the following day Jane assisted Shelley to get rid of the ass and buy a mule for further transport. That day was beautiful. Mary and occasionally Jane rode in the fine August weather. They stopped for the night at Guignes, continuing to Provins on 10 August. They were quite unprepared for the shock of seeing what had been, until recently, a battlefield. At Nogent and St Aubin, they found the houses reduced to rubble. They arrived at Ossey-les-Trois-Maisons at nine o'clock at night, and Jane's enquiries about a place to stay were met, at the first cottage where she asked, with 'unmeaning laughter'. However, they eventually found 'a kind of an auberge', which could offer a bedroom full of 'four-footed enemies'—rats—and a man invited Jane, whose position in the party seemed to him inexplicable, to go to bed with him. She eventually rested on the bed of the other two, which the rats did not invade, being scared, as Mary joked, by the threats Shelley had made to the man who wanted to sleep with Jane.[27]

Shelley had sprained his ankle during the previous long day's walk and had to ride the mule all day on the 12th, while the girls trudged in the hot sun. They arrived at Troyes, where they decided to sell the mule and saddle and buy a travelling-carriage for all three. In spite of Jane's persuasive French, they lost money on this transaction. On Sunday 14 August they pushed on, in their new conveyance, to Bar-sur-Aube. Shelley, seeing an enchanting small girl, wanted to take her into the carriage. Not surprisingly her father refused. Wanting to be like the others, Jane now began to keep a journal; her entry for that day described a beautiful evening walk.[28] According to Mary, Jane wanted to stay at each place they visited as they pressed on towards Switzerland. Mary was more critical, disliking almost everything in France, in spite of having a rare clean bed to sleep in at

Pontarlier, but Jane's spirits rose continually, and reached sheer delight at her first view of the Alps from Neuchâtel.

Then—oh then come thç terrific Alps. I thought they were white flaky clouds what was my surprize when after a long and steady examination I found them really to be the snowy Alps—yes, they were really the Alps—Peaked broken, one jutting forward, another retreating, now the light airy clouds rested a few moments on their aspiring fronts and then fled away that we might better behold the sublimity of the scene.[29]

Jane believed that Switzerland was 'the land of my ancestors', and this dazzling vision 'my native mountains . . . which I love to consider my own country'.

For Jane, Shelley could do no wrong; he seemed to her almost a being from another world, 'as if he had just landed from Heaven'. One incident that seems relevant to this is described with particular emphasis in Jane's journal.

On our way to Pontarlier, we came to a clear running shallow stream, and Shelley entreated the driver to stop while he from under the bank could bathe himself—and he wanted Mary to do the same as the bank sheltered one from every eye—but Mary would not—first, she said it would be most indecent, and then also she had no towel and could not dry herself. He said he would gather leaves from the trees and she could dry herself with those but she refused and [said] how could he think of a such a thing. The driver always looked at Shelley with a wondering stare as if he thought he was rather crazy—and 'very likely that was the cause of his being rude to us', and refused to stop so Shelley could not bathe himself in the open air and in the middle of the day—just as if he were Adam in Paradise before his fall.

This was on 19 August. They slept that night at Neûchatel. The next day they were dismayed to find neither letters nor money waiting for them at the Poste Restante. Shelley managed to borrow money from a banker, but the loan only came to just under forty pounds. However, it was enough to hire a diligence, and they pressed on the next day to Soleure. On the way some sort of quarrel took place, and Mary wrote in her journal that Shelley talked with Jane about her character.[30] She was perhaps irritable at being a third party, valued only for her skill as interpreter. There were signs that for all of them the novelty and excitement of the adventure were beginning to wear thin, in spite of the thrilling Alpine scenery and the beauties of Lake Lucerne. Mary regretted that they had quitted her father so abruptly, although she did not blame Shelley for this. On their journey through France, however, Mary conceived, and at 16 faced the demands of a new life.

Mary had the serious cast of mind which she had inherited from Mary Wollstonecraft and William Godwin. Jane, spontaneous and impulsive, had an apparently almost childlike enjoyment of life, although there was less than six months between them. Whatever Shelley said to Jane about her character, it certainly seems that he and Mary both thought her too inexperienced to be told the truth about their financial situation. At Brunnen on 24 August, they hired lodgings in a house by Lake Lucerne, but then Shelley and Mary realized that with their lack of money they would not be able to pay the rent. The only remedy was to make their way back to England. They did not fully explain why to Jane, who consequently wrote on 26 August: 'Boring morning. Project of going back to England pressed.' She added in her journal next day: 'Get up at five. Bustle, toil & trouble. Most laughable to think of our going to England the second day after we entered a new house for six months—All because the stove don't suit.'[31] Though sometimes superficial, Jane was no fool, and the excuse which the other two had invented about the stove obviously sounded fishy to her. She repeated suspiciously, 'How wild the people will think us—All because the stove did not burn rightly.' Apparently, they left the house, early and secretly, probably without paying.

Water travel was so cheap that they could afford to go back almost the whole way by boat, first across the lake to Lucerne, then along the river Reuss, and finally down the Rhine. At the inn at Lucerne, Le Cheval Blanc, Jane read *King Lear* for the first time, and scenes from Shakespeare's play gave the impressionable and over-strained 16-year-old the 'horrors'. She wrote: 'Quite Horrified—I can't describe my feelings for the moment—when Cornwall tears out the eyes of the Duke of Gloster.' Four days later, when they were all on the Rhine, she steeled herself bravely to re-read the play and to defy the 'horrors'. On 27 August she copied, 'What shall poor Cordelia do—Love and be silent', with the spontaneous exclamation, 'Oh this is true—Real Love will never [sh]ew itself to the light of broad day—[i]t courts the secret glades.' This sudden outburst reveals Jane's overwrought excitement in the presence of Shelley and Mary's love affair and her longing for admission to their charmed circle.

Mary's seventeenth birthday, 30 August, had a lovely sunset. According to Jane's lyrical description, 'The West was a long continued strip of Yellow dying away with a lovely pink which again mellowed itself imperceptibly into an amazing horizon of the deepest purple—The Rhine was extremely rapid—The Waves borrowed the divine colours of the sky.'[32] The whole scene reminded her, she wrote, of the many-coloured water-snakes in *The Ancient Mariner*. Jane's journal is full of such sudden flashes of bright and delighted colour, and she responded swiftly to each changing scene—a clearing sky after a storm, or sunset on the river—as though she herself took part in it. Her journal is a record of vivid, fresh impressions. She was further delighted by the scenery on the banks of the Rhine, each vista more wild and romantic than its predecessor.

> The Banks of the Rhine are very beautiful—The River itself is narrow and runs between Mountains which though not high are of every different shape & description—Ruined Castles are here very numerous & many most romantically situated. Ruins have a fine effect & henceforth I shall hardly think any scene complete without them—I think we passed no less than twenty Castles & about 5 towns.[33]

The same type of description of the Rhine journey occurs in Mary's journals too, impressions of which she was to make good use two years later in her account of Frankenstein's travels down the Rhine. Mary's reactions are more sophisticated, but Jane catches the innocent novelty of the experience.

The three were not occupied on their journey solely by writing their journals, they also composed fiction. Shelley was writing a story called 'The Assassins', Mary one called 'Hate', and Jane was busy, in a desultory way, on 'The Ideot'. 'This has been for years a favourite Plan of mine—to develop the Workings & Improvements of a Mind which by Common People was deemed the mind of an Ideot because it conformed not to their vulgar & prejudiced views.'[34] Perhaps her concern with 'vulgar & prejudiced views' reflected her disgust at a group of Germans in the ship's cabin—'a most horrid set'. Only two were in her view more civilized men; having a little English, they stopped to talk to the English party on deck and sang them a number of German songs. The musical Jane appreciated this very much, especially when one of the men, a schoolmaster, sang 'an animated German Song' when the boat was going through a dangerous defile in the river, which distracted her from the frightening sounds of waves over the rocks.

They reached Holland on 9 September at the frontier town of Nijmegen, which Jane called Nimeguen, and welcomed as being 'like an English town but most uncommonly neat'. She praised Holland and what she saw of the Dutch for their lack of 'German licentiousness'. All her impressions at this stage are arbitrary and often animated by personal prejudices, though she later became a shrewd judge of foreign habits. Now this 16-year-old authority appeared to Shelley as a pupil, in his words, 'a nice little girl'.

At Rotterdam, they bargained with the English captain of a ship to take them to Gravesend for three guineas each, though in the end he had to wait for most of the money until after they had landed in England, where Shelley could borrow from friends. The crossing was violent and dangerous; Jane recorded cheerfully, 'Every one of the passengers was sick except myself.' On 13 September they landed, having been away for six weeks.

2 Claire and Byron (1814–1816)

The first question was how the Godwins would receive the returned runaways. Their attitude obviously meant a great deal to Jane. Many years later, when she and Mary were both middle-aged, and the Godwins both dead, Jane wrote to Mary recalling their rejection. 'You must recollect what a coldness Papa and Mama took to Shelley . . . they fell into a most violent state of disapproval of him.'[1] Even after that space of time, she remembered the distinct attitudes of Godwin and Mrs Godwin: 'Papa took to being very chilling, haughty and stern, and Mama to being lively and furibonde,' that is, in an animated state of fury. It is typical of Jane to find a French expression for her mother's anger. She added, 'They quite overawed me.' The return was also dominated by what had brought the runaways back so ignominiously from their impulsive adventure and its joys: lack of money.

They arrived in England at Gravesend on a fine, calm morning, which was at once overshadowed by money worries. Shelley still owed the captain their fares for the crossing, and had also to find a waterman who would wait for payment—'our kind Boatman', as Jane called him. To pay these debts, Shelley had to call on his wife Harriet; she handed the money over, assuming he had returned to legal matrimony. That night, however, he, Mary, and Jane all slept at the Stratford Hotel in Oxford Street, and on visiting Harriet again the next day, Shelley made it clear he had no intention of giving up his new life with Mary. To Jane, once more, he could do no wrong, and she commented on Harriet's 'strange Behaviour'.[2] They moved that evening to lodgings at 56 Margaret Street, in Cavendish Square, and Jane, exhausted, went to bed early. Two days later, at about six in the evening, they saw Mrs Godwin and Fanny look in at the window. Shelley rushed out to them, but they refused to speak to him. Thus it was learnt that the Godwins had not forgiven him; although later that evening, pebbles at the window announced the arrival of Jane's brother Charles, who stayed quite happily till three next morning. He revealed that the Godwins even had a plan to put Jane in a convent to remove her from Shelley's influence. Shelley wrote to

Godwin, who refused to enter into any communication with him, which Jane found 'very chilling'.

Shelley was trying to persuade Harriet that their marriage had been founded on mere friendship, unlike the passionate love he now felt for Mary. ('Curious accounts of Harriet', Jane commented obliquely.) Meanwhile he acted as a kind of tutor to Jane, teaching her Greek and suggesting suitable reading. Her enthusiasm knew no bounds. She bought a copy of Anacreon's poems, although she had only just started learning the characters of the Greek alphabet and a few elementary verbs. She listened to Shelley reciting the epic poems of Southey. Every scheme Shelley proposed seemed good to her. He unfolded a design to carry off his own sisters from school, just as he formerly had Harriet. In her journal, Jane wrote 'Project the plan of carrying off poor Eliza and Helen', assuming, because Shelley did, that they were being oppressed by their perfectly normal boarding school at Hackney. This was part of the need of youth to revolt, which Shelley taught her so effectively. Shelley took Jane with him to visit his sisters at Hackney, but he failed to persuade them to adopt what Jane now called 'our Plan' and run away from school. At 16, Jane was still delighted to go to a pond in the Vale of Health, beyond Primrose Hill, and 'make Paper Boats & sail them'. Shelley delighted in these childish games, but was less enthusiastic when, two weeks later, he found himself confronted by a moody schoolgirl. Jane's adolescent feelings swung beyond her control. Now she got up late, came downstairs in an ill temper and quarrelled with him, but later regretted it and wrote in her journal:

> How hateful it is to quarrel—to say a thousand unkind things—meaning none—things produced by the bitterness of disappointment—(I hate these feelings) . . . Shelley comes into my room & thinks he was to blame—but I don't—.

She made vows—'these shall not be broken'—to keep her temper, but as she grew up the light and darkness of her storms grew with her. They were never left behind, even in maturity.

On the night of 7 October, there was an alarming incident. Mary had gone to bed early, and there is no doubt Shelley deliberately played upon Jane's nerves, as he liked to do with his own sisters; perhaps meeting them again had reminded him of this. After a conversation by the fire, during which, according to Shelley, Jane stated 'her conception of the subterraneous community of women', her late night 'horrors' reached a pitch best described in her own words:

At one the conversation turned upon those unaccountable & mysterious feelings . . . that we are sometime subject to. Shelley looks beyond all passing strange—a look of impressive deep and melancholy awe—I cannot describe it I well know how I felt it—I ran upstairs to bed—I placed the candle on the drawers & stood looking at a pillow that lay in the very middle of the Bed—I turned my head round to a window & then back again to the Bed—the pillow was no longer there—it had been removed to the chair—I stood thinking for two moments—how did this come? Was it possible that I had deluded myself so far as to place it there & then forget the action? This was not likely . . . I ran downstairs—Shelley heard me & came out of his room—He gives the most horrible description of my countenance—I did not feel in the way he thinks I did—We sat up all night—I was ill—At day break we examined the room & found every thing in the State I described.[3]

Shelley himself added lurid details, with Jane shrieking and writhing, so that he had to rouse Mary to comfort her. The main facts are, however, suggested by Jane in her own account. Her comment on the movement of the pillow contains a hint of the truth. 'Was it possible that I had deluded myself so far as to place it there & then forget the action?' If Jane were suffering from the symptom of hysteria known as 'disassociation', it was perfectly possible that she moved the pillow herself and then forgot about it. Whether Shelley induced or encouraged her hysteria remains possible though unproven, but it seems likely he did, perhaps as a sublimation of erotic feelings about her. When, a few nights later, on 14 October, she walked for two hours in her sleep and reported similar trouble with the pillow, he commented almost cynically about the behaviour of Jane's pillow, 'who being very sleepy tried to get into bed again but fell down on his back'. Shelley may even have alarmed himself by the success of his experiment. Certainly Jane herself was frightened enough to write 'I can't think what the deuce is the matter with me—I weep yet never know why—I sigh yet feel no pain.'[4]

That morning, 14 October, Jane had quarrelled violently with Shelley. She afterwards reproached herself, yet believed she had derived some good from the incident—possibly from Shelley's remarks—as she commented: 'To know one's faults is to mend them—perhaps this morning though productive of very painful feelings has in reality been of more essential benefit to me than any I ever yet passed.'[5] On the other hand, her feelings were very much hurt by

Shelley's criticism; in her journal, she writes almost pleadingly, 'How I like good kind explaining people.' Shelley's own journal recorded his despair at 'Jane's insensibility & incapacity for the slightest degree of friendship', but admitted that he failed in 'maintaining any measure in my severity'. It appears that the feelings of this 16-year-old schoolgirl were being sorely tried and that Shelley, in some perverse way, enjoyed the power he had to affect her. Jane's journal records nights when she either went to sleep abnormally late or did not sleep at all, sitting up with Shelley while Mary went to bed.[6] Mary herself wrote in her journal for 18 October, 'Shelley and Jane sit up and for a wonder do not frighten themselves.' The pattern of life which had seemed so promising when all three were abroad, now looked frightening. Jane's journal reveals that Shelley could hardly control his own obsessions and fears of 'suspicious men'. She was therefore bewildered by his power over her feelings and his verdict that her mind was 'unformed'. Only Mary seemed to maintain her normality.

At this time Jane became healthily critical of Shelley. On 3 November, when she received a short note from him saying he was unhappy, she felt moved to exclaim, 'God in heaven, what has he to be unhappy about!' On the next day she added, 'I am much disappointed in Shelley to-day—I thought him uniformly kind and considerate but I find him act as weakly as other people.' Mary, naturally, blamed Jane rather than Shelley and commented in her journal, 'Jane very gloomy—she is very sullen with Shelley.'

By Wednesday 9 November, Shelley had arranged to receive a considerable loan from a money-lender, and was now able, safe from arrest, to live openly with Mary and Jane. On that day, they all moved to lodgings at 2 Nelson Square, Blackfriars. On 10 November, perhaps encouraged by this new independence, Jane asserted her own individuality by adopting a name she considered more romantic, 'Claire', though at first in the less appealing form of 'Clara'. From this moment, then, one should refer to her as she wished, as 'Claire Clairmont'—perhaps after Claire, the lively dark friend of the lovers in Rousseau's *La Nouvelle Héloïse*.[7] With the new name she took a new, adventurous identity, shaking off the homely past. Although she was always known to her own mother and to Godwin by her original name of 'Jane', she now regarded St Clare's day as her saints' day, and indeed celebrated it when abroad.

Knowing that Jane—or Claire, as she now called herself, was discontented with Shelley, the Godwins offered her a home at Skinner Street and sent Fanny Imlay to reason with her and help her pack. Claire said she would gladly come home for a week to assist in the washing, 'or on any occasion when she might be useful',[8] and duly arrived at Skinner Street on 13 November under the wing of Fanny Imlay. Yet she was back at Nelson Square by 15 November. She had insisted that she would only accept any job found by her parents on definite conditions—'that she should in all situations openly proclaim and earnestly support a total contempt for the laws and institutions of society, and that no restraint should be imposed on her correspondence and intercourse with those from whom she was separated'. This meant a return to Shelley, whose principles she had imbibed too deeply to give them up.[9] On 21 November, Charles Clairmont reported that Mr and Mrs Godwin's reaction to this was 'indifferent'. On 24 November, Claire, probably shaken by the complex events of the last week, was ill with an inflammation of the liver. She was bled, the standard treatment, and leeches were applied by a Dr Currie who may have been the lecturer of Guy's Hospital who taught Keats a year later. At all events, Claire recovered quickly.[10]

Claire's mother, whether or not she was 'indifferent' toward her, certainly believed Shelley's influence on her was harmful. She wrote to Lady Mountcashell in Italy, one of the Juvenile Library authors, reporting remarks Claire had made during her stay at Skinner Street. She had said that an old enemy of Shelley, Leeson, was intending to ambush him in the street with a knife. She may even have reported the rumour that Godwin had sold Mary and herself to Shelley for eight hundred pounds and seven hundred pounds respectively. This may have started as a joke, never meant to be taken seriously. The only certainty is that, at the time when Claire was temporarily at Skinner Street, Shelley, nursing the ailing Mary, suffered from 'disquieting dreams'; but what these were, he never revealed.[11]

Shelley still regarded Claire as a young pupil whose mind needed to be formed by his ideas and by reading prescribed for her, yet he had begun to treat her personally as an equal. He appreciated her liveliness and wit and enjoyed her company. Mary, six months gone in pregnancy, naturally resented this; Claire was frankly pleased that Mary's pregnancy forced her to rest so frequently, leaving herself as companion to Shelley.

It was in this way that Claire came to join Shelley, early in 1815, on what was for him an important expedition. On 6 January, Shelley's grandfather, Sir Bysshe Shelley, died, and Shelley went to his family home at Field Place near Horsham for the reading of the will. He took Claire with him as far as Slinfold, a neighbouring village, while he went on to Field Place. There, refused entry by his outraged father, he sat ostentatiously on the doorstep, reading Mary's copy of *Comus*.[12] The settlement of Sir Bysshe's will took four months, at the end of which Shelley was for a time free of financial worries.

While Shelley's financial problems were solving themselves, Mary continued to have a difficult pregnancy. On 22 February, a baby girl was born, two months prematurely; 'not expected to live', Shelley noted.[13] On 6 March, after a hopeful fortnight feeding the baby, Mary recorded bleakly, 'Find my baby dead.' She was distraught, and it was Claire who went with Shelley to arrange the burial—no one knows where.[14] 'I think about the little thing all day', wrote Mary,[15] and later, 'Dream again about my baby'. In the grip of grief, she found Claire's tactless liveliness unendurable. Shelley attempted to find Claire a job which would take her out of the house, but without success. While Mary was 'wretched in health and spirits', Shelley began the idea of an interesting experimental love affair between her and his Oxford friend Jefferson Hogg. Mary responded cautiously—'we have known each other for so short a time'—but the suggestion conformed to Shelley's ideal of free love.

This plan for friendship and love in common has led critics to see a corresponding affair between Shelley himself and Claire. The Godwins, who resented Shelley's influence, certainly believed she was in love with him, but with little solid evidence to support their theory. Mary's own journal shows no sign of specifically sexual jealousy, but elaborate sarcasm, referring to Claire as 'the lady' and her husband's 'friend'. Her irritation with Claire may simply show her realization that Shelley, immersed in his own thoughts, found Claire more cheerful company than his sad, sick wife, on his long walks in Kensington Gardens. Nevertheless, when he took Mary for a brief spring holiday near Windsor, they agreed to send Claire away from London. In May Shelley saw her off on the coach for Lynmouth in Devon. 'The business is finished', commented Mary.[16]

Mrs Godwin had played her usual active part in this. She forwarded to Shelley a family letter complaining of 'unfavourable gossip' if Claire returned to Skinner Street, and implied that he had deprived her daughter of a home. Shelley, in a fateful decision, undertook to be responsible for Claire, to provide for her in his will as well as to 'form her mind'. He was the more willing because he already privately considered her mother 'a vulgar commonplace woman . . . not a proper person to form the mind of a young girl'. The journey to Lynmouth was a mark of his new responsibility, which, unlike many duties, he faithfully maintained.

From Lynmouth, Claire wrote to her stepsister Fanny Imlay at Skinner Street the first of many lively letters which have come down to us. The mixture is very much in character: romanticism with a welcome dash of humour was never far from Claire. She described Lynmouth as a place of

> a few cottages, with little rosy-faced children, scolding wives, and drunken husbands—I wish I had a more amiable and romantic picture to present to you, such as shepherds and shepherdesses, flocks and madrigals; but this is the truth, and the truth is best at any time. I live in a little cottage with jasmine and honeysuckle twining over the window.[17]

She goes on to contrast peaceful Lynmouth with the atmosphere at Skinner Street and the rages of her own mother, which Fanny too had experienced: 'After so much discontent, such violent scenes, such a turmoil of passion and hatred, you will hardly believe how enraptured I am with this dear little quiet spot'.

Knowing Fanny's depressions, inherited like Mary's from Mary Wollstonecraft, she added later in the same letter, 'Now, do not be melancholy, for heaven's sake be cheerful; "so young in life, and so melancholy"'. Although Claire here in preaching contentment to Fanny indicates her own peace of mind there are signs that she looked back on her stay at Lynmouth as a time of loneliness; she too had known, it seems, what Fanny called 'the dreadful state of mind I generally labour under', for she was to write later, 'a life of sixteen years is already too much for me to bear'.[18]

Claire was constantly at a loose end throughout the rest of the year. In October she visited Ireland with her brother, who was investigating prospects of a distillery business over there. Shelley sent her a money order for two pounds at the Enniscorthy Post Office, Wexford. Early in 1816, she was back in London where on 26 January Mary gave birth to Shelley's son, William. Claire could now visit Skinner Street, where the atmosphere seemed calmer. Presumably, her mother was pleased that she was no longer living with Shelley and

Mary, and hoped she would shed Shelley's influence. Unknown to her mother, however, she was preparing to involve herself in a fresh entanglement, this time completely on her own initiative. Mary and Shelley seemed happy in their plans for a continuing life together. Could Claire set up a similar poetic partnership of her own? Her answer was dramatic and typical of her impulsive nature.

Claire's experience of modern poets had so far been confined to Shelley, appreciated by a small circle of radical intellectuals. She saw, though, how Mary had succeeded in attracting him; but Lord Byron, the object of her attention, was a poet of a different nature. For the past few years, since the overnight success of his *Childe Harold*, he had been an idol. His poem *The Corsair* (1814) sold ten thousand copies on its first day of publication. He was importuned by all sorts of women. On sheer impulse, Claire decided to be one of them, and boldly wrote to him in March 1816, proposing a relationship and enclosing a story she had written, possibly 'The Ideot' of 1814. Byron was accustomed to receive letters from young ladies of literary pretensions (dismissed as 'Miss Emma Somebody with a play entitled "The Bandit of Bohemia"'), yet even he may have been surprised by the frankness with which 'E. Trefusis' addressed herself to him from an assumed address:

> An utter stranger takes the liberty of addressing you . . . It may seem a strange assertion, but it is none the less true that I place my happiness in your hands. If a woman, whose reputation has as yet remained unstained, if without either guardian or husband to control, she should throw herself on your mercy, if with a beating heart she should confess the love she has borne you many years . . . could you betray her, or would you be silent as the grave?

A cool reply failed to discourage this determined correspondent, who requested Lord Byron to receive her 'on business of peculiar importance. She desires to be admitted alone and with the utmost privacy.' In these terms did the enamoured Claire, aged all of 17 years, make her bid for the famous poet's attention. It turned out to be the most important decision of her life. Not until her old age could she write more calmly about it, 'I was young and vain and poor . . . The result you know.'

In many ways, she could not have chosen a worse time. Byron had married just over a year earlier, on 2 January 1815. His wife, Annabella Milbanke, had borne a daughter and then separated from him, for reasons not to this day completely understood. Byron's own feelings had received a devastating shock, which obsessed him for long afterwards, and left him incapable of falling in love with anyone. He summed up this state of mind in a letter to his half-sister a few months later: 'She—or rather—the separation—has broken my heart—I feel as if an Elephant has trodden on it—I am convinced I shall never get over it—but I try.' He added, 'I breathe lead.' Obviously, Claire had neither knowledge nor understanding of these complex emotions when she wrote to Byron.

Byron reluctantly agreed to see her, and she visited him in his green room at the Drury Lane Theatre. There he found she was not yet 18, very pretty, plump and dark with sparkling black eyes. He also found she had a charming singing voice, which drew from him one of his best short lyrics. Dated 28 March 1816, it shows the charms that Claire held for Byron before she became his mistress.

> There be none of Beauty's daughters
>   With a magic like thee;
> And like music on the waters
>   Is thy sweet voice to me:
> Then as if its sound were causing
> The charmed ocean's pausing,
> The waves lie still and gleaming,
> And the lulled winds seem dreaming:
>
> And the midnight Moon is weaving
>   Her bright chain o'er the deep;
> Whose breast is gently heaving,
>   As an infant's asleep:
> So the spirit bows before thee,
> To listen and adore thee;
> With a full but soft emotion,
> Like the swell of Summer's ocean.[19]

One lyric, however, hardly means love, which remained unmentioned in the poem. Byron continually insisted, 'I am not in love—nor have any love left for any.' Curiosity remained, however, and was further aroused by a surprising letter:

> Have you any objection to the following plan? On Thursday Evening we may go out of Town together by some stage or mail about the distance of ten or twelve miles. There we shall be free and unknown; we shall return early the next morning. I have arranged everything here so that the slightest suspicion may not be excited.

There had been many young ladies, but few of such aplomb. Byron accepted, mainly 'by way of novelty' from the recent painful rejection by his wife. It seemed to mean nothing to him but that.

What did it mean to Claire? Briefly, her dreams became reality. Years later she remembered her first experience of sexual love as 'perfect'. Soon after their night together, she scribbled on the margin of a note from Byron 'God bless you—I *never* was so happy.' She had already fallen, like most women, under the spell of his magnetic charm. 'I shall never forget you,' she wrote, 'I shall ever remember the gentleness of your manners and the wild originality of your countenance.' After their first night, and, according to Byron 'a good deal of that same', her letters all talked about love. They are full, however, of expressions of her humility towards him, 'I do not expect you to love me; I am not worthy of your love. I feel you are superior,' and 'believe that of all human evils none can affect me except offending you.' There is never any evidence that their feelings are on an equal footing. She remained for him 'that odd-headed girl—who introduced herself to me'. She developed towards him a mixture of deference and possessiveness which he ultimately found irritating.

It was no novelty for Byron to suffer from the possessiveness of women. Lady Caroline Lamb had assumed she owned him during their hectic love affair; she sent him locks of her blonde pubic hair, with frank accounts of how she had cut it off. Byron's wife Annabella assumed that she had traced his bouts of violent behaviour, often the results of excessive drinking, to actual forms of insanity, though her diagnoses were based on lay reading of medical journals which she did not understand. Claire did not attempt to dominate him in such ways. Her main drawback, in his eyes, was that she tried to extend a casual night's sexual pleasure to a long-lasting relationship. Where he was weary and indifferent, she overwhelmed him with youthful ardour: 'people of eighteen always love truly and tenderly'. She played the card of her friendship with Shelley, whose *Queen Mab* Byron admired while still not knowing the author. Claire introduced Mary to Byron, with a view to contriving a meeting between the two poets, but since both were heavily preoccupied at the time in settling legal affairs prior to departing for the Continent, this would have to wait for a while. She planned, mistakenly as it proved, to engineer this meeting as a method of tightening her grip upon Byron, in the face of his obvious discouragement.

On 3 May 1816, Claire went abroad once more with Shelley and Mary. On 6 May she wrote to Byron and told him that she had persuaded Shelley to meet him at Geneva. She in fact adapted her own travel plans to accompany Shelley, and thus used both poets' wish to meet each other as a bait to secure herself another meeting with Byron. Her objective was not only to meet him, but also to make him see her as more than a night's bedtime entertainment; for she felt unease about her own position with him: 'I know not how to address you; I cannot call you friend for though I love you you do not feel even interest for me . . . were I to float by your window drowned all you would say would be "Ah voilà!"'

Her instinct was all too correct. Byron, though he was glad of the opportunity to meet Shelley, was reluctant to do so since it would entail a further meeting with Claire, whom, he continually reiterated, he did not love. His letters always take a slightly contemptuous tone about Claire. To him, she is 'a woman who had scrambled eight hundred miles to unphilosophize me', or, even later to a man friend, Kinnaird, 'I found her with Shelley and her sister at Geneva. I never loved nor pretended to love her, but a man is a man, and if a girl of eighteen comes prancing to you at all hours, there is but one way . . .' There is evident sarcastic contempt in the words 'scrambled' and 'prancing'. Claire's persistent pursuit had irritated him. He had probably regarded her as someone like Susan Boyce, the minor actress at Drury Lane with whom he had spent a casual night a few months earlier. Miss Boyce had effaced herself. But Claire showed no sign of doing so, and would be waiting for his arrival at Geneva.

On 14 May, Shelley, Mary (with baby William), and Claire arrived at Lake Léman, and Shelley took a cheap set of rooms for them at Dejean's Hôtel d'Angleterre in the Genevan suburb of Sécheron. Beyond the blue lake they saw the line of the Alps, and, distinct from all other mountains, the snowy dome of Mont Blanc. They hired a small sailing boat and drifted about the lake every evening. Meanwhile, Byron was making a leisurely progress through Europe, calling at the battlefield of Waterloo on the way. Shelley was already relaxing on the twilit lake near Geneva, idyllically described by Mary, who wrote how they 'seldom returned till ten o'clock' and were then 'saluted by the delightful scent of flowers and new mown grass, and the chirp of the grasshoppers, and the song of the evening birds'.[20]

The Shelley party were following this happy programme when Byron arrived on 25 May, bringing with him his valet, Fletcher, and his young travelling physician, Dr William Polidori. Weary from the journey, Byron put his age in the hotel register as a hundred. Coming in from the evening on the water, Claire, delighted that Byron had really arrived, wrote him a short note, which was both flippant and flirtatiously loving. 'I am sorry you are grown so old. Indeed I suspected you were 200 from the slowness of your journey. I suppose your venerable age could not bear quicker travelling. . . . I am so happy.'

Byron, for his part, showed no such happiness that Claire had 'scrambled' to Geneva to wait for him. On the next day, he simply went out with Polidori to enquire about suitable lodgings in the surroundings of Geneva. He showed no signs of having received Claire's note. She wrote a complaint, and, as she had done before in England, made an assignation with him.

> I have been in this weary hotel this fortnight and it seems so unkind, so cruel of you to treat me with such marked indifference. Will you go straight up to the top of the house this evening at half past seven and I will infallibly be on the landing place and show you the room.

Next morning, seeing Byron and Polidori coming in from a boat, she led the Shelleys to the quay and introduced the two poets. Claire had now performed her part and, she hoped, put Byron under an obligation to her.[21] It is true that Byron hastily invited Shelley to dine that evening without the women, but Polidori, who also dined, made the entry in his diary for 27 May that Shelley 'keeps the two daughters of Godwin, who practice his theories; one L.B.'s'. It seems that Byron had responded to Claire's assignation, and, in his own words, 'could not exactly play the stoic' with her.[22]

Byron's real interest, however, was the company of Shelley, whom he found a fascinating person, '*truth* itself—and *honour* itself—notwithstanding his out-of-the-way notions about religion'. The two men determined to live as close as possible to one another. It appears that Claire was not consulted in the arrangements they made. Both wished primarily to leave the fashionable Hôtel d'Angleterre and settle on the other side of the lake, where their doings would be isolated from the spy-glasses of English visitors already beginning to manufacture fantastic legends about them. Byron discovered a pair of houses on the other side of the water, which seemed promising. Both nestled on a slope below the village of Cologny. Byron's Villa Diodati was plain, with columned portico, yet not as small as the Shelleys' cottage, the Maison Chappuis in the area called Montalègre, a little farther down towards the lake.[23] The two houses were separated by a vineyard. A boat, which Byron and Shelley had bought, lay at anchor nearby in a small harbour. It was properly rigged and keeled to face sudden squalls, for the month of June brought rough weather with frequent thunderstorms—'Rain; puffs of wind', as Polidori recalled. The peaks of the Jura, which they now faced, were lit up by vivid flashes of lightning.

The change in weather suited Claire, since Byron was therefore not always out in the boat with Shelley. She took to making the short walk through the vineyards up to the Villa Diodati, though often frustrated in her hopes of an act of love by the presence of Polidori. Often, too, Mary and Shelley were with her, and conversation between the two poets excluded Mary and Claire. On the night of 18 June, the scene in the large room at Diodati took a dramatic turn. As Polidori recorded, 'L. B. repeated some verses of Coleridge's "Christabel" of the witch's breast; when silence ensued, and Shelley, suddenly shrieking and putting his hands to his head, ran out of the room with a candle.' Polidori followed, threw water in Shelley's face and managed to calm him after his vision of a woman who had eyes instead of nipples. Byron was faintly incredulous at Shelley's behaviour—'I can't tell what seized him—for he don't want courage.' Claire, who knew only too well Shelley's late-night delusions and agitations, having been drawn into them herself, left no comment. On this, or on some similar evening when the talk 'became ghostly', Byron suggested they should all write ghost stories. The challenge was taken up by Shelley, Byron himself, Polidori and, eventually, by Mary. Hers resulted in the only lasting literary outcome of this scheme, her intensely gripping *Frankenstein: or the Modern Prometheus*, which has fascinated all ages since.

Claire's own story was soon abandoned[24]—perhaps because she had her own real-life drama at this time. This she apparently confided only to Shelley, but when the weather improved in the last week of June, and Byron and Shelley went out for a few days' tour on the lake, Shelley passed on the vital news:[25] Claire was with child by Byron. Byron received the news without enthusiasm—'Is the brat *mine*?'

Apparently Shelley had expected an unsympathetic reaction, for with great instinctive generosity he had already set about making legal provision in his own will for Claire's child, as well as a considerable legacy specifically for Claire herself. On 24 June Shelley had drafted a will, and the section of this which concerned Claire read:

To Mary Jane Clairmont (the sister in law of Miss Godwin) £12,000, one half to be laid out in an annuity for her own life, & that of any person she may if she pleases to name any other, the other half to be at her own disposal.[26]

This seems to show clearly that Shelley left Claire not only six thousand pounds for herself, but also a further six thousand pounds to provide an annuity for her unborn child so that it would not have to rely on its father for money. When Shelley signed a will based on this draft, which he eventually did on 24 September, the provisions relating to Claire were the same, and were repeated in a later will of 18 February 1817, which read

I give and bequeath to Mary Jane Clairmont . . . the sum of Six thousand pounds of like lawful money and also give and bequeath . . . the sum of Six thousand pounds . . . to lay and invest the same in the purchase of an Annuity for the term of the natural life of the same Mary Jane Clairmont and the life of such other person as the said Mary Jane Clairmont shall name (if she pleases to name one).[27]

Byron, for his part, continued to regard Claire as no more than a useful copyist and a convenient provider of casual sex. Shelley and Mary were aware that Byron's continual rebuffs were making Claire unhappy, and asked her to join them on a trip they were planning to Chamonix and Mont Blanc (having secured a Swiss children's nurse, Elise, to look after their small son William). True to character, Byron was glad to see her go and did not bother to say goodbye.

On 21 July, the three set off together, making for the dramatic valley of the Arve, with its waterfalls glistening like silver in the sun, and the glaciers hanging from the mountains, ridged and pure white, almost to the verge of the roadway. Claire and Mary rode on mules, while Shelley walked. They stayed the night at Sallanches, and pressing on the next day, arrived at the Hôtel de Londres, Chamonix, dead tired, at seven o'clock on the evening of 22 July.[28] The next morning, Shelley inscribed their names in the visitors' book at the inn.

He entered 'Sussex' as his own birthplace, 'London' for Mary's, and 'Clifton' for Claire's. It is often said she gave 'Clifton' as her own birthplace, but it was Shelley who did so. He also entered 'L'Enfer' as the destination of himself and Mary, 'England' for their origin, and in the column for 'observations' wrote some Greek verse which may be translated 'I am a lover of mankind, democrat, and atheist.' Some hand unknown has added another Greek sentence which may be translated 'The fool hath said in his heart, there is no god.'

In the hotel register, Shelley gave Mary the designation of 'Mad. M.W.G.' (Mary Wollstonecraft Godwin), and Claire the designation 'Mad. J.C.' (Jane Clairmont). Someone later heavily scratched out Claire's entry. It has been guessed that this was Byron, who visited Chamonix himself on 30 August, but Polidori, who travelled with him, specified that Byron's hotel was the Hôtel d'Angleterre, not the Hôtel de Londres: in any case, Byron spent very little time at Chamonix. What Byron is known to have erased was one of Shelley's many declarations of atheism, and Shelley's 'atheist' entry here is untouched by any later hand. One plausible suggestion is that the entry was erased by Mary, who may have resented the idea that Shelley was travelling with 'Mesdames', herself and Claire. She may even have cancelled the entry in the momentary irritation she was so often to feel about Claire's place in their lives. At the next place where Shelley made an entry, the mountain hut at Montenvers, he designated his two lady companions as 'Madame son Epouse', and 'la soeur', possibly following some protest by Mary.

On the matter of Claire's pregnancy, Mary was kept in the dark, probably at Byron's request. Her journal entry for 2 August recorded 'S. and C. go up to Diodati. I do not for Lord B. did not seem to wish it.' This was because they were going to discuss with Byron how the child should be brought up.

The substance of this discussion was given many years later by Claire in a letter of about 1870 to E. J. Trelawny: 'Before we parted at Geneva he [Byron] turned over with me the situation.'[29] Byron's suggestion was that the child should be brought up, when it was born, by his half-sister, Augusta Leigh. Claire objected.

> To this I objected on the ground that a Child always wanted a parent's care at least till seven years old . . . He yielded and said it was best it should live with him—he promised faithfully never to give it until seven years of age into a stranger's care. I was to be called the Child's Aunt and in that character I could see it & watch over it without injury to anyone's reputation.

This ultimately unworkable compromise was the best Byron would offer at the moment, probably as a way of getting rid of Claire, who was to go to England for the birth. As Byron offhandedly wrote to Augusta Leigh towards the end of the year, 'P.S.—I forget to tell you—that the *Demoiselle*—who returned to England from Geneva—went there to produce a new baby B.—who is now to make his appearance.'

3 *Allegra (1817–1818)*

The Shelley party—Shelley himself, Mary, their child William, Elise, (William's Swiss nurse), and Claire—left Geneva on 29 August 1816, arriving in England on 8 September. They crossed the Channel to Portsmouth and set off for the West Country, avoiding the Godwins (who knew nothing of Claire's affair with Byron) for fear of revealing her pregnancy. In Bath, where they settled, the Shelleys, with William and Elise, lived at 5 Abbey Churchyard, while Claire awaited her own child's birth at 12 New Bond Street, where she passed under the name of Mrs Clairmont. Nevertheless, Mary's repressed irritation with Claire continued, and in December she specified what she called '*absentia Clariae*' as most desirable.[1] Encouraged by Shelley, however, Mary found relief in writing her novel, *Frankenstein*.

Claire, for her part, wrote frequently to Byron, begging 'Now pray answer me kindly and do not put any little sarcastic speeches in it.' Her letters received neither acknowledgement nor reply. 'If you do not like to write to C., send me some kind message for her,' wrote Shelley to Byron, knowing her loneliness.

That autumn, Claire's problems were put in perspective by an event that was a shock to them all, and which throws light, incidentally, on the background of Claire and Mary. On 9 October, Fanny Imlay, unobtrusive as always, left London early on the coach for Bristol. On arrival at Bristol she wrote letters to Godwin and to Mary. The letter to Mary arrived at Bath that evening, and at once caused alarm. Mary wrote in her journal: 'In the evening a very alarming letter comes from Fanny—Shelley goes immediately to Bristol—we sit up for him untill two in the morning when he returns but brings no particular news.' Shelley failed to find Fanny in Bristol on 10 October but found traces which sent him next day to Swansea. He returned on 12 October 'with the worst account'. Fanny had been found dead in the Mackworth Arms Hotel, Swansea, where she had taken a fatal dose of laudanum on the night of 9–10 October. Her suicide was reported in the *Cambrian* newspaper for 12 October.[2] She left a suicide note wishing everyone who had been connected with her 'the blessing of forgetting that such a creature ever existed'. Godwin the Philosopher took this wish to surprising lengths. He forbade Mary to go to Swansea, or claim Fanny's body. No member of the family went to her anonymous pauper funeral, and Godwin later put it about that she had died of a fever following a severe cold.

Fanny's suicide suggests that she suffered from familial depression; her mother, Mary Wollstonecraft, had herself made two serious suicide attempts, one by taking laudanum, and Mary Godwin, her half-sister by the same mother, likewise suffered from depression. Mary's depressions were not always recognized as such, even by those nearest to her, but they frequently followed some tragic event, like the loss of her baby early in 1815. This familial trait was perhaps the underlying cause of Mary's resentment of Claire. It is often said that Mary's feelings were caused by Claire's tactlessness or insensitivity, but the most likely cause lies in their contrasting heredity—Mary anxious and sensitive to rebuffs, Claire recklessly bold and volatile.

Claire's reactions to any event were often expressed with violence. Her note to Byron on Fanny's suicide is typical.

> Fanny (the daughter of Mary Wollstonecraft and Imlay) has died, and her death was attended by such melancholy consequences as (at least for me) can never be forgotten . . . I never passed such wretched hours. Everything is so miserable that I often wish myself quite dead.

But Claire had great resilience, and threw off her sorrows. This capacity was much appreciated by Shelley, who felt the weight of suffering Mary endured; Claire's lively company, in contrast, always proved his resource when under stress.

Shelley soon had to face an appalling personal crisis. On 10 December 1816 his wife Harriet's body was found in the Serpentine. The event made such an impression on Claire herself that she was able to recall it and the events leading up to it, in a letter written in good faith, sixty years later.[3] The letter suggests that Harriet, in Shelley's perpetual absence from her, had taken a lover and was with child by him. Claire's letter continues:

> Her lover was a Captain in the Indian or Wellington Army I forget which and he was ordered abroad. His letters did not reach her—with her sister's concurrence she retired for her accouchment to live with a decent couple in a Mews near Chapel St her sister without telling either Harriett's or her own name, placed her there saying she was her lady's maid, was married and that her husband was abroad as a Courier.

In these lodgings her sister visited her and found her wretched. Harriet felt her lover intended to abandon her as Shelley had done. Claire went on:

> She went into the park and threw herself into the Serpentine—Her body was not found till next Morning—was taken to St. George's workhouse, an inquest held—and the verdict returned—An unknown woman found drowned.

Claire was able to remember Harriet's story in such detail because it made a deep impression on her. Poor Harriet's situation in many ways resembled her own, about to bear an illegitimate child by a man who seemed not to love her. Her fighting spirit gave her courage for the impending birth, now barely a month away, yet gave her, too, a profound feeling for Harriet's fate.

Shelley's first reaction was to blame everyone else for Harriet's tragedy, and—protecting his own overwrought nerves—to believe the most scandalous stories about Harriet herself. These were fostered by the Godwins, anxious that Mary should become Shelley's legal wife, now that he was no longer a married man. They achieved this largely because Shelley was persuaded by his lawyer—wrongly—that the ceremony would ensure him custody of his two children by his first marriage. For this and many other reasons, Shelley and Mary were married in London on 30 December. If the Godwins thought it strange that Claire was not at the wedding, they were silent about it. She, of course, was about to give birth.

In fact, her baby was born a fortnight later, on 12 January 1817. Safely delivered, it was a little girl. Shelley wrote to Byron to apprise him that Claire had presented him with a daughter. 'I have good news to tell you,' he wrote, 'Claire is safely delivered of a most beautiful girl.'[4] Byron, in his self-centred way, had always assumed he was about to become the father of a son, but in any case thought little of the matter. He was chiefly occupied by his new book, containing the third canto of *Childe Harold*, which Claire had copied for him at Geneva; though Byron remembered being 'half mad during the time of its composition', it now seemed to him 'a fine indistinct piece of poetical desolation'.[5] Shelley, throughout the year, continued to give Byron news of his little girl, her blue-eyed beauty and her health. At the same time, to have an unaccountable infant in their home plunged the Shelleys into difficulties. They said the little girl was 'the child of a friend in London', but this fiction could not last for ever, especially now that Mary and Shelley, since their marriage, were much more in touch with the Godwins. Claire, on the other hand, was utterly fulfilled by the little girl, whom she called Alba, and loved to see her playing with William Shelley.

On 27 February, Shelley and Mary, without Claire, went to Marlow on the Thames. Mary entrusted her baby to Claire and Elise, who were to make him some nightgowns. Shelley took the lease of a small estate called Albion House, though they did not move in until 18 March.

At the beginning of April Godwin visited the family at Marlow for four days. During this time Alba was left with the casual Leigh Hunts at Hampstead. On 6 April, when Godwin had left, the Hunts arrived with their four noisy children, bringing a baby girl of 3 months, described as 'a little cousin'. Claire kindly offered to help them by taking care of this baby, who was of course Alba. The Shelleys, in their simplicity of heart, hoped to deceive their neighbours by this artless ruse. The walled garden, where the visiting Hunt children played with the babies, was shaded by a cedar tree. Across the coach road, a field path led to where Shelley's skiff was moored on the river. On the far shore, paths wound through water meadows and wooded hills. This was a place and time of intense pleasure. Mary read by the fireside, the children talked an incomprehensible language of their own, the cat and kittens slept under the sofa. Claire spent most of her days playing with Alba, walking in the countryside, and finishing the story she had begun in the 'ghostly' evening at Geneva.[6] Shelley failed to find a publisher for her, though Mary's completed *Frankenstein* triumphed on its own merits. Claire showed no jealousy. A sure source of happiness for her was the time she spent singing and practising music. Shelley ordered a piano, which arrived at the Marlow house on 29 April.[7] In the evenings, Claire played and sang by candle-light. Her singing inspired Shelley's poem 'To Constantia Singing', of which the second stanza is perhaps the most frank.

> I have no life, Constantia, but in thee
> Whilst, like the world-surrounding air, thy song
> Flows on, and fills all things with melody:
> Now is thy voice a tempest swift and strong,
> On which, as one in trance, upborne,
> Secure o'er rocks and waves I sweep,
> Rejoicing, like a cloud of morn.
> Now 'tis the breath of summer's night,

> Which, where the starry waters sleep,
> Round western isles, with incense-blossoms bright,
> Lingering, suspends my soul in its voluptuous flight.

Claire, casually in passing, drew poems both from Byron and from Shelley; Byron's poem pays a charming compliment, Shelley's stanza reveals deep feeling.

Claire was overcome by the experience of having her own little girl. The force of maternal love was an experience beyond her imaginings. Her letters to Byron are full of happiness with his little daughter, Alba, with her 'pretty eyes of a deep dazzling blue'. Claire's love for Alba made her fearful of sending the little girl, as she knew she had promised, to live with Byron. On 30 September 1817, Mary wrote to Shelley, who was visiting the Hunts in London, about Claire's attitude to this. 'Claire although she in a blind kind of manner sees the necessity of it, does not wish her to go and will instinctively place all kinds of difficulties in the way.' Mary had already decided that the Shelleys themselves must take the child to Byron, or at any rate be responsible for bringing her to Italy. Otherwise, they would find that 'the fair prospect of Alba's being brought up by her father is taken away'.[8] The Shelleys must therefore go to Italy, which for their own reasons they wished to do, although they were by now a considerable family: a second child, Clara Everina, had been born on 2 September. Two nursemaids would be necessary to cope with these two and with Claire's Alba, since a baby was then carried 'in arms' until it learned to walk. Also circumstances prevented them leaving immediately; they all still lingered at Marlow, unable yet to sell the leasehold of Albion House.

A close neighbour and friend at Marlow was the satirical novelist Thomas Love Peacock. Claire may well have served as the model for Stella in his *Nightmare Abbey*:

> . . . a female form and countenance of dazzling grace and beauty, with long flowing hair of raven blackness, and large black eyes of almost oppressive brilliancy, which strikingly contrasted with a complexion of snowy whiteness. Her dress was extremely elegant, but had an appearance of foreign fashion.[9]

Peacock was so attracted that he proposed to her, but she refused, her life perhaps filled with love for her child. Yet she trusted Peacock and valued his friendship all her life.[10]

In the New Year, Claire took up her journal again. Godwin, who came down to stay on 20 January 1818, commented, in a letter to his wife, how attractive Claire now looked, further evidence of her happiness at Marlow. Alba again was left with the Hunts during his visit. Godwin had brought with him his own 14-year-old son William: 'William teazes me all day. He is a strange Creature,'[11] Claire commented. They went for walks and played chess. On 25 January came the news that Albion House had been sold. There was nothing now to prevent Shelley from taking his miscellaneous family to Italy, where Alba would be handed over to Byron. As a preliminary, they all went, in various stages, to London.

On 9 March 1818, Claire had Byron's daughter baptised at St Giles-in-the-Fields. At Byron's insistence, little Alba was christened 'Allegra', which Byron claimed was a Venetian name. Claire, however, stressed the link between herself and the child by having her baptised 'Clara Allegra'—the 'Clara' possibly also echoing the name that Shelley had chosen for his own daughter. The full certificate therefore reads 'Clara Allegra Byron, born of Rt. Hon. George Gordon Lord Byron ye reputed Father by Clara Mary Jane Clairmont.' The father's residence was entered as 'No fixed residence. Travelling on the Continent,' and his rank was entered as 'Peer'. At the same ceremony, Shelley's William and Clara were also christened,[12] probably at the insistence of Mary Shelley.

Claire adored her child with primitive, instinctive devotion. She took a sensuous pleasure in Allegra's beauty, her brilliant blue eyes, her curls, her stubborn Byron chin. She wrote proudly to Allegra's father:

> My affections are few and therefore strong—the extreme solitude in which I live has concentrated them to one point and that point is my lovely child. I study her pleasure all day long—she is so fond of me that I hold her in my arms till I am nearly falling on purpose to delight her. We sleep together and if you knew the extreme happiness I feel when she nestles close to me, in listening to our regular breathing together, I could tear my flesh in twenty thousand different directions to ensure her good.

Byron may have felt the appeal for tenderness in this letter; he certainly felt the implied threat of such scenes, which he later called Claire's 'Bedlam behaviour'.

A few days later, the whole party set off for the Continent. It was a collection of three small children, William, Clara, and Allegra, and five adults, Shelley, Mary, Claire, the Swiss nurse Elise, and Milly Shields, a nursery maid from Marlow. The excitement of going abroad made Claire ecstatic; Dover by night seemed 'almost like a fairy city from the multitude of lights that are sprinkled here & there over the hills'. Next morning, on the beach, Claire dipped Allegra, her first sea-bathing.[13] Claire's youthful exhilaration lasted the whole of this journey to Italy, and almost made her forget that its purpose was to surrender Allegra to Byron, with whom she obstinately believed herself to be in love. 'My dearest Lord Byron best of human beings you are the father of my little girl and I cannot forget you.'[14] She was living in a dream: 'Why might not the father and mother of a child whom both so tenderly love meet as friends?'

This dream coloured all her progress south: the stormy though luckily swift crossing to Calais, Calais itself, where Shelley bought a carriage for the party, and the journey through the Alps to Italy and its soft, warm air.[15] Claire wrote: 'The fruit trees covered with the richest blossoms which scented the air as we passed. A sky without one cloud—everything bright & serene—the cloudless sky of Italy—the bright & the beautiful.' She saw the beauty of nature through the transforming glass of Shelley's imagination. His delight in changing scenes and seasons became hers. Italy's cities, Turin and Milan, were equally delightful to her. Milan Cathedral enchanted her. 'I can conceive of no building that partakes more perfectly of the nature of air & heaven. The carved pinnacles whiter than snow rise into the cloud.'[16] An even greater delight in Milan was a visit to the Opera House and the superb performance of a ballet based on *Othello*. This, she wrote:

> embodies the idea I had formed of the ancient dances of the bacchantes. It is full of mad and intoxicating joy, which nevertheless is accompanied by voluptuousness . . . the Desdemona is a lovely creature. Her walk is more like the sweepings of the wind than the steps of a mortal, and her attitudes are pictures.[17]

She also found time at Milan to read nine plays by Molière and a life of Tasso. Claire spent as much time as she could with Allegra, now 15 months old, before surrendering her to Byron. Each afternoon and evening, she took her for a ride round the city Corso. Later each evening, she usually played chess with Shelley, who was negotiating by letter with Byron on her behalf. Byron insisted that he could not possibly come from Venice to fetch his daughter himself. Suspecting that Claire would use Allegra to work on his feelings, he refused outright to meet her, 'for fear that the consequence might be an addition to the family'. Shelley rebuked him for this attitude.[18] 'Nothing but discomfort', Claire noted in her journal, after Shelley had received Byron's discouraging letter. Shelley himself was more explicit in his reply to Byron:

> C., as you may imagine, is dreadfully unhappy . . . You write as if from the instant of its departure all future intercourse were to cease between Claire and her child. This I cannot think you ought to have expected, or even to have desired . . . What should we think of a woman who should resign her infant child with no prospect of ever seeing it again, even to a father in whose tenderness she entirely confided? Surely, it is better if we err, to err on the side of kindness than of rigour.[19]

He admitted that Claire had written unreasonable letters to Byron, but he felt this was natural considering a mother's feelings. At all events, Allegra left Milan with the Swiss nurse Elise for Venice on 28 April, and arrived safely there during the first week in May. By this time, Claire and the Shelleys had left Milan for Pisa after a stormy journey through the Appenines.[20] At Pisa on 8 May they received a reassuring letter from Elise, writing that they had arrived in Venice and that Allegra was safely with her father.[21]

Claire wrote nothing at the time about her parting with Allegra, yet fifty years later she could still describe the pain: 'In the spring of 1818 I sent my little darling to him. She was the only thing I had to love—the only object in the world I could call my very own: and I had never parted with her from her birth, not for an hour even.' This had been perhaps her first experience of adult emotion. She had coasted along the surface of life on a high tide of imagination: a girl with a great poet as her lover, a youthful mother playing with her child like a beautiful toy. She maintained the dream to the last, driving round the Corso with Allegra as though happiness could have no ending; but when the time of parting came, Claire became in reality a mother who had lost her child. All the promise of a brilliant position in life for Allegra could not weigh in the balance for Claire; she wrote plaintively 'so dreadfully had he made me suffer, the chill of Death fell upon my heart'. Yet meanwhile, life must be lived.

After only a couple of days in Pisa, visiting the Leaning Tower and the Baptistery, Claire and the Shelleys moved on to Leghorn and the small but sociable English colony there. The leader of this circle was 48-year-old Maria Gisborne, widow of an English architect of liberal tendencies named Reveley.

Before her first husband's death, she had helped Godwin to nurse the infant Mary, and Godwin had actually proposed marriage to her when Reveley died. She, however, rejected Mary's widower father and married John Gisborne a year later.[22] Gisborne was a businessman of greater intellect than first appeared. The Gisbornes went to trade in Italy, and had been in Leghorn since 1815. With them was Maria's son by her first marriage, Henry Reveley, who had trained as a marine engineer under John Rennie, and who by this time was about 30 years old. He had a workshop for engines in Leghorn, which greatly interested Shelley.

Mr and Mrs Gisborne, Henry, Shelley, Mary, and Claire made up a small family party. The Gisbornes advised the Shelleys, who disliked the town of Leghorn almost as much as they had disliked Pisa, to take a house in Bagni di Lucca, one day's ride from Leghorn. Bagni di Lucca, to which they moved on 11 June with Claire,[23] was a charming place, a small spa resort on a little hill not far from Lucca itself, with summer villas among the wooded slopes and fresh springs, much favoured by English visitors. Claire, Mary, and Shelley all took up horse-riding in the surrounding countryside. Claire, who adopted the new activity with typical enthusiasm but little immediate skill, had a number of falls; she paid very little attention to them, however, delighting in the flowery meadows and the chestnut woods through which they rode while listening to the birdsong. The delightfully warm, fine weather suited their health. They were happy in their lodgings, the comfortable Casa Bertini, and satisfied with its staff, blissfully unaware that the skill and efficiency of the general factotum, Paolo Foggi, extended to cheating them.

Claire fretted continually to see Allegra. She persuaded Shelley to take her to Venice, and on 17 August they left, taking with them the useful servant Foggi, an act they were later to regret. They arrived after a hard three-day journey in the blazing peak of the Italian summer. Allegra, they found, was not with her father, who was having a riotous time with various Venetian mistresses, but had been deposited with the English consul-general's wife, Mrs Richard Belgrave Hoppner, at the consular building. It was here that Claire saw Allegra again, after a lapse of two and a half months. The child seemed paler than usual, though as Shelley said, 'as beautiful as ever'.

Hoppner and Shelley agreed that Claire's visit should be concealed from Byron. When Shelley called on Byron at his Palazzo on the Grand Canal to arrange future visits, he therefore pretended first that he was alone, and that Mary and Claire were in Padua. In fact Mary was still at Bagni di Lucca. Byron, seeing a way to avoid a risky encounter with Claire, invited Shelley to bring Mary, Claire, and the children to his own country villa in the grounds of a ruined castle at Este in the Euganean Hills. Shelley accepted the offer; he and Claire, with Elise and Allegra, at once settled in the villa with its view of the plain of Lombardy and the changing clouds. To maintain the fiction, Shelley wrote immediately to Mary and asked her to leave Bagni di Lucca at once with the small children and come by forced stages to join them, leaving before dawn. Preoccupied with his plan, he failed to foresee the disasters that could follow. 'Bustle' and 'Packing' recorded Mary's journal for 30 August, her 21st birthday.[24] Little Clara, who was cutting her teeth, developed dysentery on the hot, jolting journey. By the time they reached Este on 5 September she was weak, exhausted, and dehydrated almost to a skeleton. Shelley, though 'somewhat uneasy', determined to take the baby to Venice to consult a doctor, but on the crossing by gondola she had convulsions. While Shelley went to look for a doctor, Clara died in Mary's arms in the hall of an inn. Claire learned of the tragedy in a letter from Shelley.

Claire, knowing that Mary regarded her as the underlying cause of this tragedy because it was related to her insistence on seeing Allegra, took Allegra and returned to Este. Mary may well have blamed Shelley too, for his willingness to subordinate their own family to Claire's clamorous demands.[25] Certainly, the heart-breaking consequences of the way in which Shelley had risked the health of their baby caused one of Mary's deepest and most sustained depressions, which lasted until the birth of a further child, Percy Florence, a year later in November 1819. Even then, Mary felt herself estranged from Shelley at times by a fitful coldness when she felt herself freeze. Claire, with her changing moods, occasional outbursts of anger, and healthy resilience, was better adapted to his vagaries.

The many fine poems Shelley now began to write reflect his sense of melancholy and self-reproach for Clara's death. *Julian and Maddalo* seeks consolation in its description of Allegra.

> A lovelier toy sweet nature never made;
> A serious, subtle, wild, yet gentle being,
> Graceful without design, and unforeseeing;
> With eyes—Oh speak not of her eyes!—which seem
> Twin mirrors of Italian heaven . . .

This poem, and what Shelley called 'all my saddest verses raked up in a heap', his *Lines written in the Euganean Hills*, were probably begun in Este at this time.[26] They herald a new advance in Shelley's poetry. Twenty years later, Mary Shelley wrote of this period that 'many hours were passed when his thoughts . . . became gloomy, and then he escaped to solitude, and in verses, which he hid for fear of wounding me, poured forth morbid but too natural bursts of discontent and sadness'.[27]

On 13 October 1818, Shelley tried to get Byron to allow Allegra to stay a little longer at Este with Claire; but Byron, perhaps chary of the influence of Claire on their child, refused to extend his permission.[28] Shelley eventually returned Allegra to the Hoppners on 29 October, and after a short visit, the Shelley party, taking Milly and Elise with them, left for Ferrara and then Bologna on their way to Rome. They reached Rome on 20 November, after a gruelling journey across the Appenines, and spent a week there together. Shelley then went ahead to secure lodgings in Naples. When Mary and Claire arrived in Naples on 1 December they were delighted by the rooms he had hired, which had a splendid view over the Bay of Naples. On 8 December they visited Pozzuoli to see the volcanic material at Solfatara and the bubbling pits of lava there. They visited the coast by boat and after a long day's expedition returned to Naples by moonlight. Shelley commented: 'What colours there were in the sky, what radiance in the evening star, & how the moon was encompassed by a light unknown to our regions!'[29]

The next major expedition, on 16 December, was the ascent of Mount Vesuvius, with its smokey, purple plume. Mary and Shelley rode on mules, while Claire, who did not feel well, was in a palanquin, carried by four men. After the long scramble through the ashes in the gathering dusk, they made their descent guided by torchlight and what Shelley called the 'horrible cries' of the guides. In the same letter, but with a swing of mood, he wrote that the ferocious southern Neapolitans 'began to sing in chorus some fragment of their wild but sweet national music'.[30]

The pleasure of Mary and Claire was marred when Shelley found himself overcome by what he called 'intense bodily suffering'. Claire, still ailing when they reached home, took to her bed for the day. Mary commented 'We are much fatigued and Shelley very ill.'

Shelley at this time was obsessed by the contrast between the natural beauties of the Italian landscape and the Italian women, 'disgusting with ignorance and prostitution'.[31] This prejudice, it seems, was absorbed by Claire, for when Byron later suggested that Allegra should be educated in Italy, Claire responded with a horrified condemnation of 'the state of ignorance and profligacy of Italian women'.[32]

The stay in Naples was marred for Shelley by Mary's continuing estrangement after Clara's death and her continued depression. As a result, on impulse he took a desperate and, as it proved, dangerous step. On 27 February 1819, without consulting Mary, he signed before a Neapolitan magistrate a false statement that Mary had borne him a child two months earlier, on 27 December 1818, and named the child Elena Adelaide Shelley.[33] This child, whom Shelley, in later letters, referred to as 'my poor Neapolitan', 'my Neapolitan', and 'my Neapolitan charge'—though never, significantly, as '*my child*'—was, it certainly appears, a Neapolitan orphan. Shelley registered Elena as his and Mary's, and placed her with foster parents to prepare for her legal adoption later into Shelley's own family. His idea was that an adopted girl-child might lift Mary's 'deep feeling of misery' at the loss of Clara. This is slightly more credible if one remembers that in August 1814, Shelley and Mary, on their journey towards Besançon, had wanted to adopt a French girl, Marguerite Pascal, but failed to persuade the child's father.[34] In Naples, Mary played no part in the adoption; would an unknown foundling have comforted her for the loss of 'my little Clara' who 'pined a few weeks and died'? This was never put to the test. All that Shelley's obscure manœuvre achieved was to lay himself, Mary, and also Claire open to later threats of blackmail. These arose two and a half years later, through their scheming servant, Paolo Foggi, who had accompanied them to Naples, and who had, it transpired, made their Swiss maid, Elise, pregnant. They married him off to Elise in January 1819 and dismissed both. Shelley's unconventional ideas did not extend to people of the servant class.

4 *No Permanent Township* *(1819–1820)*

The Shelley party returned to Rome on 5 March 1819 and instantly felt a lift in their spirits. Claire, taking up her journal again, recorded the delightful weather and sights. 'Walk in the public gardens—Go to the Fontana di Trevis and to the Pantheon now called La Rotunda—Walk with Shelley to the Capitol, to the Forum & the Coliseum—A beautiful & mild Spring Evening.'[1] Later that evening she revisited the Pantheon, and saw it by moonlight in the mild, milky weather.

Mary, too, was affected by the atmosphere of their pleasant surroundings at 300 Corso, where a parade of cheerful street-life passed by every evening. She had a further cause for happiness: on 9 April, she announced by letter to Maria Gisborne that she was expecting another child, a comfort at last to her grief over the death of little Clara.

Claire, meanwhile, was lyrical about her own daily walks with Shelley.

Go to the Capitol and the Coliseum—We range over every part—along the narrow grassy walks on the tops of the arches—above us on the nodding ruins grew the wallflowers in abundance—the Coliseum resembles a mountain, its arches and recesses appear as so many caves, & here and there are spread as in the most favoured of Nature's spots, grassy platforms with a scattered fruit or thorn tree in blossom—I think there can be nothing more delightful than a daily walk over the Capitol to visit the ruins of the Forum. In ancient times the Forum was to a city what the soul is to the Body.[2]

In the evening of 19 March, Claire went again to the Coliseum with Shelley and saw it, as she wrote in her journal, 'under the grey eye of twilight'.

Claire's usual evening visits in Rome were to the apartments of the Signora Marianna Dionigi. The *conversazione* of the elderly, widowed intellectual took place at 310 Corso, only a few doors from the Shelleys. Claire went up the dark stairs to the lady's informal rooms on almost every other day until the Signora left Rome on 27 April for her little villa in the country. Mary did not like her, but Claire was delighted by her and the interesting people she met in her circle. She especially appreciated the Signora's knowledge of music. Claire took piano and singing lessons nearly every day from an Italian music master called Bandelloni, whose moderate fees were paid for her by Shelley. She practised with enthusiasm, and he found her voice of even beauty through its whole range, 'like a string of pearls'. She also learnt fluent Italian, found it easy to talk with Italians of every degree, and was amused by her compatriots who could not. Her journal recorded:

In the Evening go to the Conversazione of the Signora Marianna Dionigi, where there is a Cardinal and many unfortunate Englishmen, who after having crossed their legs & said nothing the whole evening, rose up all at once, made their bows & filed off.

Shelley's response to classical Rome was to take up the idea of a lyric drama, *Prometheus Unbound*, with which he had been experimenting for the past few months. Inspired by his walks about Rome, he completed three acts of the work, with its philosophic speeches and intensely musical lyric interludes.

In spite of Shelley's creative happiness, there were, as always in his life, sinister and inexplicable incidents. Both Claire and Mary refer in their journal entries for 5 May to 'S's adventure at the Post Office'. According to a later account, Shelley, in asking for the poste-restante letters, was approached by a tall, military-looking stranger who exclaimed, 'What, are you that damned atheist Shelley?', and promptly knocked him down. This incident may have arisen from gossip about Shelley's rash claims to atheism in hotel registers at Chamonix, three years before.[3] It is not certain what in fact happened;[4] the word 'adventure', used by Claire and Mary, hardly suggests a knock-down attack.

On the day after the suppositious incident at the Post Office, the Shelley party moved from 300 Corso to Via Sestina, just off the Spanish Steps and the piazza of Trinità dei Monti. It is not clear whether the two events were in fact connected. We know that while walking in the Borghese Gardens a fortnight earlier, Claire had met Miss Amelia Curran, whom she had met previously at Skinner Street with the Godwins. Miss Curran lived alone, and her main occupation was painting. Claire and the Shelleys called on her in her lodgings at 64 Via Sestina, and found her an enjoyable companion with Irish sprightliness and Radical opinions. Claire began to sit for a portrait by Miss Curran, who eventually painted not only her but Shelley, Mary, and the small boy William. In her repeated visits she discovered that the house next door in the Via Sestina had rooms to be let. Thus they came to be next-door neighbours of Amelia Curran.

The sittings took longer than they expected, and Claire, like many sitters, was not fully satisfied by the results. The portrait shows her bright cheeks and curling raven hair, but it lacks the vitality which was her chief charm; indeed, it almost resembles a wooden doll. Miss Curran herself was doubtful about her likeness of Shelley, which was sentimental and idealized. The tragedy of these prolonged portrait sittings is that they delayed the Shelley family's departure from Rome, with disastrous effect. Mary had written to Maria Gisborne on 9 April that they were delighted with Rome, and that nothing but malaria would drive them from it for many months,[5] but unfortunately, typically of the Shelley household, this awareness of the dangers of malaria was forgotten in the excitement of new friendship with Amelia Curran. The Tiber marshes were becoming stagnant in the increasing heat, and, unknown to the Shelleys, the malarial mosquitoes were breeding. On 25 May, William, aged 4, the gentle, affectionate Willmouse who had played with Allegra, and whom everybody loved, fell ill with the high fever, sweats, and chills of malaria. Claire had not been present during Clara's fatal illness, but now she was at hand to share the nursing, the search for remedies, and Mary's frantic fear that she might lose yet another child. Claire sat up with Willmouse during his sleepless, restless nights, grateful for the presence of Mr Bell 'one of the first English surgeons'; she even allowed herself to hope, during the chills of evening, that the little boy might recover. On 2 June, 'William very ill—Mr. Bell calls three times—I sit up.' On 5 June, she wrote on Mary's behalf to Mrs Gisborne, 'Our poor little William is at present very ill and the Shelleys well were it not for the dreadful anxiety they now suffer.' William, like Clara, developed convulsions, or lay in exhausted silence. On 7 June he died. Claire was so moved by his untimely going that she could only enter under the date in her journal the words 'At noon-day'. Writing later to Mrs Hunt, Mary Shelley exclaimed: 'May you my dear Marianne never know what it is to loose [sic] two only & lovely children in one year.'[6]

The Shelley family and Claire left Rome on 10 June, travelling north for cooler weather. Reaching Leghorn on 17 June, they settled at the Villa Valsovano, three kilometres south of the town, and renewed their friendship with the Gisbornes. Claire attempted to support Mary, who was once more in the depths of grief. 'Everything on earth', she wrote to Amelia Curran, 'has lost its interest to me.'[7] Miss Curran was ordering a tomb for William in the Protestant cemetery, Rome, where, though Claire could not know, eighteen months later, Keats was to lie. For consolation, she again took up her music, this time taking lessons both in accompaniment and singing.[8] Shelley, of course, paid for them, as well as for the outstanding Rome lessons, which he had left unpaid in his anxiety.

On 4 September, Claire's brother Charles, who had been travelling in Spain for the past fifteen months, arrived at the Villa Valsovano to stay with the Shelleys. His visit was particularly welcome to Shelley because, influenced by Maria Gisborne, he was at the time making a study of the plays of a Spanish poet, Calderon. There is no doubt that Shelley's 'Calderonizing' helped to colour his Shakespearian-style tragedy *The Cenci*, and partly because Charles's presence helped to increase the influence of the Spanish poet, Shelley was inspired to finish his own dramatic work. Charles's cheerful nature helped to counteract Mary's grief at William's death—'I should have died on the 7th of June last', she said, when the future looked utterly empty.[9] More specifically, when Mary on 9 September received one of her father's 'philosophical' letters, warning that sorrow would leave her 'a prey to apathy and languor of no use to any earthly creature' and that in consequence her friends would cease to love her, he was able, from his knowledge of Godwin, to attempt to redress the balance. Further letters from Godwin complained abusively that Shelley had not given him enough money for his needs and urged her to force him to give more, though the final total of loans was forty thousand pounds. Godwin's correspondence was so distressing to Mary that Shelley decided to intercept the letters.

In order for Mary to have her next baby under the care of the English physician John Bell who had attended William so conscientiously, if in vain, the Shelleys on 30 September set off for Florence, taking Claire and Charles with them. On 10 November Charles left for Vienna, where he hoped to find employment as a teacher of English, although he had meanwhile fallen in love with one of the daughters of their landlady in Florence, Madame du Plantis of Via Valfonda 4395. On 12 November, at that address, Mary gave birth to a son, Percy Florence Shelley, and was, as she said, no longer childless. 'Poor M begins (for the first time) to look a little consoled', wrote Shelley thankfully. Claire attended the birth of Percy Florence, and shared in the rejoicing at his safe delivery; she was to adore him to the point of folly throughout his childhood and youth, and beyond. In the general relief she enjoyed herself with the lively young Plantis daughters. She also took up music lessons once more, with Gaspero Pelleschi. She admired him as a composer as well as a teacher, and invited him in the evenings to the Shelley lodgings in the Via Valfonda. There he played and sang, much to Claire's pleasure. Via Valfonda had happy associations, and fifty years later Claire would return to live there.

Mary was delighted with her little boy, and had no gloomy forebodings. 'His health is good and he is very lively and even knowing', and her two-hour labour had been easy, in spite of the fact that Dr Bell was not present after all. The only complaint was the exceptionally bad winter weather in Florence, heavy rain which later turned to snow. 'Here is fine Tuscan weather!' Mary exclaimed early in the New Year, 'Wind! Frost! Snow! How can England be worse?'[10] Claire, adaptable as ever, in spite of 'a very very severe frost', cheerfully played at snowballs with the du Plantis family.[11] Her music teacher told her that there had not been such a severe winter in Florence for seventy years, but she felt strong and well and kept up her lessons with him nearly every day. She was also reading the first two cantos of Byron's *Don Juan*, but did not comment on them. Byron himself was in Ravenna, where he was living as the lover of a simple, affectionate, and very pretty married gentlewoman, Teresa Guiccioli. Claire on 12 January 1820 noted her daughter's 3rd birthday. The pretty child was herself at Ravenna, being thoroughly spoilt by Teresa and her servants. Allegrina, as her father called her, was flourishing 'like a pomegranate blossom'. Claire, referring in her journal to Percy Florence Shelley, wrote of him as 'our little babe', and seems always to have maintained an almost maternal attitude to this last, happily surviving child of Shelley and Mary.[12]

The Shelleys, having changed their plans and places of residence so often since they came to Italy, now decided to choose one spot and stick to it. 'We are tired of roving', wrote Mary,[13] and Claire felt so too. They decided on Pisa, which had the advantage of a distinguished Italian physician qualified in Paris and London, Vaccà Berlinghieri, and now professor of medicine in this, his native town. Shelley and Mary, with Claire, left Florence on 26 January 1820. After a rough journey down-river in freezing wind, they first stayed at the Tre Donzelle in this old-fashioned town, and strolled about looking for lodgings, which they found at Casa Frassi Lung'Arno.

Claire's chief friend in Pisa, who became one of the best friends of her life, was Mrs Mason of Casa Silva, the centre of a lively and cultivated social circle. This lady, whom Claire called her 'Minerva', had been a pupil of Mary Wollstonecraft and had published books in Godwin's Juvenile Library. Her name was really Lady Margaret Mountcashell, but having left her husband she went by the name of Mrs Mason. She lived under this name as common-law wife of George William Tighe, known as 'Tatty' because of his Irish enthusiasm for the cultivation of the potato. Claire had an affectionate friendship with their two small girls, Lauretta, aged 10, and Nerina, aged 4. Mrs Mason, in her turn, treated Claire almost as a grown-up daughter. At Casa Silva, early in their acquaintance, they had some stimulating political discussions, and Claire had 'a horrid dream about Skinner Street'.[14] Reading and music occupied Claire—she had found in Pisa an excellent music teacher called Zanetti[15]—and on 8 February she went with Shelley and her music-master to Rossini's opera *Cenerentola*.[16]

Shelley had already had cause to consult the Pisan physician Vaccà, who had advised him to take more healthy exercise. Claire was inclined to be flippant about the professor's diagnosis of her lymph nodes after the hard winter. 'Vaccà calls & says I am scrofulous and I say he is ridiculous.' It might have been better if she had taken his remarks seriously. He suspected inflamed glands in her neck might be tubercular, and she herself later admitted there were tubercular tendencies in her own family. For the time, Vaccà kept an eye on her health, calling frequently and also meeting her socially at Mrs Mason's.[17]

On 14 March, the Shelleys and Claire moved to the top floor of Casa Frassi, where they had more room; Shelley could have a study, and the small Shelley boy more space for play. Claire's days in the Casa Frassi were well filled. Directed by Shelley, she read classical authors such as Anacreon and Aeschylus in Greek, Plutarch in Latin. Her reading in French and Italian was extensive. She went to operas by Mozart and Rossini. To her lessons in music from Zanetti Claire now added dancing lessons by another local teacher, Legerino.[18]

These music and dancing lessons, provided by Shelley, were among the most valuable gifts that he could have given Claire. With her natural skill in music, her innate ability to learn languages, and her accomplishments, Claire was able to maintain what she most valued in life, the prospect of independence. She could move confidently at any level of society. The general education offered by Shelley gave her, whatever happened, qualifications as a governess in families of good standing. Not that Claire knew that in two years Shelley would be dead, and that she would have to stand or fall by her own efforts. As a reminder that Claire should be self-reliant, the news came that Peacock, whom she had rejected in 1818, had just married.[19]

On 12 June, Claire, for no apparent reason, wrote 'Oh Bother' in her journal. Mary, in hers, was more explicit, though, in her way just as cryptic. She wrote 'Paolo', followed by a drawing of a crescent moon. This last symbol was her code-sign for some trouble concerned with Claire.[20] The secret trouble threatening both women was an attempt by their rascally ex-servant, Paolo Foggi, to blackmail Shelley. It is not certain what this blackmail concerned, but it seems likely Foggi suggested that Shelley's so-called 'Neapolitan' was in fact an illegitimate child of Shelley and Claire. Shelley later said Foggi had attempted to extort money 'by attempting to accuse me of the most horrible crimes'. Shelley, unexpectedly prudent, went to an Italian lawyer at Leghorn, who successfully frightened Foggi and made him withdraw his accusation. Mary commented to Maria Gisborne, 'Our old friend Paolo was partly the cause of this—by entering into an infamous conspiracy against us . . . That same Paolo is a most superlative rascal—I hope we have done with him but I know not.' Claire says nothing of Paolo or indeed of the whole affair. Mary, who was still feeding her baby, thought the fright over the blackmail had affected her milk and had given Percy Florence an attack of diarrhoea; this was an added alarm, though luckily soon over.[21]

More to the point, the Paolo scare intensified the bad terms on which Claire and Mary lived. On 4 July, Claire wrote in her journal:

> Heigh-ho the Claire & the Ma
> Find something to fight about every day—[22]

To Mary, Claire was a potential danger to any settled or peaceful existence. On the other hand, to outside observers, such as Claire's 'Minerva', Mrs Mason, the Shelleys were disturbing to Claire's independent development.

In spite of making jokes and writing sprightly rhymes, Claire was less well than she had been in Florence the previous winter. Possibly, she was now beginning to discover the truth of Professor Vaccà's diagnosis. Her temperament was uncertain, her reactions extreme. She referred to Byron as 'my *damn'd Brute*' and to a 'Brutal letter' from him about herself.[23] Admittedly, Byron could be brutal, especially on the subject of Allegra. He persisted in condemning Claire's 'atheism', choosing to forget that she appeared as 'atheist' solely in Shelley's deliberately provocative entries in hotel registers. For many reasons, then, Claire was in an unsettled state of mind and of health, and the kindly Mrs Mason was troubled about her.

Mrs Mason's solution was that Claire should separate herself from the somewhat feverish company of the Shelleys, above all from Mary Shelley's brooding dislike. It would be better for her to live apart with a well-educated Italian family, and so acquire an entry into good Italian society. Mrs Mason proposed that Claire should live as a paying guest with certain duties in a well-known family in Florence. This was the household of Professor Antonio Bojti, a distinguished physician and surgeon. He was friend and doctor to the Medici ruler of Florence, the Grand Duke Ferdinand the Third, and lived opposite his patron, across the square from the Pitti Palace.[24] Claire would move in good society and company, a solid background very different from that of the Shelleys and their haphazard lives.

Claire now learnt how the Shelleys were regarded by other English expatriates. The Gisbornes had lent the Shelley family their house in Leghorn while they were temporarily in England, and on their return, Shelley had found his erstwhile friends strangely cold to him. They had visited the Godwins while in England and heard Mrs Godwin's usual diatribe on Shelley and how he had ruined Claire's chances of leading a good or useful life. While Shelley himself was indignant at this, their view in many ways confirmed that of Mrs Mason. To Claire in her overwrought state, it seemed there was a conspiracy by everyone to separate her from Shelley. It may have been in May 1820, while she was in this mood, that Henry Reveley, Mrs Gisborne's son by her first marriage, proposed to Claire and was refused. The decorous Reveley, much under his mother's thumb, would have been a singularly unlikely husband for Claire.

Whatever the causes, Claire was disturbed when she first went to the Bojtis in October 1820. Otherwise, it seemed that Mrs Mason, anxious for her well-being, had made an admirable choice. Professor Bojti was only 42 and had a young and lively family—several girls and a small boy (the 'Bimbo'). Claire would teach the children

English as part-payment for her board and lodging. Bojti, originally from Rome, had been in Florence in the service of the Grand Duke since 1805. The professor had married a German wife, and his mother-in-law, 'die Grossmütter', lived with them in Florence. Claire added to her stock of languages by learning German 'Begin to learn the German verb *ich bin* (I am).'[25] As her knowledge of German grew, she may have begun to form the idea that she might eventually join Charles in Vienna.

Claire travelled to Florence with Shelley on 20 October, and, having moved into the Bojti house on the next day, said good-bye. She was unwilling to leave him, and he was reluctant to lose her lively company. 'Your absence', he wrote, 'is too painful for your return ever to be unwelcome.' His first letters to her emphasize that he is feeling physically ill without her, and seemed confident that she shared his sufferings. He will not part with her. He is only letting her go, it appears, because Mrs Mason has advised it, and he reminds her that she is only at the Bojtis for a trial month. There is no doubt she felt lonely before she had fully settled down, however friendly and kind the Bojtis might be. 'I am not well today' she wrote, as outside the rain fell in torrents. After a week in their house, she entered in her journal a sentiment which she was after to repeat about her life: 'Think of thyself as a stranger & traveller, on the earth, to whom none of the many affairs of this world, belong and who has no permanent township on the globe.'[26]

5 *The Fiery Comet (1820–1822)*

Claire's feelings of isolation proved only temporary. She settled to life with the Bojti family, taking the older children, Louisa and Annina, for walks in the terraces of the Boboli Gardens, among the small evergreen trees, statues, and fountains. She also strolled with Ska Bojti in the busy, lively town. In letters to Mary she at first complained of dullness, but her sense of humour was still acute, and she enjoyed visits to the opera and ballet with her friendly hostess. She also let her excessive blame of Byron overflow into amusing caricatures, picturing him drinking coffee with a mistress stinking horribly of garlic.

Shelley took a gloomy view of Claire's absence and pounced avidly on gossip from fellow-Florentines who thought Claire's expression sad; 'they tell me you looked very melancholy and disconsolate'. Such comments perhaps served to reassure him that she was missing him. Yet the truth was somewhat different: she felt at home with the doctor and his wife, and very soon became one of the family. After dinner she walked with the elder daughters on the Lung'Arno, and in the evening played with the children and their friends. On All Saints day she allowed some Shelleyan mockery into her journal. ('The words for piety, decorum, behaviour, respect for the opinions of the world are nothing but the coverings people put upon their souls when like Adam & Eve placing the fig leaf they are ashamed of its deformity.') This sounds nothing like a disconsolate exile from home. Even rain all day did not depress her; she wrote tersely, 'I work. Read Hyperion of Keats.'

There was one special reason why Shelley took a gloomy view of Claire's absence. He was continually depressed by nephritis, sudden inflammation of the kidneys, during which he would roll in agony, to the alarm of those who saw him. These attacks left him desiring Claire's lively and cheerful conversation, 'your sweet consolation, my own Claire'. For this and many reasons he deeply missed her, finding little relief in Mary despite their love. His nearest companion was his cousin, Tom Medwin, who had come to stay now that Claire's room was free. Shelley, as he often did, grasped at vague plans for sailing to the East. He tried to involve Claire in this, asking her to find out Arabic grammars for him, but mainly, one suspects, to interest her in his life and schemes. Mary and her small baby are hardly mentioned in his letters to Claire.

On 21 November, her trial month being up, Claire returned for a holiday to the Shelleys at Pisa. Here she met Tom Medwin. Among other things, his description of her shows how life without the Shelleys in Florence had developed her personality. He commented on her appearance and nature at this time:

> She might have been mistaken for an Italian, for she was a *brunette* with very dark hair and eyes . . . She possessed considerable accomplishments—spoke French and Italian, particularly the latter, with all its *nuances* and niceties . . . Though not strictly handsome at that time, for she had had much to struggle with, and mind makes its ravages in the fairest, most, she was engaging and pleasing, and possessed an *esprit de société* rare among our countrywomen.[1]

He also thought Claire older and more experienced than she was by several years.

Just over a week after Claire's return to Pisa she was taken by an Italian friend to meet a remarkably beautiful young Italian girl, Teresa Emilia Viviani, daughter of the governor of Pisa, who had been placed by her parents in the Convent of St Anna pending a suitable offer of marriage. According to Medwin, she was striking: 'Her profuse black hair, tied in the most simple knot, after the manner of a Greek Muse . . . Her features possessed a rare faultlessness, and almost Grecian contour.'[2] Emilia chafed at her confinement in the convent, and compared herself to a captive lark in a cage. Claire felt that Emilia was just the person to excite Shelley, as his first wife Harriet Westbrook had done a few years earlier, beautiful and apparently in some way wronged; she told Shelley of her beauty.

Claire returned to Florence on 23 December, after a farewell visit to Emilia at the convent on the previous day. She left Emilia to provide inspiration for Shelley. To Claire this was in the nature of things. As she wrote, 'a great Poet resembles Nature—he is a creator and a destroyer; he presides over the birth & death of images, the prototypes of things . . . which like the fire of Vesta should burn perpetually bursting by fits into flame & strength according to the subjects.' Meanwhile, Claire had her own problems. Though she was manifestly happy with the Bojtis in Florence, her health was not good, and Dr Vaccà renewed his warning that a gland in her neck might be infected. The gland was opened and drained on New Year's Day 1821, of course without anaesthesia, probably by Dr Bojti himself. 'My gland is opened—I am ill all the day,' wrote Claire tersely; but after recovering from the operation, her health proved much better. She went out into society, and began to enjoy herself in the lively atmosphere of Florence, especially among the extensive Russian and Polish colony; she also made a large number of new Italian friends.[3]

Claire next appears in the setting of a poem by Shelley. This was *Epipsychidion*, which he wrote at white-heat in February. It is the largest piece of semi-disguised autobiography he ever attempted. Dedicated to Emilia Viviani, Emilia symbolizes the Sun. Mary provides a different kind of inspiration under the guise of the Moon. Claire, herself, erratic but also in her manner inspiring, appears as the Comet.

> Thou too, O Comet, beautiful and fierce,
> Who drew the heart of this frail Universe
> Towards thine own; till, wrecked in that convulsion,
> Alternating attraction and repulsion,
> Thine went astray and that was rent in twain
> Oh, float into our azure heaven again![4]

It is hard to say how much is extended allegory and how much the genuine effect on Shelley of Claire's variable nature—the 'alternating attraction and repulsion' of which the poem speaks.

On a factual level, Shelley's poem may reflect his sense of isolation from Claire, now in Florence. Claire herself was less affected by Shelley and his idealized love, Emilia, than by any news of Byron and Allegra. On 15 March, she noted in her journal, 'Letters from Emilia, Shelley & Mary with enclosures from Ravenna.' The enclosures contained the news that Byron intended to place the 4-year-old Allegra for her education in the convent at Bagnacavallo, north of Ravenna. As Byron wrote to his half-sister, he intended Allegra 'to become a good Catholic—& (it may be) a *Nun* being a character somewhat wanted in our family.' A jest to Allegra's father was a disaster to her mother. This renewed in Claire the utmost indignation. All her resentment against organized religion, taught by Godwin and fostered by Shelley, was fanned by Shelley's own belief that Emilia was a 'prisoner' of convent education. 'Spent a miserable day' is Claire's comment.[5] Shortly afterwards, in March, she was overcome by one of her uncontrolled rages. She laid aside the German exercises on which she had been working diligently under the tuition of the Bojtis and wrote a furious letter to Byron; it was full of prejudices, threats, and plans, which she must have known she would have been unable to fulfil.[6]

She began by reminding Byron that they had previously agreed, though 'verbally it is true', that their child 'whatever the sex' should never be away from one of its parents. Their agreement, she violently stated, had now been broken by Byron's proposal to place Allegra for her education in a convent. 'I therefore represent to you that the putting of Allegra, at her years, into a convent, away from any relations, is to me a serious and deep affliction.' With mounting fury, she proceeded to a general attack on convents and convent education, and its known effect on Italian women. 'Every traveller and writer upon Italy joins in condemning them, which would be alone sufficient testimony, without adverting to the state of ignorance and profligacy in the Italian women, all pupils of convents.' To Byron, lover of a convent-educated Italian woman, Teresa Guiccioli, Claire then proceeded to spell out the faults of such women. 'They are bad wives,' she wrote, regardless of lack of proof, 'Most immature mothers; licentious and ignorant, they are the dishonour and unhappiness of society. This then,' she rounded off her indictment, 'with every advantage in your power, of wealth, of friends, is the education you have chosen for your daughter.' She accused Byron of depriving Allegra 'of the protection and friendship of her parents' friends (so essential to the well-being of a child in her desolate situation) by the adoption of a different religion and of an education known to be contemptible'.

She then proposed her own plan for Allegra's education. After accusing Byron of neglecting Allegra—'the purity of your principles does not allow you to cherish a natural child'—she states that Allegra must have the benefits her mother can procure for her. She then outlined these benefits. 'I propose to place her, at my own expense, in one of the very best English boarding-schools, where, if she is deprived of a home and paternal care, she at least would receive an English education, which would enable her to be benefited by the kindness and affection of her parents' friends.'

This proposal by Claire was not very different from an alternative that Byron had put forward a year earlier, which Claire dismissed in her journal as 'concerning green fruit & God—a strange Jumble'.[7] Yet in fact Byron had stated his plans for Allegra quite clearly: 'I shall either send her to England, or put her in a Convent for education . . . But the child shall not quit me again to perish of starvation and green fruit, or be taught to believe that there is no Deity.' Claire's alternative to a convent education for Allegra had therefore been made by Byron himself a year earlier, though with characteristic sarcasm towards the Shelley ménage. He had already outlined the same plan to Augusta Leigh—'into a convent or England and put her in some good way of instruction'. Claire had seized Byron's own idea in order to put herself in the right and show herself as a loving mother. There was also a new-found independence in Claire's contributions to the argument. Whereas she had once written to him 'I am so awkward and only feel inclined to sit at your feet',[8] Claire now felt ready, while keeping up a pretended humility in her letters to him on the subject of Allegra, to defy Byron openly in outspoken terms.

There was little hope of the parents agreeing. Claire's chief argument was that by Byron's plan Allegra would be cut off from her mother 'by the adoption of a different religion', Catholicism. On the other hand, Byron himself was at least favourable to the Catholic faith. Only a year later, on 4 March 1822, he wrote:

> I am no enemy to religion, but the contrary. As a proof, I am educating my natural daughter a strict Catholic in a convent of Romagna; for I think people can never have *enough* of religion, if they are to have any. I incline, myself, very much to the Catholic doctrines.[9]

Claire's attacks on Catholicism could only anger him. He sincerely believed that Allegra should be brought up as a Catholic, and that she would not be thereby 'condemned', in Claire's words, 'to a life of ignorance and degradation'. It was the impasse of two stubborn people, opposing two fixed prejudices.

Yet there was no doubting Claire's sincere anxiety for the welfare of her 4-year-old child. Her desperate enquiries to Byron showed her trying to visualize Allegra's situation in every way. How far, she asked, was Bagnacavallo from Ravenna? Was it inland or near the coast? It stood, as she must soon have found out, a small town, whose walls and towers rose from fields green with vines and spinach. Between this and Ravenna, about fifteen miles to the south, were low-lying marshes in the flat land. From March 1821, Claire began to imagine Allegra's situation in everything she did, or even what she read. On 12 April, reading of Dante's joy at refinding a copy of his *Divine Comedy*, she commented: 'So would it be to me if I recovered Allegra as if I had come back to the warmth of life after the cold stiffness of the grave.'[10] She began, in her restless sleep, to have dreams of Allegra being unaccountably restored to her own keeping. Later in April, she dreamed that Tatty (Mr Mason) had been to Bagnacavallo and brought back Allegra with him. She dreamed of her joy, and how she had exclaimed to Shelley, 'Now she shall never go back again.'

Claire's letters to Byron about Allegra aroused his suspicions that she would use the child to obtain some hold over him. A year earlier, in a letter to Hoppner, Byron had shown himself annoyed at receiving 'the most insolent letters about Allegra', and had commented, 'see what a man gets by taking care of natural children'. He wrote of what he called Claire's 'Bedlam behaviour', and added with sarcasm, 'To express it delicately—I think Madame Claire is a damned bitch—what think you?' Byron clearly saw Claire's natural anxiety over Allegra as something sinister, although Shelley tried to persuade him otherwise. In the light of Byron's harsh comments, Claire's insinuations that he did not care for a natural child seem understandable. Her 23rd birthday appeared 'odious' to her, and three days later she recorded, 'I suffer low spirits.'

Claire's anxiety about Allegra did not, however, destroy her feelings about the fate of others. On the same day, 21 April, as her irrational dream about Allegra's return, she learnt from the Shelleys that on 13 February John Keats had died in Rome. Having met the young poet at Leigh Hunt's and read, in his book of 1820, *Hyperion*, *Isabella*, and *Lamia*, she was clearly moved by the tragedy of that death: 'Thus has been extinguished the brightest promise of genius which England had seen for many days.'[11]

When Shelley, in a later letter, advised Claire to 'seek in the daily and affectionate intercourse of friends a respite', he was perhaps thinking of the benefits he himself was receiving from two new friends, also known to Claire. These were Jane and Edward Williams, whom she had met with the Shelleys at Pisa in the previous year, just before her return to Florence. These new additions to the Shelley circle were introduced to the Shelleys by Medwin. Jane was still married to a man called Johnson, a captain in the East India

Company, whom she had soon deserted. Now she and Williams were lovers, and very charming people. Shelley, free from his infatuation with Emilia Viviani, soon became even more infatuated with Jane, though he had at first written her off as 'apparently not very clever'. Edward was, from the first, a delightful companion. Unable to marry Jane, and believing her when she said her husband had done her some unspecified 'irreparable injuries', Edward Williams did everything to make up for Johnson's alleged brutality. He himself had retired from the army on half-pay on 28 May 1818. In Continental society, where few questions were asked, they were safe to exist as Captain and Mrs Williams, with their 1-year-old son.

Claire was attracted to Edward and Jane whenever she visited Pisa. She and Jane shared a love of music and, most particularly, singing. As with the Constantia poems to Claire at Marlow, Shelley wrote some of his best new Pisan poems to Jane and her singing. He and Mary established a warm and open friendship with Edward and Jane.

On Saturday 23 June 1821, Claire went to Leghorn where she would spend her summer. She travelled with Shelley and Edward Williams. Leghorn began with 'very heavy dark weather'; Claire read, walked, and bathed daily in the official baths in the harbour. By 5 July she thought this dull and turned to an almost unheard of activity for a woman: 'take my first lesson in swimming'. Her teacher, a German holiday acquaintance, seemed enthusiastic. Fearless, Claire found the sea exciting: 'The waves extremely high—The waves jump down my throat', or when she bathed at six in the morning, 'Water of an icy coldness'. On a blowy day she recorded 'the foam of the sea dashing up in the distance over the rocks' looking like 'masses of white cloud upon the horizon'. Her journal entry for 1 August carries the short, triumphant entry 'Swim by myself.'

Next Friday evening Shelley came to Leghorn to visit Claire. On Saturday morning she was up at five: 'August 4th. S's birthday 29 years. Row to the harbour with S. . . . There we sail out into the sea. A very fine warm day. The white sails of ships upon the horizon looked like doves stooping over the water . . . S. goes at two.' The glow of simple pleasure lights up the day. In such moods Claire was an ideal companion.

Claire was incapable of boredom. During her months of leisure at Pisa and Florence, she held fears for Allegra at bay with continuous reading, a book always at hand. Her choice shows the influence of

Shelley's conversation. She took satirical pleasure in the *Quarterly Review* notice of Southey's *The Life of Wesley* and wrote:

When Wesley preached, violent outcries, howling, gnashing of teeth, frightful convulsions, frenzy, blasphemy, epileptic and apoplectic symptoms were excited in turn on different individuals in the Methodist congregations. Wesley declared they were produced either by the holy ghost or the agency of evil spirits.

She added, in an echo of Shelley's cool tones, 'How very desirable Religion appears to be.' In politics she read the radical Tom Paine on *The American Crisis* and *The Rights of Man*, her stepfather Godwin's *Political Justice*, Ségur's three volumes on the comparative position of women in various societies, and John Locke's *Essays Concerning Human Understanding*. She regularly translated German and Italian classics into French or English, and in June 1820 'Begin also Latin which I pray may continue.' Regular exercises followed, and the pleasure of reading Virgil. She even tackled Tacitus with the help of a crib. For amusement, too, Claire drew on the Shelleys' choice of books: Scott's *The Abbot*, which Mary had read, and *Melincourt* by their friend T. L. Peacock. In the mornings she translated from the German, Kotzebue's *Tales* or Schiller's *Kabale und Liebe*, and after dinner leafed through Edgeworth's *Memoirs*, recommended by Mary.

Keats's *Hyperion* she recognized as a great poem, and she was found reading it more than once. It was one taste she had in common with Byron, who commented on Keats, 'His *Hyperion* is a fine monument & will keep his name.' It was a pity Byron and Claire could not have shared only their appreciation of poetry rather than their daughter Allegra. At about this time, the end of July 1821, Claire read Shelley's poem on the death of Keats, *Adonais*,[12] in which he seems to foretell his own death, or at least the manner of it. She had gone for a holiday from the Bojti family to Pisa and Leghorn, was staying with the Masons, and twice visited Shelley at Bagni di Pisa. The sea-bathing at Leghorn seems to have had a good effect on Claire's health; she rose at six in the morning, walked, and swam; then copied, transposed and practised music, and filled the day with society.

Shelley meantime went to stay with Byron in Ravenna between 6 and 22 August. Here he received some unwelcome news. This was the story which the Shelleys' former servant, Elise, prompted by Paolo, had related the previous year to Mr and Mrs Hoppner: the accusation that Claire had been Shelley's mistress, and had borne a child by him in Naples in December 1818—Shelley's 'Neapolitan charge'. Shelley refuted this in an immediate letter to Mary, and Mary wrote at once to Mrs Hoppner denying the story. Byron, however, already prejudiced against Claire, believed the story, on the hostile grounds that it was 'just like them'. This comment was not reported to Mary, who mistakenly thanked Byron 'for his kind disbelief'. Claire herself was told nothing. In fact, she knew nothing of Elise's accusation until February 1822, when Elise met her in Florence and withdrew all that she had said.[13] She was eventually persuaded to deny the story to Mrs Hoppner.

Claire returned to the Bojtis in Florence early in November 1821 and plunged once again into all the pleasures of Florentine society, going to the opera and to plays in Italian at the Cocomero Theatre. November was so exceptionally warm that Claire recorded in her journal, 'I leave off my flannel garment and am not incommoded by the cold.'[14] She spent a great deal of time practising the piano, though she did not reach the standard she set herself—'do little else but practise and that badly'. In general, however, she was living a busy, useful, and sociable life in Florence, where she now had many friends of all nationalities. This happiness she owed to Shelley's generosity as much as her own nature.

Shelley had also found time, when staying with Byron, to visit Allegra in the convent school at Bagnacavallo; he was able to bring back reassuring news, though tinged partly with his own prejudices. Allegra, with whom he spent about three hours, 'is grown tall & slight for her age, and her face is somewhat altered—the traits have become more delicate & she is much paler: probably from the effects of improper food.'[16] Here Shelley is unable to stop his enthusiasm for vegetarian diet. However, he admits in the convent's favour:

> She has a contemplative seriousness which mixed with her excessive vivacity which has not yet deserted her has a very peculiar effect in a child. She is under very strict discipline as may be observed from the immediate obedience she accords to the will of her attendants—this seems contrary to her nature; but I do not think it has been obtained at the expense of much severity.

He comments that on the whole Allegra's manners and behaviour seemed greatly improved. 'I had brought her a Basket of sweetmeats, & before eating any of them she gave her companion & all the nuns a portion—this is not much like the old Allegra.'

However, 'the old Allegra'—and she was still less than 5 years old—broke out before Shelley left. She became excited and rang the bell to summon the nuns from their cells, though no one seemed to mind very much or become cross with her. When Shelley asked her if she had a message for her father, she replied that he should visit her, and bring 'la mammina with him'—almost certainly a reference not to her mother Claire, but to Teresa Guiccioli, whom she had seen acting 'la mammina' in Byron's house in Ravenna. Shelley tactfully withheld this information from Claire, whatever he himself made of it.

6 *Deaths by Land and Sea (1822)*

Byron's movements, always important to Claire, were now entirely ruled by his liaison with Teresa Guiccioli. Her separation from her elderly husband was sanctioned by Pope Pius VII so long as she lived with her father. As Byron wrote to his half-sister on 5 October 1821, when the father was exiled from Ravenna on suspicion of anti-government plots, they had to go to Pisa, '& there I go to join them'.

He set out on this expedition with large wagons full of personal possessions, including his menagerie. When Shelley had stayed with Byron at Ravenna in August, he had commented on the number and variety of these animals: 'ten horses, eight enormous dogs, three monkeys, five cats, an eagle, a crow, and a falcon; and all these except the horses, walk about the house, which every now and then resounds with their unarbitrated quarrels'.[1] The cats are mentioned as especially noisy. To this Shelley added: 'I find that my enumeration of the animals in this Circean Palace was defective, and that in a material point. I have just met on the grand staircase five peacocks, two guinea hens, and an Egyptian crane.'

Even if Byron did not take the whole entourage from Ravenna to Pisa, it must have made a large travelling load. By a coincidence not so strange, since Claire had to leave Pisa for Florence to avoid Byron, on 1 November 1821 her diary records: 'we passed Lord B—— and his travelling train'.[2] Her carriage had to draw to one side at Empoli to let Byron's magnificent coach and four followed by crowded wagons pass on their way to Pisa. The pale, handsome head in the coach window was her last sight, as it proved, of Allegra's father. She went on to describe the thick white fog which shrouded Florence on her arrival at Casa Bojti that day.

Byron's journey, to be near Teresa Guiccioli and her father in Pisa, confirmed Claire's previous suspicion that he had left Allegra in the Bagnacavallo convent in order to be rid of responsibility for her. He apparently cared more for his mistress than he did for his natural daughter. Claire became a prey to gloomy forebodings.

On 18 February 1822, she wrote to Byron, 'I assure you I can no longer resist the internal inexplicable feeling which haunts me that I shall never see her any more.'[3] She announced, thinking of plans to join her brother Charles in Vienna, that she would shortly leave Italy 'for a new country to enter upon a disagreeable and precarious course of life'. She insisted that she could not possibly do this 'without having first seen and embraced Allegra'. She went on to appeal passionately to Byron, 'My dear friend, I conjure you do not make the world dark to me as if my Allegra were dead.'

Having received no answer from Byron to these tempestuous appeals, Claire thought of wild schemes for snatching Allegra from the convent. These involved the help of Shelley and a forged letter. She received shocked replies from both Mary and Shelley. Mary concentrated on allaying Claire's alarm about Allegra's health at the convent. The district where Bagnacavallo was placed, she urged, with some exaggeration, enjoyed the best air in Italy. 'Considering the affair reasonably, A. is well taken care of there, she is in good health, & in all probability will continue so.'[4] Mary instanced a number of disasters, including deaths, which had always occurred in the Shelley circle in springtime. She therefore advised strongly against Claire taking any decision in early spring; writing to Claire in March, she superstitiously concluded:

The aspect of the Autumnal Heavens has on the contrary been with few exceptions, favourable to us—What think you of this? It is in your own style, but it has often struck me. Wd. it not be better therefore to wait, & to undertake no plan until circumstances bend a little more to us.

Mary advised Claire to argue 'in your own style', but this did not in any way convince Shelley. Mary had already warned Claire that any attempt to involve Shelley in the kidnap of Allegra might lay him open to a duel with Byron. Shelley himself now wrote to Claire in the most remarkable and direct terms about the whole plan.

I know not what to think of the state of your mind, or what to fear for you—Your late plan about Allegra seems to me in its present form pregnant with irredeemable infamy to all the actors in it except yourself; in any form wherein *I* must actively cooperate inevitable destruction—I *would not* in any case make myself a party to a forged letter. (I *could not* refuse Lord Byron's challenge; though that however to be deprecated would be the least in the series of mischiefs consequent upon my fraudulent intervention in such a plan.) I say this because I am shocked at the thoughtless violence of your designs, and I want to put my sense of their madness in the strongest light.[5]

He added that she should follow a different way of life, and 'seek in the daily and affectionate intercourse of friends a respite from these perpetual & irritating projects'. The tone of this letter establishes that Shelley, though concerned for Claire, was not led by her. His strong advice reveals deep and wise friendship.

Shelley's sobering letter had its effect on Claire. A week later, on 30 March, he felt able to write appealing to her reason.

> No exertions of yours can obtain Allegra, and believe me that the plans you have lately dreamed, would, were they attempted only, plunge you and all that is connected with you in ruin irredeemable—But I dare say you are by this time convinced of it.[6]

As mark of Claire's respect for Shelley, nothing was ever heard again of the 'kidnap' plot for Allegra.

Shelley evidently did not want Mary to know that he and Claire were exchanging letters regularly, for he instructed Claire to address him at the Pisa Post Office under the unlikely poste restante name of 'Joe James'. It is not known what Claire thought of this curious command: but, probably from her enjoyment of anything suggesting mystery or intrigue, she obeyed it willingly.[7]

Meanwhile, Claire had begun work on a translation of Goethe's memoirs. This was a paid commission arranged by Shelley on behalf of Byron, who believed the work was being done in Paris. When Byron learned that he had been deceived and the true identity of his translator, he was, not unreasonably, angry. As Claire wrote, he 'grumbled and demurred and does not know whether it is worth it and will only give 40 crowns', Mary urged her to continue but she eventually dropped the project.

On 10 April 1822, Shelley wrote to Claire, again with the Bojtis at Florence, suggesting that she should come and stay at Pisa for the summer.[8] His purpose was to calm and console her, and he promised it would not involve her with Byron; 'The Williams's and we shall be quite alone, Lord Byron and his party having chosen Leghorn, where their house is already taken . . . no one need know of where you are; the Williams's are serene people, and we are alone.'[9]

Claire was delighted by the idea of spending a peaceful summer in such company. She accepted gratefully an invitation from Mary and arrived in Pisa on 15 April to join the party.[10] The company of Edward and Jane Williams was an additional attraction. From the first, Claire spent a great deal of her time with them. On 23 April, all three went together to the Bay of Spezia to look for a house in the village of Lerici for their summer holiday. They saw several, but none was suitable. Then, while returning home, they noticed a dilapidated house standing in waste ground by the sea which might well be adapted. This was the Casa Magni. Yet it and every other consideration was swept away at Pisa on the following day, 25 April.

It was Edward Williams who first heard from Shelley that Allegra had died in the convent of Bagnacavallo, of an attack of typhoid. Shelley looked shattered. His one impulse was to hide this from Claire until they reached a different house, preferably the one she and the Williams had already seen at Lerici. They moved to Lerici hastily to set up negotiations for the Casa Magni. Claire was kept in ignorance of Allegra's death, and the Casa Magni was taken for both families on 30 April. In the evening Claire heard Bagnacavallo mentioned. The abrupt pause in conversation as she entered, with her previous forebodings about the child and her conviction, as she had told Byron, that she would never see Allegra again, told Claire all. According to Shelley, she received this appalling news with surprisingly calm dignity. She herself wrote later, 'I found a stern tranquillity in me suited to the time.' Her current journal, however, remained blank for five months. Shelley, who thought she might go mad at the news, was relieved, though later, when she could cry, she poured out her inner feelings in a letter of furious accusation to Byron, which he read but promptly sent back to Shelley. At first Claire wanted to visit the little coffin at Leghorn on its passage to England, where Byron had decided to send it. This transaction was arranged through Teresa Guiccioli and an English resident there called Dunn; finally Claire had to satisfy herself with Allegra's miniature and a lock of her hair.[11]

Byron himself had made his own rather strange choice of the final resting place for Allegra's coffin. Always haunted by the memory of his own boyhood at Harrow, he specified: 'I wish it to be buried in Harrow Church—there is a spot in the Churchyard near the footpath on the brow of the hill looking towards Windsor—and a tomb under a large tree (bearing the name of Peachee or Peachey).' He also decided there should be a memorial tablet *inside* the church, bearing the inscription:

In memory of
Allegra
daughter of G.G. Lord Byron
who died at Bagnacavallo
in Italy April 20th, 1822,[12]
aged five years and three months

with a quotation from the second book of Samuel. In fact, by order of the churchwardens, no tablet to Byron's illegitimate child was permitted within the church; the body, though, was buried as he wished outside in the churchyard near the entrance, the grave unmarked. More than half a lifetime would pass before Claire learned where her daughter's body lay.

It seemed that the memory of Allegra haunted Shelley. Walking with Williams on the terrace of the Casa Magni, Shelley seized his arm and stared out on the moonlit sea. When Williams asked if he were in pain, Shelley replied, 'There it is again—there!' What he had seen, in hallucination, was a naked child which kept rising with clasped hands out of the sea. Claire herself had no such visions. In fact, on 16 May, Shelley was able to write to Byron, 'Claire is much better; after the first shock she has sustained her loss with more fortitude than I had dared hope . . . I can only suggest, on the subject of Claire, the propriety of her being made acquainted through me of the destination of the remains.'[13] It seems, from later evidence, that this was not done.

Claire went back to Florence to collect the remainder of her luggage from the Bojtis. She was there, and at Pisa with the Masons, for a fortnight. On 7 June she returned to Lerici. She made friends with Jane Williams and grew fond of her two small children. By an effort of will, she controlled her emotions. Shelley noticed that she seemed braver and calmer after Allegra's death than during the months of feverish schemes and gnawing anxiety in which she had anticipated it.

Claire could not sink into mourning, for a family crisis soon made sudden and urgent demands on her. On 16 June, Mary, who was three months' pregnant, miscarried at eight o'clock on a Sunday morning after a week's ill-health. No medical help was at hand, and Mary was sinking under extreme weakness from loss of blood. Shelley's promptness was remarkable. Ice was brought to the remote house; Claire was afraid of applying it to the fainting patient, but Shelley, decisive as ever in a crisis, filled a hip bath with ice and sat Mary in it. Claire supported and comforted her until the bleeding gradually ceased; they had probably saved her life.

During Mary's convalescence a friend arrived at Lerici, who gave life a new turn. At Edward Williams's lodgings the previous winter, Claire had met the most picturesque though not the most reliable of their Pisan circle, Edward John Trelawny. This romantic figure was a retired naval man, though his rank of 'Lieutenant' was the product of his imagination. Trelawny had been rejected for a lieutenant's commission, and this false naval title was, in fact, part of his mythical persona. A great admirer of Byron's poems, Trelawny invented for himself a past like a Byronic hero. The Shelleys were impressed by him: Claire, having known Byron herself, perhaps less so. However, she appreciated Trelawny when she first met him during a brief visit to Pisa from 22 to 24 February 1822, and remained friends with him for the rest of their long lives. During his visit to Lerici, from pride and self-control, she appeared her old self.

One of Trelawny's chief contributions to the interests of Shelley and Edward Williams had been to bring them, earlier in 1822, the model of an American-type sailing boat. Shelley and Edward were enchanted to have this 'perfect plaything' for the summer, and sent orders to Trelawny's nautical friend, Captain Roberts at Genoa, to have such a boat built full-size in the shipyards there. It arrived at Spezia on 12 May and at once became the centre of their attention. Shelley and Williams spent much of their summer on this vessel, named the *Don Juan*, and even Mary, still ill and perpetually depressed, was happy lying with her head on Shelley's knees while he took the helm. Shelley and Williams were obsessed by the boat. Together with the 18-year-old Charles Vivian who had brought the craft from Genoa they sailed her everywhere, ignoring the electrical summer storms which attacked the bay with sudden ferocity.

In a letter to John Gisborne in London, Shelley described his pride in the boat, and their constant voyages:

> It is swift and beautiful, and appears quite a vessel. Williams is captain, and we drive along this delightful bay in the evening wind, under the summer moon, until earth appears another world. Jane brings her guitar, and if the past and the future could be obliterated, the present would content me so well that I could say with Faust to the passing moment, 'Remain thou, thou art so beautiful'.[14]

Shelley was re-reading *Faust* with Claire in her new-found German study, and at the mention of Goethe's poem his thoughts turned happily to her as he wrote, 'Claire is with us, and the death of her child seems to have restored her to tranquillity. Her character is somewhat altered. She is vivacious and talkative, and though she teases me sometimes, I like her.' He called her in such moods 'la fille aux mille projets'. Claire seemed for her unnaturally calm after Allegra's death; in fact she had grown into mature womanhood.

This idyllic picture of happiness at Spezia was the setting for total tragedy. The immediate cause was the long-awaited arrival at Leghorn on 1 July 1822 of Leigh Hunt and his family, by Shelley's invitation. Hunt was intending to edit a new progressive paper, *The Liberal*, to which Byron and Shelley would contribute. Shelley and Williams sailed to Leghorn in the *Don Juan* with their boat-boy, Charles Vivian, for an emotional reunion with Hunt and then waited for a favourable wind to sail the *Don Juan* back to Lerici. Weather conditions were unpromising in other ways. The heat was abnormal, with electrical storms, but Shelley and Williams were eager to sail back to their wives. On the afternoon of Monday 8 July, they set sail into a hazy sea threatening bad weather. At half-past six the squall broke. All the Italian boats ran for shelter in Leghorn at the sight, but Shelley and Williams sailed on into the storm. The *Don Juan* mishandled, its sails unreefed, went down in the Bay of Spezia with its crew of three.

At Lerici, the wives watched for the *Don Juan* to return, but 11 and 12 July passed without sign of a sail. The sea was still rough and the scirocco blew wildly; perhaps, they persuaded themselves, the boat had been driven off course and landed elsewhere. Eventually Jane and Mary took post-horses to Pisa and Leghorn in search of news, but found nothing and returned 'thrown about by hope & fear'.

They had left Claire in charge of 3-year-old Percy Florence and Jane's two babies, with instructions to open any letters delivered to the house. On 19 July Claire broke the seal of a letter to Trelawny from his naval friend, Captain Roberts, which reported that two bodies had been washed ashore near Viareggio. Claire now faced the duty of telling Mary and Jane that their husbands were drowned. She could not summon up courage alone, and scribbled a despairing note to the only friend at hand, Leigh Hunt.

I pray you to answer this by return of my messenger—I assure you I cannot break it to them, nor is my spirit . . . capable of giving them consolation, or protecting them from the first burst of their despair. I entreat you to give me some counsel, or to arrange some counsel by which they may know it. I know not what further to add, except that their case is desparate in every respect, and death would be the greatest kindness to us all.

Ever your sincere friend, Claire

Their problem was solved by Trelawny. Returning from his searches, he entered Casa Magni about seven in the evening to say all was over; their husbands' bodies had been found. He did not attempt to console the young widows with conventional phrases, but poured out his praise of Shelley until Mary was 'almost happy to be thus unhappy'.

None of them could bear the waves beating under the windows of Casa Magni or the wind howling ceaselessly off shore. They packed up ready to return to Pisa: three women and three children alone. Shelley, for so many years the constant friend and protector in Claire's life, was gone for ever; she would now have to find her own way in a leaderless world. The independent spirit she prized so much was all she had to guide her.

PART II

Travels of Claire (1822–1841)

7 *To the North (1822–1823)*

The deaths of Allegra and Shelley left Claire a lone remnant of the Romantic Age. Her letters and journals, volatile textures of light and shade, record her battles as revolutionary in a world of reaction, servant in households of strangers, an Englishwoman abroad, a foreigner in England. She survived by a vivid response to life, learning in spite of early grief to be 'happy without happiness'. In the respectable middle-class world of the mid-century, she survived as a figure from a freer past, with lingering hopes of Shelley's vision:

> The world's great age begins anew,
> The golden years return.

The deaths of Shelley and Williams left Mary and Jane as alone as Claire. Trelawny, unasked, stayed with the women at Lerici, attempting to keep up their spirits, while he rode to and from Viareggio coping with officialdom. He saw the bodies buried on the shore in quicklime, as quarantine laws demanded, though he planned a later funeral. This done, he escorted the women and children back to Pisa. Here, on 20 July 1822 they settled into the Tre Palazzi di Chiesa on the southern Lung'Arno.

Claire and the young widows clung together for the rest of the summer. 'We have one purse,' Mary wrote, '& joined in misery we are for the present joined in life.'[1] She dreaded the nights, still more the lonely mornings. Daily life was monotonous and empty of outward events. Their rooms looked south, away from the town, towards the salt marshes where the river Arno flowed to the sea. Yet they cannot have been quiet, with three very young children: Percy Florence born in November 1819, Medwin Williams in February 1820, and Rosalind Williams in March 1821. Claire, at her best in a crisis, took care of their clamorous demands and attempted to comfort their mothers. Children's needs are real and admit no delay; their meals and baths, their laundry, their walks and play imposed a timetable on the empty, aching days. Claire developed a maternal, possessive love for these three infants whose lot she shared. Each child had lost a father; she herself had lost a child.

When Byron, as the most generous concession he could make, had offered Claire the alternative of making all arrangements for the funeral of Allegra herself, she was, so Shelley had written to Byron, 'bewildered; & whether she designs to avail herself further of your permission to regulate the funeral, I know not. In fact, I am so exhausted with the scenes through which I have passed that I do not dare to ask.' He added, however, 'She has no objection (this much she has said) to the interment taking place in England.'[2]

The burial at Harrow followed, though without the wall tablet to Allegra mentioning the name of Byron. The simple, unmarked mound outside the churchyard had to suffice for the little girl who had been the centre of Claire's life and emotions for the past five years. Claire, however, remained marked by the memory of her child until deep into her own old age.

Beside the two young widows who attempted to comfort each other, Claire had to bear her own grief in her own way. Her fiery temperament converted sorrow to anger. As she wrote:

> The flames of a deep sullen resentment for unmerited misfortunes burned within me and I bid defiance to the dark visitings of misfortune and to the disastrous hauntings of Fate. I said to fate You cannot inflict more than I will proudly bear.[3]

This was not a philosophical way to meet sorrow, but it was Claire's way. The resentful memory of Allegra's wronging never left her. Though buried in the changing scenes and hard work of everyday life, it returned to haunt her in the lonely nights.[4]

> She was the only thing I had to love—the only object in the world I could call my own: and I had never parted with her from her birth not for an hour even . . . never, never, neither here nor in Eternity can I, nor will I forgive the injuries he inflicted upon my defenceless child . . . I . . . went about wildly from one to another, imploring them to help me get her out and received everywhere . . . the advice to be patient and wait more favourable events. In this life, one dies of anguish many times before one really dies.[5]

Across the river, the marble Palazzo Lanfranchi was filled with carriages and horses, servants, animals, wine, and books. Byron sat writing his masterpiece *Don Juan* with a bottle among the papers on his table.[6] He delegated the burial of Allegra to his publisher, John Murray. For a short time the grave was known; Mr Gisborne saw it in

October 1822, when he escorted a new boy to school at Harrow. Yet by the time Shelley's son entered Harrow in 1832, it had vanished in the turf; Mary lodged for four years in the town then without mentioning it. It was 1869, and Claire herself 71 years old, before she learned that Allegra had been buried with Church of England rites and lay in consecrated ground at Harrow.[7]

In the depths of their shared grief, the three at Pisa had forgotten to inform Mary's or Shelley's father of Shelley's death. Each learnt the news at second-hand and each responded in character. 'Tho' we have it from the Public Prints only at present,' wrote Sir Timothy to his lawyer, 'such catastrophes are apt to be too true.' Once a proud and hopeful father, life with his elder son had prepared him for the final unpleasant surprise. Godwin, 'an unfortunate old man and a beggar', took the tragedy as a personal grievance. 'That you should be so overcome as not to be able to write is, perhaps, but too natural,' he wrote to his widowed daughter; 'but that Jane could not write one line I could never have believed.'[8] The life and death of Allegra had of course been concealed from the Godwins. The Philosopher returned to his stepdaughter's penniless state with a certain gloomy satisfaction. 'Poor Jane is, I am afraid, left still more helpless than you are.'

Claire may once have been 'Jane' to Godwin, but she was now a very different person, and far too proud to crawl home admitting disaster. Her worst fears—the loss of Allegra and Shelley—once realized, she summoned up her courage: her only skill for survival was to teach languages. She wrote at once to her brother Charles in Vienna, and his answer was affectionate and hopeful. Claire could come and join him as a teacher of English.[9]

In September 1822 Mary Shelley and Jane Williams, with their children, left Pisa for Genoa. Jane Williams travelled on to temporary shelter with her mother in Alsops Buildings, New (Marylebone) Road. Mary, who could not contemplate the scorn of Mrs Godwin, settled in a Genoa villa near the Hunt household. From Pisa, Claire wrote Mary a letter of farewell. Their old rivalries and resentments, dating from childhood, the daily fights in Shelley's household, were forgotten in the grief which bound them. Claire missed Mary. 'You have only been gone for a few hours, I have been inexpressibly low spirited . . . To me there seems nothing under the sun except the old tale of misery.' She imagined the journey ahead, 'all the lonely inns, the weary miles', to Vienna. Knowing her own fiery impatience, she apologized in advance to Mary: 'If I should write you scolding letters you will excuse them . . . Kiss the dear Percy for me.'

Jane Williams, too, was in Claire's thoughts. On a blank page of her journal, turned sideways, she wrote phonetically the Persian words from the *Divan* of Hafiz which had so enchanted Shelley when Jane sang them to an 'Indian air' on her guitar.[10] Claire wrote to Mary: 'If Jane is with you tell her how much I have thought of her and that her image will always float across my mind, shining in my dark history like a ray of light across a cave.'[11] The beautiful simile is perhaps a half-memory of Shelley's classical teaching. 'Kiss her children also with a grandmother's love,' Claire concluded, 'Dio ti da massima ventura.'

For many women whose official virtue was no longer a marketable commodity, the most practical course was to find a protector. Jane Williams, though she received an allowance from a relative,[12] appeared to realize that lustrous eyes and clouds of dark hair were her best assets. She returned to London in September 1822, bringing a letter of introduction from Mary to Jefferson Hogg. Hogg, who had been attracted by Harriet and Mary in turn, now found Shelley's last love irresistible. Within a year Jane and her children were established in his house, where she gave birth to his daughter in a common-law marriage which lasted the remainder of her lifetime.[13] Mary's situation was better. The marriage ceremony of 1816, ironically described by Shelley as 'so magical in its effects', made her the official widow of a great poet and she declared that Mary Shelley would be written on her tomb. Secretly, though, she yearned for 'one whom I might love—who would protect and guard me'.[14]

Claire's situation was bleaker than that of the two widows and their children. Shelley had fulfilled his intention to form Claire's youthful mind in romantic idealism, and this was now tested when she had to face the future alone. For eight years, almost since childhood, she had been like Shelley's younger sister, favoured and indulged. Now she was alone, homeless, penniless, and thrown on her own resources. Looking back later, she wrote: 'Amid the thousand lines of human life, branching and intersecting in endless and infinite directions, there was not one I could choose that would lead to safety.'[15] Yet she had strengths as yet hardly tapped: energy, versatility and resource, cleverness and the will to survive. She was above all proud, obstinately determined now that she must not rely on others for protection. Mrs Mason wrote, 'I have heard nothing of Claire and am very anxious for a letter from her'. Claire did not need to ask for help, since Shelley's teaching had added love of natural beauty to her innate resources and she was therefore self-sufficient. He had written to her during her stay in Florence of his illness in 1821 'I suffer equally from pleasure and from pain—You will ask me naturally enough where I find any pleasure? The wind, the light, the air, the smell of a flower affects me with violent emotions.' Shelley's words hallowed every day's enjoyment for Claire.

The two young widows and their brood of children gone, Claire stayed alone in the suddenly silent apartment on the Lung'Arno for one of the more mysterious episodes of her life. She was officially occupied with preparations for the journey to Vienna and an unknown future. No suitable escort or lady companion, then thought essential for a young woman traveller, appeared, but Claire refused to delay. Quick-witted and bold, with fluent French, Italian, and German, she determined to take her chances in stage-coach or roadside inn and travel alone. Scandal had already darkened her name for eight years. Now, having lost everything, she had nothing more to lose. Her actions suggest a new beginning. For the first time since April, since she had inhabited that vanished world where Allegra and Shelley lived and would forever live, she began to write her journal. The opening words were 'Friday the 6th of September', and the rest of the page is blank.[16]

What this page should have contained remained hidden for exactly three years when she wrote with tender regret:

Septr. 6th Lovely weather. I think a great deal of past times today and today above all of this day three years but the sentiments of that time are most likely long ago vanished into air. This is life. So live to nothing but toil and trouble—all its sweets are like the day whose anniversary this is—more transitory than a shade—yet had it been otherwise if Inwalert had been different I might have been as happy as I am now wretched.[17]

'Inwalert' was Claire's personal anagram of Trelawny's name, and the blank page on 6 September 1822 marked the day they exchanged farewells before Claire left Pisa. She had been moved by the compassion with which he broke the news of their husbands' deaths to Mary and Jane and then escorted them home to Pisa, away from the hateful sound of waves. Trelawny seldom missed a chance of relating the events of 15 August 1822, when he cremated the bodies of Shelley and Edward Williams on the beach near Viareggio. Byron and Leigh Hunt stood by, and some dragoons to dig out the corpses, but no women. Though Shelley's face and hands were eaten away by fish, they could identify him by Keats's 1820 poems in his jacket pocket. Trelawny heaped up driftwood, lit the fire, then threw on incense, salt, and wine. As he wrote to Leigh Hunt, 'the body and skull, which burnt fiercely gave to the flames a white, silvery and wavy look of indescribable brightness and purity'. Trelawny's romancing strain ensures that Claire heard something very like this description. A year later Trelawny secured the burial of Shelley's ashes near Keats's body, by the Pyramid of Caius Cestius at Rome, drawing generations of future pilgrims to the graves of the young poets.[18] These services, shared devotion to Shelley and the magic circle he created, bound Trelawny and Claire together. An erratic friendship, with long interruptions, linked them for the rest of their lives, yet they were never closer than at this parting, still lit by Shelley's funeral fire.

The day in the gilded mists of a Pisan autumn remains mysterious. Mary knew nothing of it, believing Claire had already left for Florence. Claire and Trelawny met on the banks of the Arno. Shelley's apartment, on the unfashionable side of the river, was almost the last house on the curving quay. Beyond the city wall the broad, calm river flowed six miles to open sea. This dreamlike landscape of vapour trails and water became the scene of Trelawny's love. In letter after ardent letter he dwelt on wild embraces, in words which Claire later blacked out to defeat prying eyes. Trelawny's first editor gained the impression that the pair became lovers and omitted several erotic passages from publication.[19] Reading the letters with sympathy for Trelawny's temperament, it is hard to say what is real and what imaginary; nor perhaps does this greatly matter. He sent her a note to 'Aula Palazzo', for 'Casa Aula'; accuracy, like spelling or punctuation, was never his strong point and love unfortunately did not help. 'Linked thus together,' he scrawled, 'we may defeat the fate that separates us for a time with united hearts what can separate us—Oh no, fear not even the . . .'[20] Four lines which follow have been heavily inked out. From this cloud of romantic fantasy one fact emerges. Claire, though fond of him and bound by shared loyalties, never pretended to be in love with the corsair.

Trelawny's offer of shelter dismissed, Claire wrote him a farewell letter and made ready for her solitary journey to Austria. On 14 September 1822 she collected a passport from the British consul in

Leghorn. Five days later she took this passport to Florence. By characteristic romantic irony, on the same day, Trelawny, 'overpowered by the intense feelings' Claire's letter aroused, took a boat for Leghorn in the middle of the night during a blustery squall, 'with fond hope that the swiftness of a tempest would blow me to you'. Dwelling on memories of 'the acts of love, sweet Claire', he imagined her awaiting him in the port, only to learn with 'an agonizing certainty' that she was gone.[21] The tempest at least was a reality, for in Florence on the same day Claire recorded, 'It comes on to rain in torrents.' She walked through the storm with her passport to the Austrian Consulate for its essential Imperial visa. Soaked to the skin, she went on to buy stockings, the only new clothing she could afford.[22] On 20 September 1822, still in pouring rain, she left Florence.[23]

The first stage of her journey was from Florence to Bologna across the Appenines. 'Friday Sept 20,' Claire recorded, 'Get up at five. Pack. Breakfast. It pours with rain.' Sharp words and sentences convey the stress of travel. At ten the carriage came. The account continues:

> We set out for Bologna. During the first part of the road I was too occupied with my own thoughts to attend to the scenery. I remember how hopelessly I had lingered on the Italian soil for five years, waiting ever for a favourable change instead of which I was now leaving it having buried there everything that I loved.

After the mid-day halt, the road began to wind upwards. Claire, ignoring the squalls of rain, forced herself to walk up the steep hills, 'hoping by fatigue of body to dull the painful activity of mind'.[24] Fast-approaching autumn darkened the hills and valleys, making them more beautiful in her eyes. The 'almost immeasurable prospect' of rocks now sprinkled with groves of chestnut trees, 'mingled with the more tender green of poplars, ash and beech'. On the left, the road overlooked a rich, cultivated plain, on the right, 'smaller hills heaped in masses unto a boundary line of majestic Appenines darkened into the deepest hue by the . . . black clouds which hang upon their summits'. Mists gathered around them, thickening by seven in the evening to a dense, white fog. The coachmen got down and led the horses step by step, until they reached a cottage where, Claire writes, 'we were obliged, nay even glad, to take up our night's rest. It was very poor and so dirty, the dark, vaulted kitchen looked like a cavern of Hell. I did not attempt to go to bed but lent . . .'[25] The journal breaks off for two and a half years, leaving Claire between two words like the scene snatched passing a lighted window, momentarily but indelibly clear.

She was pursued on her journey by a wild and furious letter from Trelawny, reproaching her for leaving him. 'You! You! *torture* me Claire . . . I fearlessly opened my heart . . . considered you bound to me by ties nothing could tear asunder . . . you have used your unlimited sway over me with a remorseless and unfeeling hand.'[26]

From such overwrought passion, Claire arrived in Vienna, near the beginning of October, to Charles's brotherly welcome. He was a last link with childhood and security. 'He is so quiet, good and mild that we quite suit one another,' she wrote, with evident relief, 'and then he allows me to be wild and extravagant as I please in my theories.'[27] More caution might have been prudent, but prudence was never Claire's style.

Charles could not take an unmarried sister into his bachelor quarters, in a tall house, 1175 Auf der Biber Bastei, a bastion of the city wall, where oil lamps lit the dark common staircase day and night. Instead, he found a room for her with a landlady whom she had already met and liked in Pisa. Agreeable Frau Jeanette von Henickstein had a large apartment, where she took boarders, in the fashionable Kärntnerstrasse, leading to St Stefan's Cathedral in the heart of the old city. She welcomed Claire with a good fire and an affectionate kiss.[28] The lady boarders were intrigued by the vivacious young Englishwoman with her lovely singing voice, and one by one all five began to take English lessons. Charles was hopeful of a post for Claire in some distinguished family.

The buoyant Clairmont spirit rose. Claire wrote to Mrs Mason in Pisa that when alone she still grieved for 'my lost darling', but resolutely faced the future. 'I am not in need of money, all the expenses of my journey paid, I have over £10 still in my purse and my brother says that he will soon find me a situation, as English governesses are very much in request in Vienna.'[29] True, she missed Jane; she had become a close friend during the days of mourning, as Claire wrote: 'What I had with you where I soothed and recovered my spirit by songs and thoughts which approached or drew me to the world of imagination, so different from the real round substantial globe we inhabit.'[30] Yet everything conspired to make the future look bright.

The Vienna that Claire entered in 1822 was a city freed at last from the dark shadow of Napoleon, the horrors of war and invasion. The old ramparts still enclosed the city and its houses; the walls would not be pulled down until 1857. Their breadth formed a tree-shaded walk which looked out over open country, where village suburbs and Baroque summer palaces, imperial Schönbrunn, with the Belvedere and its terraced gardens, lay among the trees. Already, prosperous citizens were building Biedermeyer villas to enjoy the country at their city gates. 'The Viennese character', wrote Karl Werner, 'showed itself in the delight in enjoyment. The whole year was filled with small and large scale entertainments, music and dancing.' The crowded coffee houses were theatres of gossip and ideas. Vienna seemed made for pleasure. Charles took his sister for walks in the public gardens, and for conversation at his favourite coffee house, Zum Jungling.

Yet Claire's hopes of success as a language teacher in Vienna, like the charms of the city itself, were overshadowed by facts her 'wild and extravagant' theories could not comprehend. Godwin had taught his strangely assorted family to believe that reason applied to public or private conduct would infallibly improve the whole human condition. The Shelley circle, fired by his poetic flame, had dreamt of ideal communities sharing home, property, children, and sexual partners in perfect freedom. The reality of post-1815 Europe showed the opposite of these cherished ideals. One idea dominated the minds of rulers: fear of revolution. Emperor Franz II undertook the impossible task of governing personally the whole kaleidoscope of Hapsburg domains. He combined instinctive fear of change with a penchant for detail; in dangerous situations his usual response was 'Let us sleep on it.' To propel this torpid monarch was the responsibility of the chancellor, Prince Metternich.

Metternich's principle of government was clear: to crush the least sign of free thought by systematic repression. The government of the widespread empire was rigidly centred on Vienna. German language and law were forced on Italians, Poles, Czechs, and Magyars. From 1819 a series of decrees enforced censorship of books, plays, journals, teaching in school or university, and private correspondence. A special department, the Foreigners' Commission, existed to detect 'revolutionary sects with tentacles all over Europe'. To the secret police, two young teachers from a radical, free-thinking family in England represented a threat to the Empire.

During the course of December 1822, an anonymous letter denounced Charles to the Foreigners' Commission. His avowed outward purpose in Vienna was to give lessons, his real purpose, the writer claimed, was 'concealed'. The accuser mistakenly described him as son of 'the authoress of the rights of women' and a father prosecuted for sedition. Moreover, 'his sister[31] married Shelly [*sic*]—the author of Queen Mab. Shelly was a deist—was deprived of his right of a father by the Lord Chancellor of England—was the intimate of the late Lord Byron—Clairmont is not his real name.' These suspicious circumstances led to a full secret service investigation and a closely written dossier of some ninety pages. The detective in charge included in his report 'Klara Clairmont of London, daughter of a Bookseller'—Mrs Godwin was the official proprietor of the Juvenile Library—'aged 24, spinster. This Englishwoman was in Pisa with her married sister, and has come here for the first time in order to see Vienna and her brother who is professor of English here.' The document includes Claire's address with Frau von Henickstein, length of stay, and a letter of recommendation from London to a prospective employer, Herr von Schwab.[32] Through living with her stepsister at Pisa, Claire had apparently also been subject to the malign influence of the radical author of *Queen Mab* and deist.

The outcome of the Clairmont case was in the Austrian tradition. Mrs Godwin wrote to tell Jane Williams that Claire and Charles 'had been ordered to quit Vienna in five days'. More unpromising news followed in Christmas week, 1822: 'The Emperor has lately published an edict to prevent the establishment of foreign instructors both male and female, particularly the English, so that their prospects there are very gloomy.'[33] The English were especially suspect because of the tolerance shown to dissenters and free thinkers in their country. In this crisis Charles showed unexpected resource. He presented himself voluntarily at police headquarters, where the investigators found this small, slight young teacher 'argumentative about everything'. The Foreigners' Commission withdrew the order for the immediate expulsion of both Clairmonts, though they remained subject to police surveillance. The innocent-looking Charles had already mastered Viennese customs. He organized a petition in his own favour, signed by 'many householders and respectable persons', among them the aristocratic families of Esterhazy and Chotek, who wished to employ him as 'the ablest English Language Professor'.[34] In time he won the essential licence to teach and settled for the rest of his life in Vienna.

Claire recognized that, with her lack of Viennese connections, there was no hope of a teaching licence for her. She who had pursued Byron with importunate demands in the past did not reproach Charles or expect him to solve impossible problems. Their family affection remained as close as ever, yet Claire knew she must fend for herself. As autumn hardened into winter she faced destitution. Her landlady needed her room in the Kärtnerstrasse 'for family reasons', or perhaps because the rent was not paid. Claire found other lodgings.[35] In mid-winter she fell ill. Italian life had ill prepared her for the east wind from Russia which drives snow storms and half-frozen birds through the narrow streets of Vienna's inner city. Claire's account of this illness, written thirty-four years later, is predictably dramatic. 'I nearly died at Vienna when I was four-and-twenty—I grew skeleton thin—I had constant fever—I could not eat and this for months.' The style is overwrought, but the illness was indeed dangerous. Charles wrote to warn Mary that she might not see her stepsister again.[36] Generously, Mary, who had just received £33 from *The Liberal* for Shelley's *Indian Girl's Song*, sent £12, 16 napoleons, to pay the fee of a physician. Belatedly Claire had to admit that Professor Vaccà, whom she had ridiculed in Pisa when she was a wilful 21, might have been right in his opinion that her inflamed glands were scrofulous.[37]

Claire reported her doctor's diagnosis to Mrs Mason in Pisa, who later wrote: 'If she has not means . . . to enable her to remove to a milder climate and use sea-bathing—I have but a bad opinion of her health and am convinced she would require great care and a total change of scene and society.'[38] Claire's letter alarmed the Masons so much that they showed it to Professor Vaccà and a colleague, who confirmed the diagnosis. Their advice was 'to go and live in the sea (which she is so fond of) like a mermaid'. Claire's love of swimming, so rare in a woman at that date, astonished everyone. The problem of course was who should pay for this attractive prescription.

Charles was only beginning to establish his practice as a language tutor. The Godwins were unpromising, to say the least: on 1 May 1822 they had the bailiffs in their house and the following winter were still bankrupt.[39] Mary was seeking an increased allowance for her small son from Sir Timothy Shelley and was herself sunk in profound depression—'my heart is truly iced', she wrote in one of the posthumous letters to Shelley which filled her journal.[40] The Masons, Lady

Mountcashell and Mr Tighe, maintained their illicit household on a modest income and had two daughters to launch on the Italian marriage market. Jane Williams and Hogg discussed Claire's predicament and reached apparently the same comfortable conclusion, 'the Giaour—Byron—would provide for the mother of his dead child'. Hogg 'could not doubt it'. Mrs Mason took it on herself to request 'a small annuity' for Claire from Byron; she was shocked to receive a curt letter of refusal 'with a sting in the tail'.[41] Neither she nor others could have imagined Byron's unforeseen and lasting grief at the death of Allegra. 'While she lived,' he confided to Lady Blessington, 'her existence never seemed necessary to my happiness; but no sooner did I lose her than it appeared to me as if I could not live without her. Even now the recollection is most bitter.'[42] Claire's furious letter, which had so exasperated him, now carried an extra reproach. The whole affair was galling. In any case, Byron's attention was now firmly fixed on the London Greek Committee and the struggle to free Greece from the Turks. On 23 July 1823 he embarked for Greece on his last journey.

In Claire's precarious existence, one resource remained. On 10 January 1823 Trelawny had written, his grievance forgotten, 'Do I pray you use me—give me proof of your belief in my entire friendship by freely using me in your service it will give me real pleasure.'[43] Claire's reply was firm. 'Do not write angrily to me for nothing can alter my determination.' Trelawny would not give up. If they met again, he wrote in April, Claire would end by staying with him. Even if she were to suffer poverty, sickness, or sorrow, he reminded her, 'you have no cause to despair—for you have one faithful bosom that . . . will receive you and press you to his bosom with the same undiminished ardour he did when he first pressed you there . . . I live in hope that ere long we shall meet without restraint.'[44] Similar letters followed in May, June, and July 1823, but when they arrived Claire had already left Vienna. 'Tell me of Claire, do write me of her', Trelawny once again implored Mary.

Claire had pulled through her illness despite the Italian doctor's fears, and with the first signs of spring began to recover her zest for life. 'I have had a letter from Claire and therefore will not delay telling you that she seems a little better,' wrote Mrs Mason.[45] She went out and about exploring the streets and courtyards of Vienna. In this police state, music, which Claire wrote 'comes nearer my soul than poetry or philosophy or patriotism or even love', was the one language freely spoken. Since she kept no journal in these months, it is impossible to say exactly which performances she heard. Yet two years later she could sing arias from Mozart operas she had attended and play Beethoven sonatas well enough for public performances. She seems not to have learnt any songs by Schubert, who had died in Vienna four years before she arrived there.

With returning health and energy, came the urgent need for Claire to earn her own living. Claire's nature was obstinate, but the Viennese fiasco was decisive. After the hopeful beginnings, work in Austria was barred to her for want of a teacher's licence. While European society was set in post-war reaction, no family would choose to employ Godwin's stepdaughter, Byron's discarded mistress, Shelley's disciple as a governess. She must seek out a post where her radical connections were unknown and her past could be concealed. Claire's next move startled even her own family, accustomed to her impulses.

At a social gathering, she met another foreign visitor to Vienna. Countess Zotoff of St Petersburg was the wife of a minister at the court of Czar Alexander I. She had two handsome daughters, of 14 and 16, and was seeking a governess to add polish to their accomplishments before they came out in court society. Charmed by Claire's ironically ladylike appearance, she offered her the position of teacher of English, music, and deportment. Claire, similarly charmed by the countess, accepted the post. As usual her imagination leapt ahead. She would act as companion rather than governess to the young ladies; 'as the girls in Russia marry early they will soon be off hand', and as their mother was 'not robust', she might choose to settle, with Claire as congenial companion, in some Mediterranean climate. Cautious brother Charles pointed out that the salary offered was small, only about seventy-five pounds in sterling, and 'Russians are not much to be depended on'.[46] He might as well have talked to the wind as to Claire in the grip of fantasy. Friends warned, entreated against what Trelawny called 'this compulsive emigration to the North', which would raise barriers of ice and snow between them.[47] Warnings were useless. Courage and obstinacy bred 'great hopes' in Claire. She had her deeper reasons too. 'I went to Russia', she wrote, 'that I might forget the visitings of my dark and wayward fate, the disastrous hauntings that seemed inseparable with my name.'[48] On 22 March 1823 Claire left Vienna with Madame Zotoff for St Petersburg. In July 1823 Mary reported one letter from Russia. Silence, without explanation or apology, followed until April 1824. The break seemed total, a blank in Claire's life.

8 *Summer in the Country (1823–1825)*

Claire's plan for travelling to Russia was bold enough to provoke Mary Shelley to rare amusement. 'I hope she will . . . persuade her *Count* to bring her to Italy,' she said. By March 1824 Mary's habitual melancholy had returned: 'hopeless—spiritless—I cannot write—I can hardly read . . . I never prayed so heartily for death as now'.[1] In this illness, anxiety and resentment fastened upon her stepsister. 'No one has heard from Claire since last July,' she wrote to Trelawny, 'this is very cruel of her since she must be aware that we must all be very anxious about her. I strive to think that her silence is occasioned only by her love of mystery or some other caprice.'[2] Trelawny also had no news. Claire wrote no surviving letters during the year she lived as governess in Count Zotoff's house in St Petersburg. Some critics have assumed disasters, which from obstinate pride she concealed.

Evidence, though scattered, presents a happier picture. St Petersburg was a cosmopolitan city with a large professional class from Europe: Scottish engineers and architects, German physicians and lawyers, French, Swiss, or English tutors. By edict of the city's founder, Peter I, who himself clipped the beards and whiskers of the old nobility, the speech, dress, and manners of the educated classes were Western. The foreign governess played an essential part in this transformation. Claire's life in St Petersburg was not the 'worse than galley slavery' Trelawny had predicted. The rigid segregation of the governess in Britain, alone in her chilly upstairs room, was unknown in the large, chaotic Russian households. Fifty servants in town, seventy in the country, and dependants encamped like nomads was the rule. Claire joined the medley of cousins, aunts, old nurses, or idle neighbours which made up the family party for picnics or charades. Her failure to write letters, which so distressed Mary, arose perhaps from a hectic social life.

Claire's first Russian pupil, the pretty Betsy Zotoff, was only a few years younger than her governess, and the two young women became friends. Their time together as teacher and student was short, since in

1824 Betsy became engaged to be married and Claire moved to a new post in Moscow,[3] but their friendship lasted. In July 1825 Betsy visited Moscow and invited Claire for an evening; next day the two went round the city together sight-seeing and shopping. The same year, four days before the Russian Christmas, Claire wrote in her journal: 'A letter came from the Countess Zotoff announcing her arrival and that of her two daughters and inviting me to dine with her tomorrow. I am delighted at the idea of seeing Betsy again.' The day of meeting was festive. 'The cold was very severe but the sun shone brightly and the atmosphere was so clear that everything sparkled in his rays; frost ice spires and steeples all seemed gay and dazzling with a thousand beams.'[4]

Betsy married Prince Czernicheff, who later became Russian governor-general of Warsaw, but she did not forget her English governess. In 1842 she was still writing to Claire and in 1844 invited her to stay for the summer.[5] This was the first of several long Russian friendships, which suggest Claire's gifts as a teacher. French, which she spoke fluently and correctly, was the domestic language of the Russian upper class, who reserved their native tongue for their serfs; she also spoke German and Italian. Claire's education in English, though erratic, had been better than average, her reading much wider and her musical talent exceptional. Despite the obscurity of her family background, she seemed to move gracefully and easily among the aristocracy of Petersburg and their children; her attitude to girls' education, learnt in the tradition of Godwin, Mary Wollstonecraft, and Mrs Mason, rejected Russian convention.[6]

> They educate a child by making the external work upon the internal, which is, in fact, nothing but an education fit for monkies, and is a mere system of imitation—I want the internal to work upon the external, that is to say, that my pupil should be left at liberty as much as possible, and that her own reason should be the prompter of her action.[7]

This method was evidently successful. After five years in Russia she was able to write to Jane with frank pride, 'I came here quite unknown . . . but I soon acquired a great reputation, because all my pupils made much more progress than those of other people.'[8]

Claire was fortunate that her first Russian year was spent in St Petersburg, one of the most romantic and beautiful cities in Europe. Some of her early impressions, as told to her stepfather, William Godwin, were recorded in his 1830 novel, *Cloudesley*. Claire felt, as any visitor to Leningrad still must, the enduring presence of Peter the Great, who had founded his new capital on islands where the three mouths of the River Neva pour into the Gulf of Finland. Her sense of Peter's character, 'aiming always at something vast', his contempt for danger or hardship, his 'violent excesses of rage'[9] were as vivid as his monument, the bronze rider on the rearing horse.

Claire spoke of pacing at moonrise along the Neva embankment,[10] when the walker sees a throng of granite bridges, towers, fantastically coloured and gilded palaces, and the glittering spire of the Admiralty, newly built when she saw it in 1823. Nor was she blind to the dark side of Russian life. When an aristocratic family was disgraced, 'some had been sent to Siberia: some imprisoned in fortresses; some only existed in their estates'. Executions were carried out publicly, in the sight of many thousands of spectators (a fact equally true in Britain at the time she recorded it). She knew also of the universal threat of torture, 'a mighty instrument in Russia for laying open secrets'.[11]

It was late June 1824 when Mary, with characteristic melancholy, at last recorded a letter from Claire: 'Poor girl. She is dismally tossed about.'[12] To her amazement, Claire was no longer in St Petersburg but had been for at least a month four hundred miles away, as governess to the children of a lawyer in Moscow named Posnikov.[12] She had gone boldly, of her own free will, not because she knew anyone there, but because 'the opportunities for foreigners are good', and she hoped to build up an independent practice as a tutor. No record survives of this unimaginable journey. We do not know if Claire travelled during the snow season, swift but bitingly cold, in a sledge drawn by three horses, with a rider galloping before to set the pace. The alternative way was by coach in summer over dusty, pot-holed roads which rain turned to deep quagmire. Timbers laid across the track shook coach and passengers, or broke the horses hooves; 'tossed about' would be a fair description of the journey rather than of Claire's state of mind.

Every foreign visitor noted the contrast between classical St Petersburg and the vast, sprawling village of Moscow. In 1812 Napoleon had advanced upon it, to meet only crackling flames; in the 1820s a new city, half-European, half-Asiatic, was still rising from the ashes.[13] Foreigners complained of the narrow twisting streets, uphill and down, the filth of staircases and corridors, the scavenging buzzards. 'Asiatic beyond any city I ever beheld,' wrote an English traveller. Pushkin captures the dazzling confusion of the city in *Eugene Onegin*:

> Street lamps go flashing by and stalls,
> Boys, country women, stately halls,
> Parks, monasteries, towers and ledges,
> Bokharans, orchards, merchants, shacks,
> Boulevards, chemists and cossacks,
> Peasant and fashion—shops and sledges.

Claire recorded her arrival at a house near Moscow. 'I was much tired and retired to rest early, but all hopes of repose were at an end after spending $\frac{1}{2}$ an hour in bed—Bugs the torment of Russia came in troops and I escaped only from them by sitting up the whole night in an arm-chair.'[14] In this city and the summer countryside of the Moscow River, Claire was to spend some of the best and worst days of her life as governess.

Here it is as well to consider Claire as letter writer. Her letters were fluent, vivid, sometimes lyrical and sometimes extremely funny: 'you write the most amusing and clever letters in the world', wrote Mary. Yet as evidence they must be read with considerable caution. Her imagination, though not quite in the class of Trelawny's, was ceaselessly active. Her volatile temperament swung from enjoyment to brooding over past griefs or present grievances, even as her pen dashed over the page. She was, moreover, a chameleon letter-writer, taking colour from the personality of her correspondent. Mary evoked regret for lost happiness, complaints of ill-health, or fears for Percy. Jane suggested feminine gossip, comic accounts of Russian life, even hints of romance. To or of Charles she wrote with childhood's loyalty, eager for news of his health, his work, his wife Toni, and their growing family. The letters are spontaneous and revealing, and the style not only full of humour and wit, but totally without literary affectation. They are best read in the light of each other and especially of her journal, which now took on new importance.

On 12 May 1825, Claire had taken up her journal again, this time in a small quarto volume bound in Russian leather. 'My Life flows so swiftly away and so unobservedly that I have need of a Journal to mark . . . its progress,'[15] she commented. But in fact her journal quickly expanded beyond the personal. Within two weeks, she had begun to explore the character of traditional Russia.

Russia has a million of soldiers . . . the mortality among these troops is dreadful from excess of fatigue and bad nourishment. At least ten and sometimes fifteen in every hundred die which is as great a mortality as in time of war . . . It is generally believed that the Russian people were always slaves. This is by no means the case. There were no slaves in Russia but such as became prisoners of war and were given to their conquerors, until three hundred years ago . . . The prisoners . . . worked for their master and he was obliged to pay their tax for them. The Government found that the prisoners or slaves' tax was much more regularly paid than that of the peasants, and therefore reduced the latter into a state of bondage, by attaching them to the soil, and exacting the tax from the master to whom they were given. This is the origin of slavery in Russia.[16]

Few Russians would utter such implied criticism of the state. Claire records 'a long talk about Philosophy' or 'a little political talk', while walking in the garden after tea with the Scottish tutor of a neighbouring family and the young German tutor of her own employers.[17] Such conversations, uncensored and unchaperoned, appeared strangely easier in autocratic Russia than in law-abiding England. Perhaps they passed unobserved in the hurly-burly of everyday life. Claire wrote of her employer in the Russian style by name and patronymic, Zachar Nicolaivitch. His wife, Marie Ivanovna, was a Kalmuck Tartar who spoke openly of her own 'ugly face', but compensated for it by what seemed to Claire an excessive 'adoration of instruction'.[18] They were not nobles but members of the rising professional classes, with whom she could feel reasonably at ease.

Claire's duties were to teach a little girl of 5, Sophie, always called Dunia or affectionately Dudinka, with two nieces of Marie Ivanovna, Catherine and Helene, who shared Dunia's education. An older niece, Olga, also lived with the family. After lessons, Claire took the children for walks on the Promenade of the Devichni Pol, or in the park of the Petrovsky Palace, or shopping for books and toys at Hutchinson's Foreign Bazaar in the *gorod*, the inner city. The pace was leisurely, and there was room for children's games. The house, in old Moscow style, was enclosed by a long, wooden fence, with its own garden, orchard, stables, coach house, servants' quarters, and paved yards.

Yet this spacious setting was filled to the brim by the conflicting activities of the huge Russian household. As Claire confided to Jane, 'never anywhere did quarrelling flourish as in Russia . . . every house is in a state of civil [war] with eternal jarring of ideas, manners and languages'.[19] European and Asiatic features danced in a gaudy haze before her eyes. When she was tired or worried the noise oppressed her: 'Their incessant squabblings frightens away every happy thought every sublime meditation . . . I seek a corner in this tumultuous house where to enjoy a moment's reverie, and I can only compare myself to some unfortunate miscreant pursued by a shouting rabble.'[20]

Such complaints called out Mary's anguished sympathy. Imagining Claire suffering as she herself would have suffered, she told Hogg, 'The climate hurts her health and the brutality of her associates her spirits.'[21] At other times, though, Claire joined in the battles with gusto. Half of her complained, the other half warmed to these passionate people.

As Claire established her journal, the May days brought Russia's late spring: a wind from the south 'soft and balsamic', showers 'soft pattering on the leaves'. The family 'drank tea in the bower in the garden'. Claire and the tutor walked out of doors; 'the blossoms of the acacia trees fall in showers upon us as we pass under their boughs'.

On 19 May, Marie Ivanovna, the children and their teachers, went by carriage to their summer home.[22] Zachar Nicolaivitch's country estate, Islavsky, lay about twenty miles west of Moscow on the river Istra which flows into the Moscow River through deep woods.[23] The property included five hundred acres of wood and water, with a small parterre of flower beds in the French style near the house. Beyond the park lay the farm, managed at Islavsky by the bailiff, Ivan, and the village where the serfs lived in wooden huts, decorated with carvings in patterns centuries old. The roads were of dust, deep mud, or ice, according to the season. The manor houses were also built of wood, sometimes disguised by painted plaster, always long and low-built, often with a chain of connecting rooms on the ground floor. Here stood the forte-piano from France, the billiard table from England, the casual clutter of Western books and journals, all the products of foreign cultures assimilated into a deeply Russian atmosphere.

In this environment, Claire began to feel at peace:

> Walk on the riverside with the whole household. Beautiful sunset. Light violet clouds surrounded by golden edges were reflected in the river, and so truly, so naturally . . . it could not be said which was the most perfect . . . grief consumed the tender bloom of youth and the whole world was a scene of

distress and struggling—but now I yield my soul up to all that surrounds me—I dare to look upon Nature as a consoling friend.[24]

Islavsky had a particular charm for Claire, in the links between the house and its natural setting in the woods. On every side hung balconies, each with its view of the estate. 'I cannot count the number of balconies there are in Islavsky and I stroll delightfully from one to another and spend a little time in each contemplating its prospect.'[25] Each afternoon the samovar was lit on the lower balcony, or in the arbour of the English garden; adults and children came and went at will, in a changing circle of idle gossip described by Pushkin

With tea and jam and endless tattle
About the weather, flax and cattle

or deep discussion, according to the mood of the moment. In one such discussion, on the French and German theatre, Claire declared boldly:

Passion is the high tide of the mind—it overleaps all bounds . . . Passion while it lasts is free . . . Passion in human nature is a Titan, on the french stage they imitate it upon such small proportions that she becomes a dwarf.[26]

Such moments created a personal creed.

Islavsky's grounds had hot-houses for fruit, a dairy, an Orangery, the children's own garden plots, where Claire planted and watered with Dunia; grain mills on the river and the pleasures of a traditional Russian bath house in the woods—high, light and built of well-scrubbed planks.

At one go to the Bath—Here I was very happy—reclining in the warmth of the soft water; and listening alone to the wind amid the trees; the green shade which the surrounding grove threw upon the room; it seemed to me as if I had laid my head upon the very bosom of Nature and were listening to the beating of her pulses and the breathing of her breast.[27]

On Sundays came the sound of bells from village churches. 'In the wood we hear the church bells ring for the mass and in the distance all the churches of the far off villages sounding also—this gave a meaning to the scene.'[28] The peasants crossed themselves at the sound, knowing the message of the peal, for the bells spoke a universal language; the great bell of the Zagorski Monastery could be heard twenty miles away. On Sundays there were no lessons; tutor, governess, and children walked in the woods. 'The sun setting from beyond the river pierced the deep woods behind the arbour in lines of golden light . . . The evening was still, except a soft wind whispering in the ear and lightly lifting every curl.' Claire found such moments 'inexpressibly dear'.[29]

June brought pleasure, for on the first of the month 'The Piano comes . . . After dinner unpack the Piano and sing.' There is a sense of quickening of tempo, of Claire waking to life and enjoyment again. The piano was needed to celebrate Marie Ivanovna's birthday, which fell on 5 June. The tutor Hermann Gambs had written a French comedy with musical numbers for the occasion, to be performed by the teaching staff with Olga Mikhailovna and Catherine, on the stage of a small private theatre in the Islavsky grounds.[30] The early rehearsals had taken place in the garden, to gales of laughter; Claire had already learnt her part, and was much pleased with the naturalness and vivacity of the style. Now, with the piano in place, the amateur company learnt the music specially composed by a prolific composer of romances and comic operas, Joseph Genischta. 'We repeat l'Impromptu at the theatre and sing'; the next day, 'Repetition both before and after dinner of the Impromptu'.[31] Not all the rehearsals were official; on 3 June 'I pass my morning very idly for M G [Gambs] is there and he makes me talk and sing with him.' Next day the composer of the score appeared, and Claire for once was silent while he sat at the piano and played the whole evening; 'we hung speechless upon his notes'.[32] There was time for one Grand Rehearsal in the theatre before twelve guests and a further 'Quantity of Officers whose names I do not know' arrived to dine. No guest was ever unwelcome in a Russian country-house. The evening continued in what appeared to be the normal way for this household:

> After dinner we play the Impromptu d'Islavsky. Then we drink tea in the Orangerie and dance. We return to the house thro' the gardens with a Polonaise. The rest of the evening passes in dancing.[33]

The polonaise was the formal processional dance which opened court balls. Every dancer knew the quadrille, the waltz, the galop, and the mazurka, in which couples dipped and swayed under the candle-lights. This country birthday party was carried through with the complete devotion the arts command in Russia. For the next two days, Claire was still excited; she 'sang and played the Marriage of Figaro', which she had seen at Covent Garden in 1818.

The impromptu had been such a success that there was general clamour for another performance. By the end of June 'they talked over in the Balcony how to arrange the play of *Esther*'. Apparently this intelligent company, at the very dawn of Russian literature, turned without question to a classical drama by Racine, so deep was the gulf between official French culture and the native language of the Russian working people. Gambs inevitably took the lead, acting two parts. This involved Marie Ivanovna drawling two lines, 'putting as much false emphasis and making more pauses than the sense would permit', while a posse of six valets in the wings tore one costume, including a beard, off Gambs and dressed him again in a quarter of a minute.[34] 'There is nothing but spouting of verses heard all over the house,' wrote Claire, 'nothing to be heard but exclamations and orders for the theatre and the rehearsal.' She was not needed to sing, so went into the garden to gather blackcurrants for the large houseparty. 'Innumerable dinners' were cooked, yet nothing was wasted. By traditional charity each household had its own 'unfortunates' to feed, or 'the beloved of God', innocent beings too simple-minded to earn a livelihood. After dinner on 22 July, *Esther* was performed and dancing followed. Next morning, Claire recorded, 'We all get up late and tired.'

A day later Claire and Gambs went for a long walk across the river, 'thro' a path overshadowed by a thick grove on both sides. We repose in a grassy nook and make garlands with grass and try our luck with blades of grass in flower'.[35] It was impossible for her not to be aware of this young Franco-German, whose lively mind invigorated the whole house. As well as producing plays, he edited a home-made magazine, the *Islavsky Gazette*, to which Claire contributed articles. In spare moments he read aloud to her—'After dinner M. Gambs reads aloud the Gazette which is very amusing'[36]—or novels, drama, and poetry in French and German, played duets or persuaded her to sing. Gambs also undertook for this crowded and polyglot household a series of lectures on European history—on Spain and the Inquisition, Greece and the Trojan war, the French monarchy from Louis XI onward, and aesthetics. Claire kept full and, for her, accurate notes, although her mind evidently strayed from the lecture to the lecturer during his first discourse on the sublime and the beautiful.

He looked very handsome—His broad white forehead and black hair, his brows arched, the extreme fire of his dark eyes, contrasted well with the delicate oval of his face and the varying colour of his cheek . . . formed a countenance rich in expressive enthusiasm and intellect.[37]

Almost every day the moody Russian summer allowed, they took long walks with the children: by the river bank to the mills, to the sand hill and the church, running races on opposite banks of the river, or to pick wild strawberries in the woods. On these walks, Chrétien-Hermann told tales of his student days, how he had fought a duel, how with friends he had climbed the great tower of Strasbourg by night and woken the sleeping city with a midnight concert on horns and trombones.[38] He had been at court in Weimar and had gone hunting at Saratov, deep in the Russian steppes, with his two dogs. 'He says it was the happiest time in his life.' Now he was writing poetry, which he read aloud. Claire wrote to Jane Williams that 'his society recalls our former circle, for he is well versed in ancient and modern literature and has the same noble enlarged way of thinking . . . What you felt for Shelley, I feel for him.'

Jane naturally assumed that this was love, but Claire insisted in reply, 'I am not in love as you suspected with my German friend Hermann.' Perhaps this denial was a form of self-defence, since the journal suggests a young woman in love. Claire had seen enough of the world to know her own disadvantages. She was the daughter of a free-thinking family in an age of increasing orthodoxy, reputedly 'sold' to Shelley by her stepfather, the discarded mistress of Byron and mother of his bastard child. There was no question of 'a good marriage' for her once her personal history was known. Ten minutes of happy passion with Byron, she was later to write, had 'discomposed the rest of my life'.[39]

For similar reasons, Jane had accepted the equivocal attentions of Jefferson Hogg; and Mary was proud of being Shelley's widow yet wrote pathetically in secret, 'cannot I yet forego the hope of loving and being loved'. None of them married. Pride sustained Claire, but she was often lonely.

Hermann Gambs's life story, by contrast with Claire's, was as clear as daylight. He was a native and graduate of Strasbourg, equally at home in French and German speech and culture. Although a protestant clergy son and eventually a minister himself, he was undogmatic, apart from a passion for liberty and equality. He had been among the crowd of hopeful tutors from all over Europe which disembarked on the quay of St Petersburg each spring when the ice broke. Adventurous like Claire, he had made his way far into the steppes, spent four years at Saratov, and was now established in Moscow.

'You may imagine how delighted he was to find me, so different from everything around him and capable of understanding what had been sealed up to long in his mind', wrote Claire to her confidante Jane. Unlike Claire herself, Hermann had nothing to hide. His admiration was frank and open. On 12 August, St Clare's day by the Western Gregorian calendar, which was 24 August by the Orthodox Julian dating, which was celebrated at Islavsky as Claire's holy day, she found a birthday cake at her place, concealing a French poem of thirty lines that Hermann had written in her honour.

> Quand elle règne sur ma vie
> Ton nom peut vivre dans mon coeur.[40]

To be loved again was revivifying:

> August 21 Fine weather.
>
> Walk in the great Alley. Again the sight of Nature rejoices me. I sit upon the Balcony at the bottom of the great Alley, and watch the wind among the trees . . .[41]

In love, life was not always serious; Claire liked to tease, as when 'MG has a new coat and admires himself in the glass', which the handsome young man accepted with good humour.

Chrétien-Hermann Gambs made a further and lasting contribution to Claire's life. For the first time since the death of Shelley, she had someone to encourage and direct her reading. She had always read sporadically, devouring an author who caught her interest: sixteen comedies of Molière in French in one month, seventeen plays by Goldoni in Italian in another. Now she kept a record of her reading at Islavsky from May to September 1826. Some was desultory, among books which lay around the house: odd numbers of the *London Monthly Review* and *Blackwood's Edinburgh Magazine*, the Romantic favourite *Paul et Virginie*, romances by La Motte-Fouqué author of *Undine*, *Lives of the Saints*, and a volume of English controversial tracts from 1813. Other reading, though, showed signs of systematic guidance. Frequently the journal records that Gambs introduced books by first reading them aloud. In drama, Claire read Racine's *Phèdre* while rehearsing *Esther*; Gambs's favourite German dramatist

Schiller's *Wallenstein* and *Wilhelm Tell*; and also a selection of Schiller's poems, including *Pegasus, Der Handschuh*, and *Die Kraniche des Ibykus*. Poetry included Shelley, of course, selections from Wordsworth, and the whole of Ariosto's *Orlando furioso* in the original Italian. A solid German education demanded some introduction to philosophy; for Claire, Moses Mendelssohn, *Phaedon* on the immortality of the soul, and Villiers *Philosophie de Kant*, defining his fundamental principles: 'never for a moment', Claire noted, 'does he admit any minor question to break in upon the devoted unity of his subject'. It was perhaps her first introduction to disciplined thought rather than free speculation.

Gambs's favourite study was European history, which was of great interest to Claire, who lived and worked in so many different countries. His library included some remarkably solid books, which he read concurrently, chapter by chapter, over a period of months. Rollin's *Histoire ancienne* in thirteen volumes occupied the weeks from September to November; des Odoard's *History of the French Revolution* (ten volumes) was intelligently accompanied by *Mémoires* of Marie Antoinette and Madame Roland, which Claire mentions reading with pleasure. Voltaire's *Histoire de Charles XII roi de Suède*, was followed by W. Robertson's *History of the Reign of the Emperor Charles V*, a massive comparative study of European societies in the century, which Claire read through the winter of 1825/6. Russian history was as yet little studied, but they found R. Lyall on *The Character of the Russians*. Finally Gambs selected '*Les Femmes* leur condition et leur influence dans l'ordre social chez different peuples', by A. J. P. de Ségur, an indication of his liberal leanings.[42] Five or six months is not long to devote to higher education, but whether from ardour or untapped intelligence, tutor and pupil achieved a creditable level of work in the time.

Hermann and Claire also had a shared interest in their work as teachers, which went on every day, except Sundays and the frequent Russian holy days, before private reading could begin. Here Claire had the easier and happier duties. She and 5-year-old Dunia formed a spontaneous affection for each other, unclouded by rigid or formal teaching. So Claire told stories and sang songs from which Dunia learnt English. A book ordered from London, *Papyro-Plastics*, demonstrated how to build and furnish a dolls' house from cardboard and papier mâché. They sowed seeds in Dunia's plot and watered the plants. Every fine day they went outdoors as much as possible for the little girl to run and skip freely, while her governess yielded to the vast mysterious power of nature in Russia. 'The whole face of the country is now beautiful. The wide space around is covered by high green corn, beyond one sees on every side the dark pine woods . . . the sun sets without a cloud, a quiet ocean of golden light.'[43]

The teaching of Johnny, an intelligent and charming tall boy, presented many more problems. His mother had 'such an adoration of instruction and knowledge' that she crammed his head with facts beyond endurance.

The Tutor and I so reason with her, and as she is uncommon weak, she always finishes by declaring she will follow our ideas; but no sooner are our backs turned than she gets the child into a corner, to teach him some important fact in Universal history—The boy is only nine years old and a great favourite of mine because he is so very frank but he is quite distorted by knowledge . . . by the time his lessons are over, his head is completely confused.[44]

John learnt four languages, but 'does not know enough of any language to express what he feels'. His imagination was so lively and his ideas so forcible that in frustration he seized and tugged at the clothing of his hearer as he fought for words. Claire found that if she held his hands, however gently, John could not speak at all. Fortunately, she was left in charge of the children when their mother went to St Petersburg for two months about a lawsuit. Gambs and Claire took the decision to reduce John's lessons by half and to let him eat his meals 'without the aid of historical recollections'. They did not try to deceive his mother:

I wrote to her . . . that in the space of two months, he had progressed so much for learning fewer words and thinking more, that I was happy to inform her, he could now say a sentence to the person opposite to him, without twisting all the buttons of his waistcoat.[45]

A governess was responsible not only for the lessons of her pupils, but for their play-time as well. The children were seldom without entertainment in this hospitable house. Four children—the cousins Helene and Catherine with John and Dunia—were always at home to make up games, with a constantly changing series of visitors' families (at one time in July, nine extra children were staying in the house). Visitors, young or grown-up, joined in. It is impossible to distinguish between adults and children in the games of hide and seek among the trees, 'hot cockles', Russian style catch-as-catch-can in pairs, swinging from a strong bough, baseball on the green in front of the house or charades—'a fighting scene takes place between me, John and Mr. Gambs'.[46]

One Sunday evening the young girls played with men at The Ring, holding a cord in a circle, while the odd one out tapped hands to secure a place. Marie Ivanovna entered in high dudgeon and then fell on the unwitting participants.

> She called all those poor young ladies by the most infamous names: who but a fille de joie would ever be so indecent as to give a gentleman a tap on his hand? And declared she would turn them all out in the street to starve. You may imagine the scene. About sixteen young ladies began to howl for forgiveness: the gentlemen stood aghast and I fell into such a fit of laughter at the strange sight that she grew furious and advanced to strike me—however some of the gentlemen interposed and saved me . . . So the thing continued till we sent for the old nurse to make peace. She came waddling in and with many Lack-a-daisies condoled with us—in vain she remonstrated with the mistress of the house and bid her remember . . . how often she had played at this game herself both before and since her marriage: but the other swore it was not in that indecent manner and began to howl also in her turn that the reputation of her house was done for. As a last remedy we sent off for the priest.[47]

This was a skilful move, for Marie Ivanovna intended to receive the Sacrament, for which an essential preparation in the Orthodox Church is to beg and receive personal forgiveness for any offence.

> Then a new scene began . . . she cried and wept threw herself on the mercy of all those she had offended, and begged pardon a thousand times, the old priest making the sign of the cross the whole while . . . This stupid scene lasted till twelve at night. And so it is almost every day.

The one person impervious to Marie Ivanovna's temperament was apparently her husband. 'Zachar Nicolaivitch says—I am now perfectly happy—My son devotes himself to his Marmot, and my wife to a Colonel.'[48] It is as though Yslaev, the amiable husband in Turgenev's *A Month in the Country*, had appeared on stage twenty years before his time.

Claire appeared by day in the lively society of Islavsky as inventive member of the revels. Yet at night, alone, she knew moods of sorrow. They came whenever something called up remembrances of the past. 'Listened with melancholy pleasure to the sound of the wind among the trees—it recalled to my mind the breaking waves upon the shores of Lerici.'[49] A summer storm on the night of 2 June brought memories more detailed, more distressing:

The lightning darted here and there by fits . . . the thunder muttered amid the howling of the wind and the beating of the rain. This made me melancholy—every gust of wind recalls Lerici and those days of storm and rain when the wind seemed raving up and down that savage place and roaming round our desolate house, as if searching every corner for our lost friends . . .[50]

Even in this remote place, unexpected news might alarm her: 'After dinner I take up the Newspaper by Accident and read there an account of a duel between Trelawny and another Englishman. In a moment my whole peace is destroyed.' Next night she saw him in a dream—'He was masked but spoke not.' Although banished as a lover, Trelawny still belonged to the magical Shelley band. Claire wrote to question Jane, yet was dissatisfied by her reply: 'What you say of Trelawny distresses me—it seems to me that you are unwilling to say what you have heard as it is of a disagreeable nature.'[51] Claire's instincts were correct, as later discoveries would confirm. For the present she was relieved by picking up an English newspaper, after breakfast on 13 September. 'I did not dare to read, yet notwithstanding with a horrible feeling of dread & yet hope—I read—that he was well . . . who shall describe the happiness I felt.'

September at Islavsky brought nutting time. 'After dinner we all go a walk to the woods to seek nuts.' They scattered among the trees, the children searching like terriers. Not all their instructors could keep up with them; the German governess's three petticoats fell down 'and she lags behind as usual'.

As they walked home they met an Islavsky servant 'upon the gallop' who told them there was scarlet fever in the village and that they must return, for safety's sake, by another route. Marie Ivanovna had already gone to beg a lodging for the children in the safety of the house of a German friend, Mme Zimmerman, a few versts away. Next day Claire took the four children there, and Mme Zimmerman gave them a kind and friendly welcome. They explored their temporary home.

It is an old wooden house built on the very edge of the cliff which descends steeply to the river—a bed of stones and sand . . . which is only covered in spring and autumn . . . By the side of our dwelling a little mountain river comes from inland and joins the Moscow River. We follow it to its source through a wild ravine between two ridges of hills . . . The sides of the hills are clothed with pines . . . The paths are narrow and intricate.[52]

Most days Claire took the children to this ravine before lessons, and they scrambled happily up and down the steep banks. The sun shone for six days, but on the seventh they woke to a country 'veiled with a thin white mist of falling rain'. Unwilling to face the racket of games indoors and convinced that the children were healthy, Claire decided to take them home. The droshsky came to fetch them and the children piled in, though Claire herself chose to walk. At Islavsky they found happy disorder, the maids in the drawing room playing cards with two visiting officers. Next day and the day after Claire noted: 'Rain in torrents.'[53] They had reached home just as the weather broke. It was the end of summer.

The Islavsky idyll was ending. It was mid-September, and having walked with Gambs up and down the great Alley in the park Claire noted: 'The groves are not yet bare, but the fresh countenance is changed to a deep brown except where the unchanging pine stretches its vigorous branches amid the fading branches of its neighbours.'[54] The changing scene foreshadowed a change in life.

In the evenings, Claire always read the children stories—from *The Parent's Assistant, or Stories for Children* by Maria Edgeworth: 'The Basket Woman', 'Tarlton', 'The Barring Out', and 'The Birthday Present'. On Sunday 20 September, Dunia missed the story; she fell sick after tea and went to bed. Next day Claire recorded, 'Dunia has been ill all night', by Tuesday, 'Dunia is very ill'; apparently she had caught the scarlet fever still spreading among the serf children. She 'spent a very bad night', and on the dark, cloudy morning of Wednesday 'a blister is applied to her throat'. The whole house was sad and uneasy.

After dinner we are alarmed at Dunia's state, one of perpetual restless listlessness. No consciousness yet perpetually tossing from side to side. I went to her at eight o'clock and did not leave her till five the next morning.

At midnight Claire woke Gambs, who set off to consult the German doctor from Ilinsky; it was thought that Dunia had developed pneumonia:

She lay in utter insensibility . . . her chest more oppressed at every moment; her cheeks of a burning pink and all round her mouth of an ashy pale . . . The difficulty of breathing increased every moment & we were obliged to hold her up to prevent her from suffocation.[55]

Gambs returned with the doctor's orders to apply leeches behind the ears and mustard plaster to the legs. 'We did so but she gently expired while it was being applied.'

Dunia, so playful and affectionate, was 5 years old: the same age at which Allegra, in her small, sealed coffin, had travelled beyond her mother's knowledge. Claire mourned both deaths in one: 'The lovely child smiling and brilliant as a star lay not in death but in a sweet stillness before us. A thousand wounds bled afresh in my heart.'[56] At six in the morning Gambs, who had been up since midnight, rode to Moscow to break the news to Dunia's father. They returned together. 'Zachar Nicolaivitch could find no rest for his sorrow; every moment he returned to look at his lost darling & then again hurried away unable to bear the sight.'[57] Claire, who did not know where her own child's body lay in the earth, shared Dunia's funeral rites as though a member of the family.

Dunia is dressed in white and laid out upon a table and tapers in tall candelabras are burning around. The angelic smile of death is soon lost . . . and a hollow leaden vacancy looks out from the once beaming countenance . . . all the peasants come to take leave of her, and the whole morning was spent in weeping and wailing . . .

Dunia's cousins watched by her body all night. On the morning of the burial, Claire got up early and went to the Orthodox church:

At eleven the funeral service began—after the mass, the priest gave a lighted taper to every[one] & after singing the funeral anthem, every one in the church approached to kiss the departed . . . Everyone shrieked & wept as the body was lowered into the grave.[58]

Grief for Dunia reawakened mourning for Allegra and rekindled emotions too quickly suppressed in the Shelleys' general tragedy. Claire walked again in the great Alley: 'the dead leaves are stirless on their branches; not a single bird in the grove . . . All nature had faded.'

9 *Hard Winters in Moscow (1825–1827)*

Three days after Dunia's funeral, Marie Ivanovna began to recover from her paroxysms of grief and the household prepared to move back to Moscow. 'Pack up,' wrote Claire on 28 September. 'Walk all round the gardens. All is solitude, silence and ruin.' Next day, when they reached Moscow, Johnny was ill with a fever. Misery, confusion, and 'nights of breathless anxiety' followed until he began to recover. Claire sat with him at night, reading his favourite Maria Edgeworth stories aloud. After ten days, Claire tells us that 'even now that Johnny is nearly recovered the whole house is topsy-turvy. I sleep upon chairs every night there being no bed to be had . . . The days pass so miserably away they leave nothing but a blank trace of misery behind them.'[1]

Still in mourning for Dunia, the house remained irresistibly, even comically, Russian. One evening in December a Mme Gerardoff called 'and disputed so loud upon holy subjects with Marie Ivanovna there was no staying in the room'. The shrieks of the two pious ladies battered Claire's eardrums: 'Each tried by raising her voice to make the other listen and as neither yielded the noise went on rapidly increasing to the very highest pitch.'[2]

Marie Ivanovna, with all her eccentricities, was warm-hearted and kind. She would not turn Claire out. Soon after Dunia's death, she had a long talk with her governess, which Claire reported to Jane Williams:

> By the death of the little girl I became of little or no use in the house and the thought of entering a new house and have to learn new dispositions was quite abhorrent to me. Nothing is so cruel as to change from house to house and be perpetually surrounded by strangers; one feels so forlorn, so utterly alone that I could not have the courage to begin the career over again; so I settled to remain in the same house to continue the boy's English and to give lessons out of doors [i.e. as a daily governess in other houses]. It is not very agreeable to walk about in the snow and in a cold of twenty, sometimes thirty degrees [below zero]; but anything is better than being a governess in the common run of Moscow houses, and I often enjoy moments of serenest calm.[3]

So Claire went from house to house as daily teacher.

At home, Claire made herself useful to Marie Ivanovna in a number of ways: sorting household linen with the new maid (she had learnt enough Russian to talk with the house serfs), washing and ironing frocks, baking cakes to a recipe from London, reading aloud in English, continuing lessons to Johnny and his cousins, Catherine and Helene. Her chief duty and chief consolation was to perform music for the family and guests in the evenings.

Music now took an increasing part in her life. Genichsta, who had contributed the music for the Islavsky impromptus and was later to be well known as a composer and conductor praised by Berlioz as a rehearsal pianist, now came to the house each week to give Claire music lessons. It seems hardly possible that she could have met his fees out of her seventy-five pounds a year, and probable that her rich and generous employers paid, though this is not stated in writing. Claire got up early, sometimes as early as five on a black winter's morning, to practise voice and piano.[4] She learned Genichsta's own Exercises for technique, the Sixth Concerto for Piano and Orchestra, by John Field, the blind Dublin composer who had settled in Russia in 1803; and Hummel's Variations on *La Sentinelle*, and on the march from Rossini's *La Cenerentola*. She writes of performing a Beethoven sonata and learning 'Beethoven's seventeenth sonata where there are triolets and semiquavers that almost drive me mad'.[5] The 'triolets' are evidently triplets, three notes in the time of two. Claire sang as well as played, and gave a recital of Schiller poems set by Genichsta, for which the composer himself played the accompaniments. 'When he ceased to play, all seemed dull, flat and void; the air seemed empty to which before he had given a soul.'[6]

Genichsta evidently liked Claire's interpretation of the Schiller songs, for five days later, on 6 December 1825, he sent her a present of all his compositions. In an age of drawing-room musicians, the chance to study with a professional was rare. Claire made the most of it, since she knew the lessons could not continue indefinitely. 'Got up early and practised. It is very cold. After dinner slept & then practised till eleven at night.'[7] The strong technique lasted her lifetime and the study deepened her musicianship. But sadly, music was not her only concern; as the Russian Christmas approached, she knew she must leave Marie Ivanovna and move to a strange house.

This winter was to see a critical development in Russia's history too: the December Revolution of 1825. The first secret societies for the reform of Russian government had been formed among young officers who travelled to the West during the Napoleonic wars and after. They saw Western political freedom, the excitement of the Carbonari plots in Italy, the final success of the Greek revolution, and they were struck by the contrast between life in Europe and life in Russia. They were an attractive group, young, brave, well educated and noble, since only the nobility had access to higher education. Their aims included freedom of speech and worship, trial by jury, and an end to serfdom. The St Petersburg group adopted the revolutionary principle, 'The source of the supreme power is the people.'[8] This was essentially an underground movement, yet in November 1825 a strange sequence of events provoked an open crisis.

In Claire's journal it is introduced briefly and casually. 'Do you know,' asks a friend one Sunday morning, 'the Emperor is dead at Taganrog!' Alexander I had gone to the Sea of Azoff in the south for his health. His rule, though ineffective, had showed liberal intentions. He had proposed a constitution for Russia and the freeing of the serfs. In practice the constitution was confined to Poland and the release to the Baltic states, yet in his reign Western liberals could feel that Russia was slowly moving with the times. His death brought a sharp frost to their hopes. Alexander's heir was his next brother, Constantine, but Marie Ivanovna's sister wrote that 'Constantine will not accept the Russian crown.'[9] In fact Constantine had married a Polish noblewoman who was a Roman Catholic, and he preferred to live with her in Poland. He had resigned the throne in favour of the military youngest brother, Nicholas. All this, in the Imperial Russian manner, had been concealed from the population, and the coronation mystified onlookers. Constantine, short, thick-set and ugly, advanced his superb soldier brother Nicholas to receive the Russian Imperial mantle, 'apparently happy in so doing'.[10] There was public confusion over which heir was the true emperor. Claire heard visitors to the house talking in whispers of 'bad news from Petersburg'.[11] No foreign newspapers were on sale. 'Nobody here receives periodicals from France,' the poet Pushkin, raging with frustration, wrote to a friend in French, 'I am condemned to live among these orangutans at the most interesting moment of our century.'

This public doubt and confusion offered an opportunity for the revolutionary groups to attack Imperial tyranny. On 14 December 1825, Nicholas I had himself proclaimed czar and drew up his troops on Senate Square, next to the gold spire of the Admiralty, to swear allegiance. Already, members of the secret reform groups had been persuading officers and men to reject the oath. By mid-day, about three thousand members of the Moscow Regiment, one Grenadier regiment, and the Marine Guards had refused to swear allegiance. The governor of St Petersburg was shot, 'by a common soldier as he was haranguing them to obedience', as Claire heard; in fact, the bullet was fired by a civilian in the crowd. The Metropolitan Archbishop Serafim in his robes and Grand Duke Michael, a royal cousin, went unheard, until finally, as night and freezing darkness closed in, the czar gave orders to fire cannon into the square. The crowd broke and fled. Nobody ever knew how many were killed, but information circulated furtively in Moscow. 'The usual people dined . . . All the guests are as usual full of consternation and surmises. Different arrests have taken place,'[12] wrote Claire, after a social gathering in Orthodox Christmas week. Nicholas I, a believer in military discipline, dealt personally with the leaders of the December Revolution. Five were condemned to death and executed, others exiled to hard labour in Siberia for life. A generation of liberal writers mourned them. The czar instituted press censorship, passports, and the 'Third Section', a secret police to monitor political subversives. At Kazan University the sciences of anatomy and astronomy were suspended as 'impious'.

Marie Ivanovna, at her dinner-table, spoke boldly of the new czar as 'a rising Nero'. Claire would have liked to applaud, but remembered from experience in Vienna that it was dangerous for a teacher to utter liberal opinions. As she wrote to Mary:

> Our political horizon here has been very stormy; there has been no end to the panic terror which has reigned for six months. Arrests and imprisonments are innumerable and all among the flower of the russian youth . . . I dare say you know more of the matter than I do, for no one here dare mention the subject.[13]

In this atmosphere of political reaction, Claire was careful to say nothing about her own family background and beliefs, even to friends in the circle of English teachers. As she told Jane, 'I had few acquaintance among the english, to those I had never mentioned a single circumstance of myself or fortunes but took care on the contrary to appear content and happy as if I had never known any other society all my days.' Claire concealed the fact that she had read Godwin's *Political Justice* or Shelley's *Queen Mab*, and hid even more deeply that she had lived in the households of both revolutionary writers. The atmosphere was hostile to them.

The principles that I looked on as sacred were objects of execration to the rest of mankind: the persons whom I cherished and revered were the objects of scorn and blame . . . their name so forbidden that, though deeply graven in my heart, it never passed my lips.[14]

Conversation was banal, avoiding any controversial topic; Claire learned to hold her tongue, though the provocation was extreme when guests 'reviled our dearest Shelley'. But she had to keep her anger to herself, as she did when she read Medwin's *Conversations of Lord Byron*, published in January 1827.

My God, what lies that book contains! Poor Shelley is made to play quite a secondary part . . . When I was in bed I wept a great deal because my reading of today had brought back Shelley vividly to my mind.—It is cruel to think how his merit was lost upon the world, how that impostor Byron was admired for his imposture.[15]

Claire also learned from Medwin's book of Byron's death. Byron had died of fever in April 1824 at Missolonghi, dehydrated by the zealous purging and bleeding of his doctors. Mary wrote about the death to Trelawny, but did not know Claire's address. Claire later heard through Mary from Byron's manservant Fletcher that on his deathbed Byron had talked of her and seemed uneasy of her fate and anxious if possible to repair it. Claire was not convinced: 'This I always thought was a lie invented by the tenderness of Fletcher's heart. I knew the man too well.'

But Claire's concern was more for Shelley than for Byron. Riled by Medwin's view of Shelley, Claire wrote her own private description of Shelley, a description which suggests neither physical nor even personal love but the poet's enduring spiritual qualities:

S. was beautiful with that kind of beauty which Bacon says is the best—'that which a picture cannot express'. It dwelt upon his countenance, it enshrined his person, and seemed to be a perpetual emanation from himself, rather than any union of exquisite proportions either in form or figure.

Returning later to the theme she added:

His whole existence was visionary, and there breathed in his looks and in his manners that high and superhuman tone which we can only conceive as belonging to a superior being.[16]

Claire apparently showed none of those deeply personal memories of Shelley to his widow, who might well have felt them intrusive. Instead, knowing Mary's concern for social standing (following her efforts to assure the status of her son), Claire described instead the extreme conformity of Russian manners under the rule of Nicholas I. As Batiushkov described society in *A Walk Through Moscow*, 'boredom and all its tortures' reigned. Claire, as resident governess, lived in high society, yet the concerns of that society were, for her, strangely restricted—'No talk of public affairs, no talk of books, no subject do I ever hear of except cards, eating and the proper management of serfs'.[17] Sometimes, to escape the dangers of political conversation, the gentlemen turned to talk of love, 'for it is the only topic upon which they can speak their minds . . . the usual nonsense about infidelity being unpardonable in women but very pardonable in men'.[18] Outside, by late November the heavy snows of winter had begun to fall, 'between the bare branches of the trees and filled up every interstice, so that [where] there was an overarching canopy of leaves now presents a roof of snow & frost work'. By the third week of December, Claire's awareness of the beauty of the winter scene had given way to complaints about the cold as she went out to teach her various pupils in their parents' houses: 'the cold returning home was intense one's breath seemed chilled in one's breast and scarcely able to force a passage against the cold'.[19] Next day she wrote: 'Unwell with the cold. Notwithstanding, went in sledge.' By Western Christmas 1825 she was ill, with inflamed eyes from the blinding snow dazzle, a neuralgic headache, and pain in the chest. Yet soon after, she was up and dressed again, taking John for sledging expeditions.

One question never answered is what Claire wore in the murderous cold of a Moscow winter. Western silk, linen, and even muslin frocks with a linen chemise and tiny satin slippers were the fashion, and the Hermitage collection of costumes shows extra garments to meet the Russian climate. These include walking dresses of fine soft cashmere, padded and quilted garments; the short spencer jacket or the long full-skirted redingote—from the English 'riding coat', or the uniquely Russian creation, double-sided woollen stoles made by serf weavers in brilliant colours on white. To go out of doors in winter, when the temperature stood at twenty degrees below zero, a heavy fur coat, hood, and boots were essential; the peasants wore sheepskins. Claire came to Austria and Russia with her former Italian wardrobe. The only outer garments she is known to have owned at this time were a shawl, treasured all her life because it was a gift from Shelley, and a fur tippet which needed mending.[20] Did she receive cast-offs, the usual perquisite of ladies' maids? Few things would have been more galling to her independence and pride. Understandably she was silent on the subject, even in her private journal.

Winter ended in Moscow as swiftly as it had begun. In May 1826 Claire wrote to Mary:

It is wonderful how soon the warm weather has begun here . . . In three weeks from the disappearance of the snow the grass was so high that it has already been mown. The change from winter to summer here resembles the illumination of St. Peters—from sudden darkness light bursts forth—a change from one excess to the other.[21]

Spring brought another and less welcome change: Hermann Gambs left Moscow for another post. Claire later admitted to Jane Williams that she missed his company. 'He went away last spring for five years to the country. I have a great friendship for him because he has the most ardent love of all that is good and beautiful of anyone I know.'[22] We know that the two partners in this *amitié amoureuse* continued to exchange letters, since Claire 'wrote to Hermann' from her bed in January 1827; yet the correspondence, if it survives, has not been discovered. It would be natural to see this as the usual summer holiday flirtation but for two facts. In December 1830 Claire wrote to Mary that *Moïse*, a French poem by Hermann, had pleased her very much when he read it to her, and added: 'If you have any literary friends in Paris to propose it to some bookseller . . . I know my friend has nothing more at heart than to appear in print.'[23]

Claire apparently continued to make efforts for the poems. Chrétien-Hermann Gambs published his three-volume *Œuvres poétiques* in Paris in 1834 and *Poésies fugitives* in Strasbourg in 1838. A second fact is that all these volumes appeared under the *nom de plume* of C. Clairmont. The choice of Claire's name as pseudonym suggests a debt of some kind still remembered by the poet. The poems are Shelleyan in sympathy, and accord well with a nephew's description of Gambs's 'fiery temperament' and his 'passion for liberty and equality'. Several of them begin with a verse dedication to a nameless feminine reader: 'Mon coeur est plein de vous, mais ma bouche est muette' (My heart is full of you, but my mouth is dumb). The poet declares that the world's indifference does not trouble him if this reader approves: 'Elle a jugé comme peut juger l'ange' (She has judged as only an angel can judge). A dramatic sketch among the poems includes an appealing character named 'Clara la Fauvette', or warbler bird. Claire's own verdict was simple and brief: 'It was the happiest time of my life; but the golden dream which I thought would be realized has vanished.'[24] By the time Gambs returned to Moscow, Claire was in Italy. Knowing she could not stay indefinitely in Marie Ivanovna's house, she spent the early months of 1826 looking for a new post, but the opportunities available were very few. An Englishwoman of whom Claire was fond had failed in the attempt to open a boarding-house at Odessa and was due to return to teaching in Moscow. As Claire told Jane:

> I expected her arrival daily and began to grow uneasy—at length someone wrote to another acquaintance of her here, that she had destroyed herself . . . the horror of entering again as governess, made her resolve on this as the only means to escape it.[25]

Claire was a born survivor, unlikely to yield to despair; yet the prospects were unpromising. A Moscow lady offered her a post as companion to travel to Podolia on the Turkish frontier, but she decided not to take this exciting opportunity ('I should certainly go'), because she was afraid of her husband, 'who is a most ferocious violent man and who is suspected of having killed his wife's brother in order to encrease her fortune'.[26] Claire would have liked to return to St Petersburg, where the Westernized inhabitants did not threaten such dangers. She hoped Trelawny might secure letters of introduction for her from 'the numerous dear female friends he will immediately have', but he was abroad and did not answer letters. Claire's mother urged her to come home, but she could not bear the thought of 'living upon others'. Determined to be independent, she accepted that 'teaching is the only thing I know'. By April 1826, her 28th birthday, she was governess in the house of Prince and Princess Paul Galitzin.

The Moscow house of Claire's new employers was on the Tverskoi Boulevard, one of a ring of streets originally enclosing the inner city. Through the centre ran a belt of grass and trees, chestnut and lime, veiling the walls of the Strasnova Monastery opposite.[27] The aristocratic houses, though built of wood, were plastered and painted in classical style, with ochre-washed walls, white columns, and pediments. Their dignity was oppressive. Tolstoy writes in his *Youth* that he remembered the sensation of visiting in the boulevard during his student days: 'as I ascended the huge staircase I felt as if I had become terribly small'. Claire had little feeling for architecture, she never wrote of an overwhelming townscape, the red walls and rainbow domes of the old Kremlin, little more than a mile from her door. Yet even so, she felt the contrast between the classical calm of the house and the raging family life within its walls.

If St Petersburg and Islavsky saw Claire's happiest days in Russia, the Galitzin mansion certainly saw her worst. By ill-fortune, she went from a cosmopolitan and friendly household to a family set in the harshest of old Russian traditions. From the first, she felt insecure, the subject of gossip among staff and visitors or the object of their prurient curiosity. She took to stratagems in order to conceal the Shelley family name—for instance, sending letters to Mary under cover to Jane Williams. Later she made an arrangement at her music shop to send and receive mail 'chez Monsieur Lenhold, Marchand de Musique à Moscou';[28] this concealed any damaging connections in the West.

In England, Claire's relations had no wish to draw attention to her. As Leigh Hunt, with a journalist's instinct for a celebrity's death, began *Lord Byron and some of his Contemporaries*, Mary wrote tactfully:

> I think if I were near you, I could readily persuade you to omit all allusion to Clare [spelt thus]. After the death of Lord Byron, in the thick of memoirs, scandal and turning up of old stories, she has never been alluded to . . . In fact poor Claire has been buried in entire oblivion, and to bring her from this, even for the sake of defending her, would I am sure pain her greatly and do her mischief. Would you permit this part to be erased?[29]

Meanwhile Claire faced hardship in Russia. Urgently needing money and shelter, she had taken the first available post without question. Foreign visitors often observed how the institution of serfdom brutalized home life in Russia. As the German-born Catherine the Great had observed, 'inclination to tyrannise is inculcated from the tenderest age by the cruelty which children observe in their parents' behaviour towards servants, for where is the home that has no traps, chains, whips to penalize the smallest mistakes?'[30]

In this cruel society, Claire attempted to understand the six Galitzin children, especially the three girls it was her duty to teach: 'I cannot seriously be angry with them, for I do not know how they can be otherwise with the education they receive.' Yet to a Shelleyan they shattered ideals of childhood: 'I never thought children could be so

1. 'Go to Miss Curran's and sit for my portrait'. Rome 1819

2. 'Allegra — a pretty little girl enough, and reckoned like papa.' Byron, Venice, 1818

3. 'One's breath seemed chilled in one's breast.'

4. Travelling sledge. In one winter fourteen thousand travellers froze to death.

5. 'The air on that beautiful warm coast is a field of fragrance.' Bay of Naples, 1831

6. 'Mrs Sanford says you must send her stays.' Paris Boulevard, 1845

7. 'How can I get the Mantilla over.'
Claire to Mary, Paris 1845.

8. 'The pleasure of seeing dear you and dear Percy.' London to Field Place, 1845

9. 'Walk in Boboli. A divine day.' Florence, with Boboli Gardens, 1827

hideous or vicious; they never cease brawling; squabbling and fighting, from morning till night, but I cannot describe them.'[31]

Claire wrote in May 1826 to Mary describing her new situation in terms of frank gloom.

I am now in another house but I am far from happy. I have three children and I have to teach them everything—from eight in the morning till half past ten at night I have not a second to myself and then you may imagine how tired I am. I often throw myself on the bed without undressing because I am completely worn out . . . All I desire is repose and it seems to me often that nothing can sufficiently quench that desire except Death which from its mere stillness always appears to me lovely and amiable.[32]

Mary understood this longing for death only too well: 'how dark—how very dark the future seems,' she wrote, 'poor dear Claire . . . my heart melted within me at the thought of her dreariness'. Mary now received a living allowance of £250 a year from Sir Timothy Shelley and invited Claire 'to share my fortune here', privately hoping that if they lived in the country together, 'the grand annoyance [nuisance] of Mrs. G[odwin] will be neutralized'.[33] Claire was touched by this spontaneous kindness, as she showed by sending Mary a little ready money from her own savings when the Shelley allowance was delayed.[34] These matter-of-fact gestures of help on both sides show the family loyalty of Mary and Claire more convincingly than their volatile and moody writings.

Prince Paul and the princess were remote but frightening figures who gave Claire the feeling that she was:

a complete slave . . . I have never one half hour to myself except Sundays and then I am full of work [needlework]. I feel at every moment like a person who has lost his way: every step taken is one of dread for fear it may lead further into danger and yet on he must; and so with me. I never know whether the most innocent of my actions will not produce a dispute—a scene—and this from the detestable nature of the people.[35]

The children, too, were frightened of their parents. If the prince and princess went away, or even out to drive, there was a perceptible lightening in the atmosphere. The princess herself was a famous beauty, and her major interest in her children apparently an insistence that their hair should be curled. Otherwise, she showed little interest as Claire wrote, 'the instant they fall into their father's or mother's way and are troublesome, they are whipped'.[36]

The Galitzin household, in the custom of the Russian gentry, removed to spend the summer of 1826 on their country estate at Nazarievna, on a small plain lost in surrounding hills dark with pine trees. Before they left, in a harsh Moscow spring, Claire wrote to Jane, prepared for the worst:

> Cold, bleak winds have brought me back if not the presence at least the feeling of winter. Pray my dear friend write to me—I am now going to the country where I shall see nothing but marsh and heath. My heart becomes as waste and desart as the wide country stretching all around me . . .
>
> Shall I ever see you and Mary in Italy again? My melancholy writes a no to that.[37]

Claire's melancholy exaggerates the bleakness of the country. The summer improved to become 'Italian', she wrote, adding that she bore up very well 'because we were often in the garden'. She had written earlier that though there were no English-style school games, 'boys may jump and play, but girls must always be in a state of etiquette which constraint spoils their disposition'.[38] With the Galitzins there were no children's games, no picnics, no reading aloud before bedtime. Yet in summer when all the children were out of doors, they enjoyed a chance to grow healthily tired and good humoured.

Even so, Claire nursed hopes of change. Having met the Professor of English at Moscow University, an acquaintance of Walter Scott's son-in-law Lockhart, Claire wrote that he had 'a great deal of friendship' for her:

> because as he says very truly I am the only person beside himself who knows how to speak english. He professes the most rigid principles . . . I however took care not to get upon the subject of principles and he was of infinite use to me.

The professor recommended Claire as tutor to the only daughter of a rich and distinguished family; 'no one can give the child the education she ought to have but Miss C.' Overjoyed at the prospect of escape, Claire accepted the post as soon as it was offered. She was counting the days to release, when suddenly, without warning or apparent reason, she writes: 'all is broken off'.

The mystery was explained in the autumn. Another English governess in Moscow, Miss Trewin, had been to London on holiday. Mrs Godwin, avid for news of Claire, 'got hold of Miss T., sought her out and invited her to dine'. On 21 August, by Godwin's diary, Miss Trewin dined at Gower Place and made the astonishing discovery that Claire had been brought up in the house of this notorious infidel. 'Miss T. came back full of my story here.' It spread through the schoolrooms of Moscow and inevitably reached the Professor's ears:

> You may imagine this man's horror when he heard who I was; that the charming Miss Clairmont, the model of good sense, accomplishments and good taste was brought up, issued from the very den of freethinkers . . . he cannot explain to himself how I can be so extremely delightful and yet so detestable . . . 'God knows' he says 'what Godwinish principles she might not instil.'[39]

All hope of escape to a better position was at an end. Claire despaired. 'I do not know how far this may extend.' She felt bitterly that her mother's curiosity had done her 'an incalculable mischief'.

The full misery of life with the Galitzin children appeared only when winter imprisoned them indoors. A letter to Jane which reached London on 22 January 1827 described her usual day. She rose early for domestic tasks, which filled most of the morning. Then,

> from eleven till four I teach my children, then we dine—at five we rise from table—they have half an hour's dawdling, for play it cannot be called as they are in the drawing-room and then they learn two hours more. At eight we drink tea and then they go to bed which is never over till eleven because all must have their hair curled which takes up an enormous time.[40]

This account is cheerless, but factual and objective. A letter to Mary of about the same date, by contrast, is an outpouring of misery and resentment too long dammed up. In style and feeling it resembles the hysterical letters she had written to Byron as a young girl terrified of danger to Allegra. 'I have been tormented to death. I am shut up with six hateful children. They keep me in a fever from morning till night.' Claire explains that the children are afraid of their parents, who have them whipped,

> but the instant they are with me which is pretty nearly all the day, they give way to all their violence and love of mischief because they are not afraid of my mild disposition. They go on just like people in a public house, abusing one another with the most horrid names and fighting; if I separate them then they roll on the ground, shrieking that I have broken their arm, or pretend to fall into convulsions, and I am such a fool I am frightened.

Claire may have hated these children, but she pitied them for the crushing etiquette which warped their natures.

> Everything is a crime; they may neither jump, nor run, nor laugh; it is now two months they have never been out of the house and the only thing they are indulged in is eating and drinking and sleeping; so that I look upon their defects as proceeding entirely from the pernicious lives they lead.[41]

Given the tone of the letter to Jane, it seems to us that the importance of the letter to Mary has been exaggerated. It was, after all, written under exceptional circumstances—Claire, by her own admission, was 'completely giddy from worry . . . in a tottering situation' and 'unable to think upon my affairs', had slept badly for weeks from 'fever at night', and was near the onset of a serious illness—yet for several generations it was accepted, apparently without question, as the sole account of Claire's experiences and emotions during her life in Russia, from her arrival in March 1823 to her final departure in May 1828. There are two principal reasons for this strange distortion. One is simple lack of evidence; Claire's journals, so full of light and shade, so charged with contrasting emotions, were known only in brief quotations from the years with Shelley, which were considered their sole claim to literary interest.[42] The second reason for the exaggerated influence of this one letter among many is the overwhelming effect it had on Mary. In Mary's nature, love entwined itself with fears and anxieties: 'I am beyond measure anxious to learn how she is.' Her Gothic imagination seized upon Claire's sufferings, and she related them in good faith to any sympathetic hearer. This established the legend of Claire's unremitting misery in Russia.

Claire's journal remained unwritten for eleven months of 1826: 'every day I have put off writing it, tired of having nothing to say and because I was overwhelmed with work'. Then, on 21 December 1826, the notebook came to life again. Claire's zest revived, and for a simple reason. The prince and princess, with their children, had gone away on a visit to the country. 'So I am as quiet as a bird roosting for the night,' wrote Claire thankfully. As if to consolidate her happiness, a letter of two lines arrived from Mary's 6-year-old son. '*Percino.* Darling boy,' wrote his step-aunt ecstatically. This child, or Claire's image of him, became her idol.

Claire decided to enjoy herself with a freedom unthinkable for the governess in any orderly British household. Guests, often friends of the absent Galitzins, arrived casually to dine, to stay overnight, to go to the Opera. Claire herself invited a Monsieur and Madame de Villeneuve to dine because they had been to Greece, a country that had long captured her imagination.

Claire's first thoughts of Greece had stirred five years earlier. Then Shelley, sharing her lodgings at Leghorn in October 1821, began writing *Hellas* to honour a city

> Based on the crystalline sea
> Of thought and its eternity;

Trelawny wrote of 'buckling on the sword in the great struggle of Liberty'. In 1823 he had sailed with Byron to Greece in an old tub chartered for the journey, 'all on fire for action and ready to endure the worst that may befall'. The worst inevitably befell.

Trelawny had joined a guerilla raiding party led by a local brigand, Odysseus Androutsos. With childish credulity he wrote to Claire 'we are sworn brothers . . . he is brave, clever and noble'. He believed this self-styled 'Governor of Attica' represented the Greek Revolutionary Government and retired with him to a cave on Mount Parnassos, as he thought, 'commanding for my Chief an important Fortress'. In fact, Odysseus, disappointed of funds, secretly intrigued with the Turkish enemy; he was captured by the Greeks and murdered in prison. Claire, reading this in newspapers, was disturbed. 'What this means I cannot make out,' she wrote in her journal in the evening of 24 June 1825. 'I cannot believe that the chief Edward has chosen is one capable of betraying his country; but I am naturally extremely low-spirited at this news, tho' I do my best to believe it is false.' Trelawny was less realistic; he still failed to recognize his 'sworn brother's' treachery and refused to surrender the cave to the official Greek army. A raiding party of seven was sent to assassinate him; in the shoot-out which followed he lost part of a jaw and the use of an arm, and for three weeks his life hung in the balance. 'I have had a narrow escape Claire,' he wrote in October 1825, 'terribly cut up—Death thought me his own . . . he let me go; and I am recovering fast from very severe wounds.' Claire, who had waited every day in fear and anxiety for the post, was relieved.

Now independent in the Galitzin mansion, she invited the Villeneuves to dine because they had recently been in Athens. She was still an enthusiast for Greek liberation, and their conversation excited her: 'it was like reading the most entertaining book or seeing a series of pictures'.[43] The Villeneuves were charmed by Claire's delight and invited her to join them on their next Greek visit. She was tempted, but experience was teaching her discretion. A marital argument gave warning of trouble ahead. 'I said sex ought to be abolished—He was of my opinion she not. They want me to go to Greece with them . . . How much I should like it, but I dare not for fear of being a burden.'[44] Even so, she dined out with all her old verve. 'Our conversation at table was very amusing. We agreed to found a state upon the Turkish model, only that the tables should be turned and the men shut up in harems and kept by the women.' This passed as a joke over the damask cloth, the glasses and the candle flames, yet Claire's laughter was rooted in bitter experience. Her idea of freedom seems far from the sober projects of the later women's movement: serious education, access to the professions, the right to vote. Her own instinctive ideal was Shelley's universal sexual freedom, with a personal revenge for the humiliations of Byron's contempt. This was the thought which brought colour to her cheeks and sparkle to her black eyes, as she led the table talk which onlookers found so attractive.

On one December evening she went by sledge to drink tea with the parents of a pupil. Moscow was mysterious in the winter light:

> The moon was up and shining with a white light upon the white snow—we went through narrow by-streets—the window shutters of the houses were all shut, the yard doors likewise, not a soul was to be seen, not even a dog baying at the moon . . . we glided along like ghosts at midnight with the utmost swiftness and silence.

The romantic side of Claire's nature yielded to the eery silence of the snow. Her childlike love of romping came into its own at a rowdy tea-party at the Pomikoffs with former pupils, boys as well as girls.

> I amused myself very much . . . I thumped all the boys which they bore with great patience. We jumped up and down on the sofa—I jogged Johnny's arm as he was drinking his tea; it was spilt and he was furious. The tall Nicolas opened his mouth and said 'Oh! My God Miss Clairmont, how you are funny!'[45]

These amusements were welcome, for Claire dreaded the Russian winter. She could not share Pushkin's love of the

> . . . glories of these frosty days
> Like secret promenades in sleighs . . .

Each year the months of snow had brought a minor return of her illness in Vienna, with obstruction in breathing, hoarseness, fever at night, and pain in the chest. She could not afford to consult one of the fashionable foreign physicians, but found an ordinary Russian doctor who spoke bluntly to her. 'You are not yet in danger . . . Some change might restore you to perfect health, but if you do not change climate I cannot answer for the consequences.'[46] This echoed the advice of the physicians in Pisa which Claire had chosen to ignore in 1822. For the first time in her reckless career, as she wrote at the New Year 1827, 'I was frightened to think I had another year to run like the last!'[47]

The return of the Galitzins brought fighting, screams and disorder; exhaustion lowered Claire's resistance: 'to stay here is certain death in a year or two'. By the end of January 1827, 'I had such a pain in my chest with talking . . . that I soon after went to bed quite worn out.' She wrote from bed to Jane:

> I have been obliged to renounce every active [?] and have been shut up in my room till the walls of it seemed to close around me and leave me scarce room to breathe . . . The question is whether I shall leave Russia or no, and my desire for independence is so great that I cannot bear the idea of returning to London to live upon others.[48]

Claire could not afford to travel south at her own expense. The only hope was to find a family who would take her without salary if she gave lessons to their children in return for expenses. Weak but resolute, she planned to look for a travelling post.

10 *Reunion in London (1828–1829)*

The previous year, on a morning call, Claire had met the wife of General Kaisaroff, who had one child—an ailing, fretful, and nervous daughter, Natalie, the source of continuous anxiety to her parents. Claire was not then free to teach Natalie, but continued to visit her mother as a guest. After dinner at the Kaisaroffs on 6 January 1827, she enjoyed a lively argument, defending liberty against a man who thought it 'a chimera'. No sooner had she left than the men around the table engaged in frank sexual speculation about her. Mme Kaisaroff saw how exposed a young foreign woman was, alone in Russian society. Next morning she invited Claire to breakfast and apologized for the scene. Claire responded with irony, 'Amiable delightful creatures! I must really take great care of my poor heart.'

Anyone may reasonably share the curiosity of Mme Kaisaroff's guests. Claire's inviting warmth, her figure, and her provocative conversation suggested forbidden pleasures, yet as a governess her reputation must be spotless; her manners had won over the critical Professor of English at Moscow University, yet below the surface, the moods and passions of her girlhood still vibrated. Later she made common cause with a niece whose own love affairs were open and unashamed. Claire was not necessarily ignorant of contraception, since she had the habit of picking up and reading chance periodicals. Shelley supported the radical journalist Francis Place, who later published 'To the Married of Both Sexes', describing contraceptive methods current in France. Claire also kept an accurate record of her menstrual days by marking her private journal each month. The question of her sexual activities cannot be finally answered but aroused curiosity, then as now. Returning from the party where she had aroused such imaginings, she wrote, 'The moon was up and quite round . . . All alone in the blue vault of heaven she looked as solitary as our sledge which slid over the white floor of snow, and no other thing was to be seen.'[1]

The next winter, when illness descended and Claire lay alone and frightened in the room which seemed to close round her, she remembered the kindness of Mme Kaisaroff and the possibility that Natalie might take a cure in the West. Once out of her sickbed, Claire dressed and left the house, apparently without braving Princess Galitzin to give notice. She walked to the Kaisaroffs' house, 'although so weak I could scarce go', and threw herself on their mercy. They took her in without hesitation, surrounding her with Russian warmth. 'They are extremely kind', wrote Claire thankfully.

This was almost the last entry in Claire's Russian journals. But, on 2 February 1827, perhaps unpacking her travel-worn possessions in a solitary bedroom, she picked up a journal book she had kept in Florence, during Shelley's lifetime. There she had copied on an April day in 1821 three lines from Dante. The great exile, driven from home, laments how bitter it is to taste another's bread, how hard to tread his staircase.

> proverai siccome sa di sale
> Lo pane altrui e come è dure calle
> Lo scendere e'l salir per l'altrui scale.

'How true', wrote Claire, an unimportant exile who dreaded strange houses,

> little did I think when I wrote these lines some years ago in my Journal book at Florence that I should feel their bitterness to the quick. None can know like me what it is to mount daily a stranger's stairs and to feel with every step that a solitary room and faces filled with strange indifference await us. The world is closed in silence to me. The voices that spoke to my youth, the faces that were then around me, are almost forgotten . . . The last consolation is torn away.[2]

The year with the Galitzins had been a time of blank silence so far as thought or feeling were concerned. Now, Claire felt, Mme Kaisaroff would rescue her from mental destitution; she was later to write: 'she gave me a home, she gave me consideration and kindness, and beyond all these, sympathy in my thoughts and feelings'. Aware of Mme Kaisaroff's kindnesses, she contracted to accompany the Kaisaroff family to Dresden for Natalie's cure.

The long journey from Moscow to Germany had three stages: by coach to St Petersburg, by ship across the Baltic Sea and by hired coach from a German port to the interior. The Kaisaroff household set off on the long journey to St Petersburg in the style of the Russian nobility, with their own carriage, multitudinous baggage, and their own engraved silver chamber pots. Once embarked, predictable troubles arose in this overcrowded ark. Natalie, the 12-year-old invalid used to her mother's undivided attention, formed a jealous dislike of her new governess which was heartily returned. In her journal, Claire privately mocked the child's nervous fears, and described their appearance as 'the Comic Muse and the Tragic Muse seated side by side in a Diligence'.

Politics was another source of difficulty. In private conversation Mme Kaisaroff appeared to be, like the Decembrists, a Russian aristocrat of liberal principles. Claire, who had lived in silence and isolation since coming to Moscow, found this intoxicating. Her response at first was wildly emotional. 'I belonged to an outcast race; our name was one of utter reprobation; it lived in my heart but was never in these many long years pronounced by my lips . . . the principles that I looked upon as sacred were objects of execration.' Now, with her new employer, who 'gave me a home and a sister in herself, once more they breathed the light of day'.[3] But her enthusiasm was to be short-lived; on the journey, Claire soon learned that Mme Kaisaroff on her own was one person, and in her husband's company quite another.

The ultra-conservative general, in the newly embellished uniform of the Imperial army, was a formidable presence. General Kaisaroff, who instructed his family and employees in 'the infinite superiority of Russia to all other countries, since it is an established truth that Liberty and Civilization are the worst of all evils',[4] rightly suspected Claire of liberal opinions. When he insulted her loudly in public, his wife listened meekly, not daring to express an opinion. As Claire explained to Mary, 'The lady is very good, but she cannot show much favour towards a person her husband particularly disliked . . . The husband is very disagreeable.'[5]

Discomfort in the carriage—'a little Universe'—completed Claire's disenchantment. 'They made up a bed for their daughter in our four-seated carriage and her feet were placed on my cushion, so that I had only a corner with my legs bent under me for four days and nights,' she complained. Slowly, Claire's fury and resentment mounted. When the party disembarked from the St Petersburg boat at the little Baltic port of Travemunde, Claire, stiff and aching, exploded into one of the passionate rages which Byron had known so well. In what he had called 'her fiendish temper', all caution, all fear for the future, was swept away. She swore to the Kaisaroffs that she would not submit in silence like a serf to their ill treatment. Rather than endure days crushed into a corner of the coach, she would leave them and make her own way to Dresden, where they must await her. Even the general seemed silenced by this storm. Only one thing frightened Claire; she wrote to Mary, 'I entreat you not to tell my mother I am entirely separated from the family I came with.' Claire knew her mother would not hear of her being out of England, but insisted none the less: 'I never will live there if I can help it . . . My desire for independence is so great that I cannot bear the idea of returning to London to live upon others.'[6]

After this announcement, Claire made one of her swift, masterful decisions. Having reached Dresden by herself and rejoined the Kaisaroff family, she was near enough to England to visit her family and friends. Ignoring the quarrel on the journey, she would request leave of absence from Natalie's mother. Relations followed the pattern Claire had described to Mary. The Kaisaroffs accepted their governess's refusal to travel in the overloaded coach as a mark of independence, and even respected her for it. Such battles were, as Claire observed, 'habitual as the bread they eat'. Madame thought no more about it and generously gave her a year's leave of absence. The usual fears about a woman travelling alone arose; Claire, well accustomed to solitary travel, disarmed convention by finding a needless chaperone, a governess from the staff of the Duchess of Saxe-Weimar. From Dresden, the two women took the Diligence, a public coach, to Hamburg, and from there a sea-passage to London. On 16 October 1828, Claire arrived at the Godwins' house.[7]

This sudden change of plan was not wholly irrational. In 1824, while Claire was in Moscow, Charles had married Antonie von Hembyze, affectionately called Tonie. She was the daughter of a senior Imperial customs official of Belgian descent, from a devout and conservative background very unlike that of the Clairmonts.[8] Mrs Godwin was furious at the match and tormented Mary with loud complaints, but Tonie accepted her husband's family with remarkable loyalty. Perhaps she thought all the English were radicals. In July 1828 Charles brought Tonie and their two eldest children, Pauline aged 3 and Clärchen or Cläri aged 2, on a visit to their London grandmother. The chance of seeing Charles with his young wife appealed to Claire; the prospect of two little nieces made a London visit irresistible.

For the first time in years, the Godwin family was reunited. The Philosopher at 72 was 'feeble and bent'; a drawing of him shows a shuffling, dilapidated old figure. His wife, in her own prosy, domineering style, was devoted to him, though they were battered by money troubles. In 1826, after a final bankruptcy in the Strand, the couple had retreated to 44 Gower Place, a narrow turning off Gower Street. Here Godwin entered what Hazlitt in *The Spirit of the Age* ironically called 'the Serene Twilight of a doubtful immortality'. Yet *Political Justice*, apparently forgotten after thirty years, had been absorbed into secular thought, and one of its monuments rose next door to Godwin's obscure refuge. In 1827, University College, known to its critics as 'the Godless College in Gower Street', opened its doors to students without requiring them to sign oaths of allegiance to the Church of England. For the first time since the Test Act of 1673, British Dissenters, Roman Catholics, Unitarians, Jews, and eventually non-Christians from the British Empire added their rich vein of talent to British life. Charles Clairmont, fired with enthusiasm, hoped on this visit to found a student hostel for the new college but failed, presumably from his chronic lack of capital.[9]

The meeting of Claire with her mother left few traces. Mrs Godwin was in Mary's eyes 'the grand annoyance' of the family, but to her own daughter she showed a tenacious, if combative, affection. To Charles too his wife notwithstanding, she extended her concern; she was a byword for managing her children's affairs, and she intended a Chair at the new University College for him. Even tolerant Mrs Mason wrote:

> Mrs. Godwin is forming plans and making interest for Charles Clairmont. I should be very glad to hear of this last obtaining the professorship as I suppose it would insure an asylum for poor Claire, if ever she found it expedient to return to England.[10]

Mary had already made Claire 'a cordial invitation to share my fortunes here', though Trelawny, who knew them both well, viewed this with caution. He wrote to Mary, 'Nor can I say whether it would be wise or beneficial to either should Claire consent to reside with you in England.'[11]

Godwin himself, though weary and stale, still wrote novels for a living. By chance, almost as soon as Claire arrived Godwin needing his yearly three hundred pounds, had embarked on a rambling narrative called *Cloudesley*. In a crisis, his family could be relied on to help: Mary contributed a brilliant description of the waterfall at Terni, from a letter by Shelley; Charles provided pages on Vienna and its forests; even Trelawny made a contribution, for after a colourful and talkative visit to Godwin the previous year he had become one of the dramatis personae. The novel opens, for no apparent reason, with the hero tutoring in St Petersburg and for this Claire was the sole source.[12] It is not clear if the Russian element was contributed in her swift, dramatic speech or equally fluent writing, yet she clearly felt a collaborator's anxiety for the book for she was later to ask how Jane and Mary liked it, and demanded to know what reception it had met with from the public.

A regular visitor to Gower Place was Claire's half-brother William, now 25 years old. After several false starts, including a period as draughtsman to Rennie, the architect who had completed London Bridge, William Godwin the younger had become a journalist. He was happily married, lived on the South Bank near the House of Commons, and earned a steady living as parliamentary reporter to the *Morning Chronicle*.[13] Neither he nor Claire could compete with the 'truly extraordinary' talents of Mary in Godwin's estimation, yet Claire stood up for him. She wrote that 'his industry, his attachment to his wife and his talents raised him, in my opinion, considerably above the common par'. She was always ready to defend those few beings she could call her own.

The surviving members of the Shelley circle were drifting apart, though all within reach. Mary, Jane, and Hogg lived in London, while Trelawny was on his first visit since 1820. The evening after her own arrival, Claire saw Mary for the first time since their parting; for nearly six years they had lived in different countries. Claire's first impression was of Mary's beauty—even though Mary had survived an attack of smallpox earlier in the year with the greatest courage; 'how rejoiced I was, how thankful you had escaped', Claire had written. She was prepared to be 'a monster to look at', but sea-bathing at Hastings had healed her scars. Claire faithfully recorded the visual impact Mary made. She struggled, with many false starts, to describe Mary's hair, 'floating in gauzy wavings round her face and throat and upon her shoulders . . . so fine the slightest wind or motion tangled it into a golden network'.[14] Even more striking than Mary's looks, which she saw without the least jealousy, was 'the surpassing beauty of her mind; every sentiment of hers is so glowing and beautiful, it is worth the actions of another person'. Yet beneath the beauty, Claire could sense the depth of melancholy.

Mary, deeply conscientious and sensitive to reproach, found herself trapped in a web of conflicting duties. From childhood she had carried the burden of Godwin's love and of his vanity of her intellect. When Shelley died she suffered the additional burden of her father's draining demands for money. She was driven to write for cash, each book a paler impression of her original brilliance. She was humiliated by the writer's trade; visitors who found her at her work table with drafts, copy, or proof for correction noticed her deep social embarrassment. The work which Mary might have given to the world—a biography of Shelley whose life she had shared and whose poems were in her keeping—was forbidden by Sir Timothy. Any public mention of the poet produced a sharp threat from the family solicitor; the annuity she needed for her son might be withdrawn. The social slights of the Shelley family cut Mary to the quick. The duty she had most at heart was to bring up Percy Florence by the standards of his father, whom Byron had called 'as perfect a Gentleman as ever crossed a drawing room'. It is not surprising that Mary was tense and worn. Claire soon learnt that she had a further, more immediate, cause of grief.

Mary was staying with her friends the Robinsons at Paddington, having left the 'green lanes and gentle hills' of Kentish Town, where the attraction had been Jane Williams; 'I long to get out to Kentish Town where I shall be near my Janey,' Mary had written in 1824. The tenderness of their early widowhood overflowed. 'I love Jane better than any other human being . . . Jane is my chosen companion and only friend . . . to her for better or worse I am wedded . . . She is in truth my all—my sole delight.'[15] But the passion of Mary's love for Jane, which had survived even when Jane and Hogg set up a family household together—'of course we shall still continue near each other'—had collapsed, and Claire's visit, though not unwelcome, did little to rouse Mary from her despair. The crash in this fervent relationship had come in July 1827. Mary learnt that Jane had written to Leigh Hunt and to the young American actor John Howard Payne as common knowledge that the Shelleys' marriage was 'not as happy as it should have been'. She claimed that Mary's coldness made Shelley unhappy.[16] Moreover Jane, so accustomed to admiration, said that Shelley had become her lover 'one evening after an Italian fiesta' at San Terenzo.[17] Pitiful scenes and wild accusations followed this, while Mary paced her solitary room driven nearly to madness. 'My friend has proved false and treacherous! Miserable discovery.' Claire did not share this surprise. She knew the Shelleys' troubles, since she shared their lives. It should be said, though, that she never wrote or uttered any public criticism of their marriage. In later life she resisted Trelawny's suggestions that she should write her own memoir of the poet. Possibly this was from family loyalty to Mary, possibly from reverence for the memory of Shelley: his 'virtue which never flagged a minute, his undying spirit, beautiful contempt of pain and Death, his carelessness of riches',[18] which became her standard. From whatever cause, Claire's public silence on the Shelleys' marriage deserves note.

In the secrecy of the blank pages at the back of her journal, Claire admitted passionate emotions. She admired Mary's fame as the author of *Frankenstein*, and respected the industry which turned out pot-boilers to support herself and her son. Her only open criticism was directed at the Byronic hero of Mary's *Lodore*.

> Good God! to think a person of your genius, whose moral tact ought to be proportionately exalted, should think it a task befitting its powers to gild and embellish and pass off as beautiful what was the merest compound of vanity, folly, and every miserable weakness.

Claire wrote to Jane Williams of her shock that Mary was willing to contribute personal memories to the tiny, flattering, Lord-loving Tom Moore for his *Letters and Journals of Lord Byron*. 'She ought not to be acquainted with Moore: it is a privilege he has no right to, having expressed so cruel and unjust an opinion of Shelley.' In her note book, Claire contrasted this with true fidelity:

> Others still cling round the image and memory of Shelley—his ardent mouth, his exalted being, his simplicity and enthusiasms are the sole thought of their being, but she has forsaken even their memory for the pitiful pleasure of trifling with triflers.[19]

The phrase 'ardent mouth' hints at deep-buried feelings. Claire considered the 'public admiration of L.B. . . . a piece of gross imbecility'. Her own devotion to Shelley was also ardent and exalted, as these secret memoirs show: 'You felt that there was a spell, a silent agency in his presence, which opened a new world of nobleness and wisdom to one's gaze.' Inevitably, Claire and Mary, bound by shared experience, felt for each other a mingled love and resentment.

One major object of Claire's London visit was to see Percy, whom she had worshipped from birth as heir to Shelley's fire and genius. She now found a cheerful boy of 9, sturdy, florid, and 'excessively fat'. He had his father's blue eyes, and Mary believed 'grows more like Shelley'. Percy was devoted to his mother, and she in turn found him 'really very good and above all tractable—which is not quite the virtue of his father's family'; but he did not like poetry, and his mother admitted that he showed 'a great want of sensibility'. Mary had hoped to find 'the art of painting in his long fingers', but Percy amiably yet firmly preferred playing out of doors, kite-flying,[20] and summer visits to the seaside, or re-enacting battles with the children of the music publisher Novello, in which he was faithfully supplied with paper cannon balls by Clara Novello, 'his abject slave'. Clearly, Claire, like Mary, had cherished unreasonable expectations; Percy was a nice, ordinary child, but had inherited none of his father's magical aura; he seemed a throwback to his grandfather old Sir Timothy who stumped round the Field Place estate, as a visitor remarked, 'in yeomanlike garb and tanned leather gaiters'.[21]

When Claire saw Percy after an interval of seven years in autumn 1828, the boy had completed his first half year at his private school, Mr Slater's, Kensington. Mary, wife and daughter of radical households, had formed an iron resolution to bring up Shelley's son as a classical scholar and a gentleman. This decision was to cost her years of poverty and toil. Charles, Shelley's elder son by Harriet, had died of tuberculosis in September 1826, leaving Percy heir to Field Place. Sir Timothy refused to see his grandson, so correspondence was conducted through the family lawyer; but Mary politely and steadily demanded her boy's rights with a promise 'not to bring dear Shelley's name before the public'. All radical influences—Godwin, Wollstonecraft, his own father's controversial writings—were banished from Percy's education. Instead he learnt classics, of which he made 'sad work', drill to straighten his spine, and dancing; from the age of 9 he had his own 'taylor's account'—in short, everything to make him a gentleman, though Mary regretted the lack of a horse. Percy appeared, as Mary rather wistfully wrote, 'everything his [Shelley's] family could wish'. An aunt from Russia who was elegantly shabby and had foreign manners, fanciful turns of phrase, and passionate endearments fitted uneasily into this gentlemanly upbringing. Percy, pursuing the traditional line of retreat from an embarrassing situation, was not interested. Claire continued to love him, without the illusion that the child returned her love. She wrote to Mary that she had been delighted with a letter from Percy,

> though I am afraid it was written unwillingly and cost him a world of pains. Poor child he little thinks how much I am attached to him. When I first saw him, I thought him cold; but afterwards he discovered so much intellect in all his speeches, and so much originality in his doings that I willingly pardoned him for not being interested in anything but himself.[22]

Another tie from the past bound Claire to the second of the Lerici widows, Jane Williams and her children. She had written freely to Jane from Russia, sent offerings of the little silk handkerchiefs the fastidious beauty liked to carry, and had not condemned her claims to a love affair with Shelley. Claire's name for Hogg was 'Blue Bag', from the blue legal portfolio he carried, and she considered this Scottish lawyer of caustic tongue and parsimonious habits a thoroughly dull figure. Claire had cherished the idea of Jane and Edward Williams as the perfect romantic couple. She had written from Moscow in frank dismay:

> Never was astonishment greater than mine on receiving your letter. I had somehow imagined you would never love again, and you may say what you like, dearest Jane, you won't drive that out of my head. 'Blue Bag' may be a friend for you, but he can never be your lover.[23]

Nevertheless, her own affection for Jane drew her, two years later, to the villa at 12 Maida Vale, Edgware Road, where 'Mr and Mrs Jefferson Hogg' were installed, with Medwin and Rosalind, now aged 8 and 7, yet still called, with Jane's slightly cloying fondness, by their baby names. A baby girl, Prudentia, completed the family. This name was not, as one might suppose, a Shelleyan affirmation of illegitimacy, but a compliment to Jefferson's highly respectable sister. This baby died at 18 months, but the name was to be inherited by a sister born in 1836. Jefferson's youthful principles were not, however, wholly extinct: when Jane's legal husband, Captain Johnson, died in 1840, setting her free at last from a contract made when she was 16, Jefferson, on Shelleyan grounds, firmly refused to marry her.[24] Yet Jane had won a home with her children around her, and Claire complimented her friends on the young family.

> How happy you are to have a little girl. It is the only thing I ever envy my fair friends . . . How I wish you would write to me, my dear friend all about yourself and your children. Kiss Meddy and Dina and the new one for me.[25]

Talented and temperamental Dina was especially engaging; already her childish drawings showed promise of the embroidery she would later create. The friendship of Jane and Claire appeared unruffled for years to come, yet in the depths a doubt stirred. Perhaps, despite her blue eyes and soft voice, Mrs Hogg was not the priestess of romantic love that Claire had imagined.

Of all Claire's reunions in London, the most fraught was her first meeting with Trelawny since their dramatic parting at Pisa. Time and his own erratic judgement had used him roughly: she knew, as he must have known, that his attempts to play 'a first part' in the fight for Greek independence had been a disastrous, humiliating failure. There was also a further complication, not mentioned in her letters. At the height of his enthusiasm for Odysseus, Trelawny had seduced and then married the bandit's half-sister, Tersitza, whose beauty in her brilliant Greek embroideries had seized his fancy. They had both been rescued after the shoot-out in the mountain cave and carried to safety in the Ionian Isles by a British naval vessel. The ship's chaplain was privately appalled to learn that the heavily pregnant bride was barely 14 years old. She was hardy, though, and safely gave birth to Trelawny's 'Greek daughter', Zella, later to be one of Claire's responsibilities. For the little family did not last long. Tersitza had developed a youthful fondness in the West for fashionable frocks and hats, refusing to wear the peasant costume her husband demanded. When she appeared one evening in Paris party frock and coiffure, Trelawny, in a fit of rage, seized his dagger and cut off her hair before the assembled guests. A Greek Orthodox divorce, by mutual consent, had followed in 1827.[26] Its simplicity caused Trelawny, for once in his life, to speak well of religion.

Trelawny's letters had followed Claire during these crowded years, forwarded from Vienna to St Petersburg, Petersburg to Moscow, Moscow to Islavsky and back, often missing her by months. Her failure to reply caused him intense agitation: 'I am fevered with anxiety of the cause—day after day I have suffered the tormenting pangs of disappointment . . . why is this dear Claire—everything or anything may have caused the painful silence but *Want of Love*.'[27]

His 'inseparable companion' was a portrait of Claire by Amelia Curran, an 'excellent likeness', which he had somehow acquired from the painter in Rome. He also possessed himself of Mary's portrait and despite her many requests kept both for the rest of his life. In the midst of the Greek campaign and his affair with Tersitza, Trelawny insisted on his love for Claire: 'My heart is filled—at this period—with the same tenderness and deep affection which filled it to bursting at our melancholy parting on the banks of the Arno—indeed dear Clare I feel too much to say more.' Apparently, 'judging you as I have a right by my own feelings', Trelawny expected Claire to share his raptures: 'Write sweet friend . . . say you are unaltered and that it will give you pleasure our meeting.'[28] Claire had made clear her ambition, approved by Shelley in May 1821, of 'embarking in some independent mode of life'[29] if she could raise enough capital. That had been one reason for going to Russia, as she explained to Jane, 'because there is no country so favourable to foreigners . . . I should work to gain a little independence, turning over every possible scheme in my mind to gain money'.[30] Independence, not protection, was Claire's dream.

The meeting of these two romantic egoists, each absorbed in a world of illusions, could not be easy. Nor were the circumstances helpful. Trelawny called on the Godwin household (Godwin, at work on *Cloudesley*, wove him into the novel as the misanthropic Borromeo),[31] and found that Mrs Godwin, who from the first had blamed Shelley for 'having deprived my poor Child of her home and made her an outcast in the world', hoping for a 'respectable career' for Claire, would not permit an unchaperoned meeting. As mistress of the house she could not be excluded. Intimate conversation was hampered by heavy building works beyond the back wall as an army of contractors raised William Wilkins' neo-Grecian University College with surprising speed. Claire felt Trelawny's disappointment at the commonplace family meeting, for she wrote:

> Is it that you find me so very uncommunicative in conversation that you wish to see if my heart will open itself more freely upon paper. You have guessed very rightly. It might have been centuries before I should have been able to express by word what I shall now tell you by paper . . . Do not think the melancholy you see sometimes from me is the sign of hopeless wretchedness, I am happy—it is only the shadow of former days which throws its deep gloom over my mind which is not yet passed away. How should I not be happy when I possess so many good friends, and see you—restored a by a miracle from out the thousand perils—with which fate had encompassed you.[32]

Meanwhile Trelawny, bitterly disappointed after all his fervid expectations by Claire's 'sister-like insensible' conversation, is said to have written to Mary complaining that Claire had 'talked of nothing but worsted stockings and marrying—the only doubt to my mind is which is worse'. This letter has not been found, but the topics are plausible enough. Trelawny made a fetish of physical hardiness and was said to sit in Hyde Park showing bare legs and challenging critics with a ferocious 'What do you want socks for?' Claire had already written to Jane Williams from Moscow asking her to see that he did not get his feet wet while in London and fall ill.[33] Marriage arose in a letter which, as his inimitable spelling shows, he copied himself:

I wish very much Dear friend to see you married—and I am sure if you were to a beutiful and young woman you would be happy and make her so.

You are fond of beuty—therefore she must be beutiful . . . to these she may early add great instruction and much natural talent . . . Only you must give yourself the trouble to look for it and that you do not do. I wish you to be settled—and happy . . . I wish you to marry that you may rest at anchor in a safe harbour.[34]

In November 1828 Trelawny left his London quarters for an optimistic visit to a rich elderly uncle at Trewithen. While in Cornwall he received a letter from Claire, since lost. Clearly he found it difficult to answer: 'How reply to such a letter—beautiful it is—but its melancholy strain vibrates on my heart and fills me with sadness how undeserved is your fate—all goodness yourself you have met with nothing but unprovoked ill.' It sounds as though the familiar London scenes had recalled to Claire the heady excitement of 17 and 18 years old, which ended in such sorrow. In reply, Trelawny could only invoke the loyalties of the scattered Shelleyan band. 'Dear Claire . . . arouse yourself—you have duties to fulfil—many love you and you owe us your love.'[35] He recalled Shelley's ideals: 'If we are to fail—let it not be without a struggle—our cause is good and let that give us hope—that we are not to live in vain.' He said nothing of Claire's longing for an 'enterprise' which would bring independence, and it was unreasonable to hope he might invest in such a venture. He had already offered to support her in 'ties nothing could tear assunder', and Claire had refused.

At New Year 1829 Trelawny wrote from his London hotel reproaching Claire for coldness and neglect. He complains that she does not write to him and continues in an uneasy, jocular manner:

you are becoming so horridly prudish . . . I consider you very fish-like—bloodless and insensible—you are the counterpart of Werter—a sort of bread and butter and worsted stockings—like Charlotte fit for suckling fools and chronicling small beer

Adieu old Aunt[36]

This letter has been felt to mark the end of their relationship and to relegate Claire at 30 to the ranks, if not of Maiden Aunts, at least of Early Victorian aunts. In fact, like so many of her own letters, it reflects a mood: Trelawny's impatience and irritation. It uses literary allusion not as description but as comic thrusts. 'Very fish-like' echoes Trinculo describing Caliban in *The Tempest*. Charlotte, who was 'cutting bread and butter', comes from Thackeray's humorous poem on Goethe's *Sorrows of Werther*. In 'To suckle fools and chronicle small beer', Iago ironically caps his verses about women. Conscious literary jokes hardly express a serious and lasting decision.

Early in March 1829, Trelawny returned to Florence; the disappointment of reality in London changed within a month to the old romantic manner: 'Is there no hopes, my Claire,' he wrote on 7 April with more ardour than grammar, 'of your ever returning here?—how I should delight in again seeing you in Italy.' In July, 'I never write a line or pass a day without wishing you by my side.'[37] Trelawny's teeming imagination had turned to 'sketching the life and character of Shelley'. Rebuffed by Mary—'there is nothing I shrink from more fearfully than publicity'[38]—he counted on Claire's help. After one letter to her, he added a postscript, written closely and urgently upon a fold of the paper:

Dear girl come away to the clear sky of Italy—and be sure of this—that what I have is thine—and whilst I have a house to shelter you it is yours, a heart—all unworthy as it is—it is yours—an arm—it shall defend you . . . come away Dear Girl and doubt not my truth—and doubt not me for whatever I am[,] I am never anything but your true friend, Edward.[39]

By the time this letter arrived in London, Claire was packing to return to her former employers the Kaisaroffs at Töplitz. She seemed to be leaving England and her official home with little regret. She was going to the German forests, not bleak Russia:

I am delighted with Germany because it has such an air of simplicity, ease and comfort. After Russia without one object to greet the eye except the bare sky and earth, the country here seems teeming with roses and gardens and trees.[40]

There had been signs of stress within the family during Claire's year-long visit. Charles, 'after an unsuccessful struggle', returned to

Vienna in November, apparently four months earlier than he had planned, leaving his family to follow. He had failed either to found a student hostel or to secure a lectureship in German at University College. However, Claire had enjoyed staying with Mary at one of her series of furnished lodgings. This one was in Oxford Terrace, Edgware Road. We know this because Trelawny addressed a letter to her there 'at Mrs. Shelley's'. When Claire's visit to Mary was over, on 27 April 1829, she decided not to return to her mother's house, and instead she borrowed money from Mary; this, as always between them, was faithfully repaid. With this she moved for the rest of her time in London into independent lodgings at 5 Carmarthen Street, Tottenham Court Road. Mary explained to Trelawny that Claire had been 'surrounded by needy and in some cases unamiable relatives'.[41] This, of course, meant Mary's bugbear, Mrs Godwin, who wanted Claire to return to England and live permanently with her. It may have been, as Mary hinted, to secure another salary for the insolvent household. Yet it may equally have been maternal possessiveness and a desire to wrench Claire finally 'out of Mr. Shelley's clutches',[42] an influence which had survived his death. There was conflict, if not open, then underground. On 8 May Claire returned to her employers at Töplitz in Germany. Looking back after the visit Claire wrote frankly, 'I should think my mother must be delighted to be no more plagued with us; it was really a great bother and no pleasure to her.' Claire valued the freedom of living abroad, and told Mary:

> Nothing but Sir Timothy's death can now bring me to England, and that is a horizon which retreats as one advances. We may die, but he won't. Backed by Providence, the old gentleman seems determined to keep his ground . . . and outlive us all.[43]

There was another 'great bother' in the air at this Clairmont reunion, unwritten yet real: Claire and Charles were perturbed by the uncertainty as to their origins. In a time of large and close-knit families, they appeared to have only one blood relation, their mother's widowed sister at Rochester. They lacked the unexciting but comfortable resource of grandparents, and their supposed father Clairmont remained merely a name. Mary Godwin's silence on this matter was deeply troubling to them.

If the Clairmonts were ignorant of their origins, later students are equally baffled. Sources of information are few. William Godwin, in an unsuccessful application to Christ's Hospital, wrote that his stepson Charles had been born at 4 Bridge Street, Bristol. Shelley, in the 1816 hotel register at Chamonix, entered Claire as 'Mad. J.C.' of Clifton. A search of Bristol parish registers—St Mary le Port for Charles's baptism and St Andrew, Clifton for Jane—reveals only that their first names were surprisingly rare and their surname nonexistent. The whole family might be as fictitious as the widowed 'Mrs Clairmont's' first marriage ceremony with Godwin, or her sworn statement to the Austrian authorities that 'her previous husband deceased the Knight Karl Clairmont' was the father of Charles. Given Mrs Clairmont's resourcefulness and lack of scruple, one baptismal entry may attract attention. In April 1806, a brother and sister Charles and Jane were recorded as having been privately baptised earlier and then omitted from the Clifton register. Their parents were identified as John and Agnes Brett, innkeepers. Since Mrs Clairmont was described by Crabbe Robinson as 'a kept Woman', she might have farmed out troublesome small children in the interests of her career, which explains the silence on the earliest years until 1808. This brings us no nearer to the real father or fathers of Charles and Jane, however, and the question remains as mysterious still as it was to them in their lifetime.

Claire left England, then, no wiser as to her origins. On 18 September 1829 she arrived at Carlsbad in the Bohemian Forest,[44] where the Kaisaroff family was still pursuing Natalie's interminable cure, extended month by month on the advice of the thriving spa physicians. Claire settled in as casually as a migrating bird. When she was a girl of 19, she had confessed to Byron that her temperament was 'inconsistent and volage', but promised 'at thirty I shall be better'. Now she was 30, experienced and worldly wise, yet life seemed uncertain as ever.

11 *Return to Italy (1829–1832)*

Mary half-envied Claire the excitement of foreign travel: 'she returns to Dresden to an agreable situation'.[1] Claire had certainly described spa life in pleasant terms.

Töplitz is a charming place, how much I should have enjoyed it if we had been together . . . It is the custom to breakfast every morning at a mile or two from the town, where one finds in every direction comfortable little inns, in the most romantic spots possible. Everybody almost dines in public at the restorateur and supper the same thing.[2]

Mme Kaisaroff and even Natalie welcomed their English governess on her return, but public outings with the general were an ordeal. Even wilful Claire was frightened to oppose his violent Russophilia. If anyone ventured to contradict him in public, he therefore dragged her forward as a supporter 'and then I am at once set down by everybody as a fawning creature or an utter fool'.[3] Seething with suppressed anger, Claire preferred to spend evenings alone 'in self defence as much as possible'.

Duties to Natalie with her perpetual ailments created a new situation; Claire was employed less as a governess than as a sick nurse to the girl: 'I was employed in rubbings, stitchings, putting on Trusses, dressing ulcers, putting on leeches and bandaging swollen glands.' These intimate services, and the fact that Natalie was truly ill, overcame Claire's initial coldness; she even began to write of her young patient by the affectionate diminutive 'Natasha'. But her account of the Teutonically thorough *Kur* was distinctly dry. 'Our recreations were, mud baths, baths of bullocks' blood, steam baths, soap baths and electricity. If I had served in a hospital I should not have been more constantly employed with sickness and its appendages.'[4]

Claire remained in touch with Mary, always anxious to know the progress of the latest book and for news of Percy. The contact was important to her: 'Your last letter although so melancholy gave me pleasure merely because it came from you.' In responding, Claire wrote a description of Dresden, where she spent the winter of 1829–30 taking charge of Natalie while her mother was away.

Here, as in Italy, you cannot walk the streets without meeting with some object which affords ready and useful occupation to the mind. The more I become acquainted with the town and see its smallness, the more I am struck with the uncommon resources in literature *e le belle arti* it possesses.

Claire was a witness to the delights of this baroque gem before it was destroyed by bombing—its cupolas, towers, and spires of copper green, its palaces, libraries, and great picture gallery set among vineyards by the Elbe—and she was charmed by it. 'How I wish I could draw you to Dresden. You would go into society and would see a quantity of things which treated by your pen would bring you in a good profit. Life is very cheap here.' She painted a picture of Mary enjoying a summer holiday at one of the spas in the Bohemian Forest 'which would enable you to bear the winter of London with tolerable philosophy'.[5]

Claire spent the winter of 1829–30 in Dresden lodgings with only Natalie for company; Mme Kaisaroff wished them to wait there until March without her.

Of Dresden. About two months and a half ago we had falls of snow for many days. It was dry and crisp, not wet and powdery as it usually is in the beginning of winter, and one tripped as lightly over it as over a new-shaven lawn. Since then alternate frosts and thaws have turned the snow into ice and every street seems paved as in chrystal. The houses rise on both sides like tall grey ramparts with snow patched summits . . .

The streets are very narrow, the houses of massy dark coloured stones and built so high they shut out the sky, the sun and the wind. Their fronts are very small, but if you look down the narrow lanes which run by their sides . . . you will see that they extend in a dead wall to a vast depth backward . . .

The street door is a massy portal barred with iron and studded with the largest iron nails; the entry is underground, is paved with flagstones and vast and damp and dark as a cellar . . . By the side of the back door is the staircase; it is of stone and pitch dark at noon day; when you have groped up the first flight your head gets a good knock from a bulky corner which projects like the buttress of some sea washed castle and you catch a glimpse of light struggling down from a window or sometimes an open grating above; as you mount past this you see through it the snowy court below and enter upon the other side into the apartments which look upon the street . . . The rest of the rooms including kitchen and offices are built upon the court . . . In summer it must be pleasant to sit in these shaded rooms and with both front and back windows thrown open, hear through one the busy hum of the market place and through the other the singing of the birds perched in the trees by the neighbouring terrace, or the flowing of the Elbe . . . But in this season of the year, the whole house seems to me like an ice cellar.[6]

This description is plain, yet Claire's innate pleasure in the scene gives it character. Fortunately for the two young women with only each other for company, Dresden, even in winter, had its own charms. 'Dresden is a very cheerful city' wrote Claire,

the streets . . . full of passengers and men working all day long at their trades in the free air. All day long I hear below my window the saw of the wood cutter, the gossip of the women at their stalls, the creaking of sledges over the snow, the fiddle of an opposite musician, the hammering of a cooper and the morning and evening hymn of the scholars of a neighbouring school . . . To me Dresden offers an eternal field for amusement.[7]

The plan had been to take Natalie to the Mediterranean for the winter as her doctor advised, but Mme Kaisaroff had gone home to Russia leaving Claire in sole charge. She had a reason for this. She was pregnant and had returned to her husband in Moscow to give birth to their child. The general hoped for a son as his heir and wanted the child born on the sacred Russian earth. To leave an invalid through the rigours of a Central European winter seems hazardous, and Claire felt the burden of responsibility. Natasha, she reported, suffered

fits of the toothache because she will not have a decayed tooth out; a dry cough which frightens me to death and two glands that swell sometimes in chorus sometimes alternately. I have reason to argue, to console, to amuse, to invent nostrums &c &c.

The general dismissed the suggestion that Natalie should winter in Italy to avert the painful ulcers in her throat scornfully as 'a womanish caprice'; Claire knew the force of his threats upon his wife. 'I forsee how things will go. When the autumn comes and the child is born he will work upon her . . . to abandon the journey to Italy altogether and send for Natalie home . . . where she may then die at her leisure.'[8] This was, of course, a Russian drama, yet hearing Natalie's day-long lamentations for her mother confirmed Claire's conviction that women and children lived unjustly in the power of men. The French Revolution had torn society apart to claim the rights of man, yet even at the guillotine women appeared either as victims or knitters. Their embittered, still unfinished, revolution lay in the future. For all she knew, Claire stood alone.

Not even sole responsibility for an invalid could spoil Claire's enjoyment of Dresden, she wrote in her journal. Mme Kaisaroff returned to Dresden and Natalie in the spring of 1830. 'I am glad she has come as the responsibility of Natalie's health was too much,' wrote Claire with relief. The awaited child had evidently miscarried or failed to survive, since nothing more was heard of it. Natalie remained the heiress of the Kaisaroff family and sole object of her mother's anxious love.[9] Plans for a winter in the south had been discussed by post in veiled terms, to avoid the family ogre. 'Neither of us can speak frankly in our letters owing to their being subject to her husband's inspection . . . We have as yet done nothing but misinterpret the circumspect phrascology in which our meaning was wrapped.' This letter shows no sign of depression; if anything, Claire seems to enjoy a plot against the joint tyrant. At one stage negotiations were almost broken off. 'On my showing great unwillingness to go to Italy . . . She now talks of going to Nice, to which place I have no objection in the world. But nothing of this can be settled till she comes.'[10]

Mme Kaisaroff did not want to lose her English nurse-governess, and at the beginning of autumn and cold weather, the household moved to Nice. The city was then in the possession of the House of Savoy but culturally it was French, and it was free from memories of Shelley or Allegra. It fulfilled Claire's longing 'to feel the sweet air of the South, to see its deep blue sky'.[11] Yet even now Claire admitted to Mary, 'I must confess that wherever I went I carried about with me my own identity, (that unhappy identity which has cost me so dear and of which, with all my pains, I have never been able to lose a particle).'[12] Mary knew the truth of this honest admission.

Nice welcomed English visitors to winter under the clear skies. In 1822 the eccentric English philanthropist Lewis Way headed the subscription list to give work to the unemployed by laying out the Promenade des Anglais. Claire was wary of English tourists who might know her history, yet her spirits, as always, rose at the landscape: the long curve of the bay, yellow thickets of wild mimosa in spring, summer's sage and lavender, the deserted rocky cape of Antibes. A notebook entry records her response:

> The whole earth seems tingling with pleasure and joy. I look upon the sun the moon and the stars as if they were new to me . . . the bare rock or the waving woods, winter and summer, spring and autumn . . . It seems to me as if Nature was holding a Jubilee and I was invited to the Banquet.[13]

Claire's delight overflowed in a letter to Mary which weighed grief and joy in the balance.

> I wish I could give you any idea of the beauty of Nice. So long as I can walk beside the sounding sea, beneath its ambient heaven and gaze upon the far hills enshrined in purple light, I catch such pleasure from their loveliness that I am happy without happiness.[14]

Her letters to Mary commonly began with apologies for delay in writing. She feared Mary might think she copied Trelawny in fitfully neglecting old friends, but no:

> My silences are quite on another principle than his: I am not desperately in love nor just risen from my bed at four in the afternoon in order to write my millionth love letter nor am I indifferent to those whom time and the malice of Fortune have spared to me, but simply I have been too busy. Since I have been at Nice . . . we were a long time without a maid, and received and paid innumerable visits. My whole day was spent in shifting my character. In the morning I arise a waiting maid and having attended to the toilette of Natalie went into the housemaid, a laundry maid and eftsoons I fear me a cook having to look to the cleaning of the room, the getting up of linen, and the preparation of various pottages fit for the patient near me. At mid-day I turned into a governess, gave my lessons and at four or five became a fine lady for the rest of the day and paid visits or received them . . . at Nice it is the custom so soon as a stranger arrives that everybody comme il faut in the place comes to call, nor can you shut your doors against them even if you were dying . . .
>
> So went on day after day. We had *dejeuners dansants*, *soirées dansantes* (diners dansants are considered de trop by order of the physicians) *bals, theatres, operas, grand diners, petit soupers, concerts, visites de matin, promenades a âne, parties de campagne, réunions litteraires, grands cercles, promenades en bateau, côteries chosies, thunderstorms* from the sea and *political storms* from France; in short if we only had an Earthquake, or the shock of one, we should run through the whole series of modifications of which human existence is capable.[15]

This list of society pleasures and Claire's tearing high spirits may well have grated on Mary, who felt herself 'friendless, alone and poor', or even 'as one buried alive'.[16] Godwin, remembering her mother's despair and Fanny Imlay's suicide, accounted for Mary's misery tersely. 'You are a Wollstonecraft!' Yet despite depression, Mary fought for the social standing to which she felt entitled, not as the author of *Frankenstein*, but as mother of Sir Timothy Shelley's heir. In the new year of 1831 she had moved from Edgware Road to Somerset Street, which commanded the fashionable address of Portman Square.[17] Here Mary began 'going a little into society' and held modest soirées, though she spoke of parties as 'too expensive'. Her poverty became an obsession—'a barrier I cannot pass', 'the bars of a prison'.[18] Objectively, she was not badly off; the £250 a year from Sir Timothy compared favourably with the £265 a year half-pay on which retired captains of the Royal Navy maintained wife and children. But she suffered a hidden expense—her father's demands for money—and it was this that drove her to the hack work that exhausted her and eroded her natural talent.

Claire was well aware of this family situation. In April 1830 she wrote to Mary: 'I tremble for the anxiety of mind you suffer about Papa and your own pecuniary resources.'[19] By the end of the year Mary's reports were worse rather than better. Claire replied: 'What you tell me of the state of family resources has naturally depressed my spirits. Stair upon stair of wretchedness is all we know; the present, bad as it is, is always better than what comes after.'[20]

Mary blamed Sir Timothy and his lawyers for her troubles—unjustly, for he was not inhumane. According to a county newspaper, in a hard winter he distributed whole wheat flour, pease, and 'forty stone of good beef' among his poor neighbours; also—in a gesture his son could have approved—'a fat sheep to the prisoners in Horsham Gaol'. Yet he had been deeply wounded by Percy Bysshe's conduct and the hostile, contemptuous letters which announced it. Like many a disappointed parent, he blamed others, in this case the Godwins.

Mary was enjoying a remission from her depression in January 1831 which she described with touching simplicity. 'I have felt peculiarly happy—as usual without any special cause—content is an unalloyed good . . . it always seems to me the dearest blessing of heaven. Yet I cannot command it.'[21] This lasted for some months, during which she felt 'peculiarly happy'. She imagined Percy attending Eton like his father and forming intellectual friendships in society. Sir Timothy considered the suggestion of Eton 'highly improper'; he feared that painful and shameful memories of Percy's father would be aroused. Mary rejected St Paul's and Merchant Taylors', but was forced to consider Harrow as a compromise. Claire indulged herself in ridiculously lofty dreams for Shelley's schoolboy son. When Mary wrote that he was 'horrifically fat', Claire instantly countered:

If he really is fat, I am glad of it. Whenever I think of him I cannot help flattering myself he will become the greatest poet and the greatest philosopher England has ever produced. That he will follow the doctrines of his father and force by his truth and eloquence the blind and ignorant creeds that infect us to retire into obscurity.[22]

Fortunately for fat, easy-going and it must be admitted idle Percy, Sir Timothy refused to increase his allowance, and this ambitious programme remained unfulfilled.

Meanwhile, Mary was not the only member of the Shelley circle to complain of poverty. Trelawny also faced money problems: his generosity exceeded his income of £500 a year. Demands for a loan came, as Claire said, 'like a stone dropping from the moon upon a man's head'. She felt, not entirely groundlessly, that he might give away all he possessed. The end she foresaw for him was quite dramatic: 'He will pile up and set fire to a pyre of wood, into this he will run headlong and nothing shall be seen of him beyond a wreath of smoke ascending from his burning tomb into the quiet blue sky.'[23] In this letter, which shows the affection of old friendship, Claire wrote to Mary 'I admire, esteem and love him'. Yet she took a firm view of their differences: 'He likes a turbid and troubled life; I a quiet one; he is full of fine feeling and has no principles; I am full of fine principles but never had a feeling (in my life).' This is exaggerated, as though to convince both Mary and herself. 'He receives all his impressions through his heart; I through my head. *Che vuole? Le moyen de se rencontrer* when one is bound for the North Pole and the other for the South.'[24]

Trelawny realized that to make ends meet he must write for money, but his plan for a memoir of Shelley collapsed when Mary, fearful of Sir Timothy's anger, refused to provide material. Perhaps in an effort to persuade her, he even proposed to her in a desultory fashion, but expressed himself 'delighted' when she refused.[25] In fact, this was the beginning of Trelawny's growing, and frequently unjust, hostility to Mary. Instead of Shelley's biography he negotiated two hundred pounds a volume with Colburn and Bentley for 'an honest confession of my life'. Claire foresaw what this would be. As she wrote tolerantly to Jane, 'when his brain is once heated, out of everything that is cast in, it forges something new; not out of willfullness but from the laws of its nature and kind'.[26]

Trelawny wrote to Claire in Dresden, but the letter reached her after long delay since it was forwarded to Nice. In it she read of the

'Paradise' he had found in which to write his autobiography, 'a villa . . . beautifully situated on high ground very near a Tower you may remember'; this was the tower in Arcetti above Florence where Galileo had housed his telescope. In the pure air, Trelawny's 4-year-old Zella was 'growing a strong and handsome girl . . . it is on the top of a mountain—and I am in as perfect solitude as you could wish me—Oh that you were here to share it.'[27] Claire probably did not know that a similar offer had been made to Mary at about the same time.

Either Claire had no time to keep a journal in Nice or her notebook was lost on her travels, so the arrival of Trelawny's letter is unrecorded; there is no question, though, that it gave her much to think about. After nine years' fitful courtship by post, she made no pretence of being in love with Trelawny, as her letter to Mary on the subject made plain. Yet he was an old friend, and her letters to Jane make it equally plain that she was truly fond of him. Moreover, Claire had her future to consider and as always must fend for herself. She had made her way back to the Mediterranean world of her girlhood, where 'the whole earth seems tingling with pleasure and joy'. Now she faced a turning point; either she must find a new position as governess in the south or remain with the Kaisaroffs, returning with them to Russia to face the general's suspicions and the killing winters. She also feared that the French translation of Moore's Life of Byron might reveal her past and damage her chances of employment.[28] Trelawny's 'Oh that you were here' suggested a providential escape. Unsurprisingly, considering all the circumstances, Claire wrote to him in December 1830 offering to come to his Villa Paradiso and take charge of Zella. Her letter survives only in a fragment quoted by Trelawny. 'You say we have an undeniable right to be happy—and that our past sufferings are our title deeds . . . to our equivalent of contentments.' Clearly Claire's 'plan', as he called it, for Zella implied a sexual offer to her enthusiastically amorous Papa.

Whatever Claire expected, it can hardly have been the letter written by Trelawny on 4 January 1831 in which he lamented 'my present *position*—my plans—my *poverty*—my *embarrassments*—my unsettled state; the impossibility of my settling myself anywhere—and my want of means'.[29] He added casually in a postscript that he thought of 'sending Zella to a friend and resuming my Arab life'. Trelawny always had a short way with his children, and Claire would later be involved in the inevitable breakdown of this arrangement.

Nor was he unfeeling, and his letter ended with confused sentences of regret and apology. 'This letter will give you no less pain in reading than it has me in writing. I cannot in the ferment of my mind write clearly or express myself better—I beseech you to think of me as favourably as you can.'[30] He signed himself, 'Still believe me your sincerely attached', but to Claire the message of his letter was plain: he was no longer in love with her.

Yet after this letter, for all its decisive sound,[31] Trelawny again invited Claire to come and live with him. During his next journey abroad, to the United States, Claire recovered her health; when Trelawny came home, he found her once again attractive. He addressed her as 'my dove-eyed Sister Luesa'. Less than three months after his return he begged her to come as 'housekeeper to my houseless self'. In 1837 he persisted, 'Are your fetters never to be knocked off . . . my fancy is ever at work hankering after your kind.' In 1838 Trelawny took a house at the top of Putney Hill and wrote: 'Claire hollo—do you hear? . . . are you alive? . . . Have you not lived long enough in your present way of life? Well then, will you come and live at Putney?'[32] Claire would not be tempted to take these offers seriously, and watched Trelawny's various amours with a mixture of affection and amusement. 'Trelawny has always got a quantity of young ladies whom he pays a platonic court to and poor things turns their heads and half breaks their hearts.'[33] Claire sympathized with these 'pretty beings, so puzzled'; Trelawny had paid court to her as well, but fled when she responded.

There was in fact good reason why a mistress and even his own child were particularly unwelcome in Trelawny's house in 1831. In the autumn of that year the publishers Henry Colburn and Richard Bentley, tardy payers, brought out in three anonymous volumes his *Adventures of a Younger Son*, that riot of imaginative writing which he insisted, or perhaps even believed, was 'an honest confession of my life'. He had already told Claire, 'My occupation is in writing—the second volume of my life is nearly finished . . . three volumes will be ready for publication in a few months.'[34] The book began with a reasonably factual account of his childhood and naval enlistment as a midshipman, but then takes off like a whirlwind. The author-hero meets a corsair, sails with him, hunts lions or pirates impartially, and rescues a beautiful young woman who is then poisoned by a jealous rival. This farrago of violence, adventure, sexual conquest, revolt against authority, and above all success embodied the unfulfilled dreams of Trelawny's lonely youth and mediocre achievement. In the grip of writer's frenzy, the least intrusion of reality was unbearable. Moreover, he knew the risks he ran if the true facts should leak out. His name was concealed even from his publishers, and only one copy of the book was sent to Italy where he might be recognized. Once the book was published, to praise and high sales on all sides, the imposture was irrevocable. As Trelawny's biographer put it, 'all possibility of shedding his fictitious past was gone for ever. He would have to live with it for the rest of his life. Each succeeding day would be a crisis.'[35] As witness to this act of compulsive creation, Claire would have been an uncomfortable reminder of reality.

Fortunately, considering their fiery temperaments, this episode seems to have left little or no ill-will between Trelawny and Claire, which suggests that her proposal was practical rather than amorous. Only three months later, on 13 April, the Kaisaroffs took Claire from Nice by sea to Genoa and on by land to Florence. Here she met Trelawny 'three or four times'. He took predictably an intense dislike to the religion and politics of her 'bigot' employers, believing they 'persecuted her . . . she looked so pale, thin and haggard . . . Poor lady, I pity her.'[36] They exchanged a few letters on dissipating 'the cant and humbug about Byron'. Meanwhile, Claire sought Trelawny's advice on her future; she would like to live alone and independently in some Italian city, where she could support herself by giving English lessons. Trelawny's reply, for a self-styled corsair, was timid. He thought Claire would be 'better in some Italian family . . . You should hesitate in giving up your present position, bad as it is—till there is something like a clear road opened.'[37] Like many progressives, he was more cautious near home. Then on 3 January 1832, without warning he left for four years' desultory roaming in the United States.

Claire was only too sure that she could find a position as governess or companion after ten years' experience. As she wrote drily:

> Many people would be glad of a well informed person, who can read to them in various languages, teach them German, write their letters, and of a lively, sprightly disposition, one who neither minds heat nor cold, nor hunger nor thirst, nor fatigue nor hardship of any kind.[38]

Her wit had always been lively; now it was becoming sharp. In future years she would seem formidable to her nieces and nephews.

For the present she concentrated on hopes of independence. There was a brisk family row with Charles, who wrote that his sister had quarrelled with Mme Kaisaroff and would come to Vienna. This was not true, wrote Claire indignantly to Mary, 'nor can I imagine how Charles could say it for a certainty'. Living with the Kaisaroff domestic staff and the faint cloud of scandal which hung about her, Claire was at a disadvantage among the fashionable English in Italy. She was introduced to Mary's acquaintance, elegant Mrs Hare, but this lady 'was so prejudiced against her from stories she had heard against her . . . that she could hardly be induced to notice her'.[40] The Russian atmosphere of the Kaisaroffs obscured Italy for Claire: 'I see neither its sky, nor mountains nor seas, nor any of its thousand minute blooms. I am shrouded in a night which shuts them out as if I stood beneath the midnight of the Arctic Pole.'[41] Claire must escape from her position as dependent in other people's houses and shake off the past: but how?

In October 1831 something happened to make these questions urgent and practical. The Kaisaroffs had moved south, planning to spend a mild winter in Naples, when a sudden death in the family recalled them to Moscow.[42] Would Claire retain the secure job she had held since Christmas 1827 and return with them, or would she hand in her notice and survive as best she could in Italy? There was very little time in which to make a decision. Perhaps the soft, warm nights, the fireflies, the purple cloud drifting from the cone of Vesuvius across the gulf made the decision for her. The Kaisaroffs said their farewells, apparently with genuine regret, and Claire remained alone in Naples. The city was hallowed for her by Shelley's praise of its 'radiance' and 'light unknown'. She had never been homesick abroad, had always wanted to explore. Her time was once again her own; in celebration she turned to her notebook and began, abortively 'The air on that beautiful warm coast.' This cancelled, she drafted:

> Earth, Sea and Sky blaze like three Gods, with animated, but tranquil loveliness, with a splendour that does not dazzle, with a richness that cannot satiate. The air on that beautiful warm coast is a field of fragrance . . . In that enchanted garden, Morning is a Rose, Day a tulip, Night a lily, and Evening like the Morning again a rose and Life is a ceaseless song . . . that one goes singing to oneself, wandering like a Bee or a Butterfly along this perpetual chain of Flowers.[43]

There followed a total silence which lasted from October until Christmas 1831. Mary, Jane, and Mrs Godwin all wrote to her '*Ferma in Posta*, Napoli', but no answers came. Mary besieged Trelawny with demands: 'Send me news of Clare [spelt thus]. She never writes herself and we are all excessively anxious about her.' Two months later Mary repeated, 'I am beyond measure anxious to know how she is and what doing.'[44] The agitation resembled that of Claire's year in St Petersburg, but this time the questions were never answered. No one can say where Claire lived or how she maintained herself in Naples. Like Stendhal, the arch romantic, she was in love with the city, by night as by day. In this dream world, where Vesuvius was erupting fire, the Godwins, Mary, even idolized Percy faded into shadows. It was not until Christmas that the family in London heard news through Charles. Naples had proved a dangerous place for a solitary woman, and Claire had finally taken Trelawny's advice to live with a family. She had delivered to Mrs Mason in Pisa two letters sent by Mary, and after an affectionate welcome she was now living with their old friends in Pisa.[45]

12 *Governess in Tuscany (1832–1836)*

The Mason family had left Casa Silva, where Claire had known them since 1819, and moved to the Via della Faggiola, Pisa. Time had brought changes. The two little girls, Laura and Nerina, whom Claire had taken to dancing class and for walks in the Cascine, were now attractive creatures of marriageable age, and a set of young men called every evening, filling the drawing room with noisy conversation. The Masons, infatuated Italophiles both, could find no fault with their visitors' racket. Mr Mason, whom his wife's friends had called condescendingly 'Tatty' because of his interest in potatoes, had completed and published his researches on the new strain of potato best suited to Tuscan soil, a solid and useful proposal for cheap food.[1] He now appeared older, slightly bent, and fatigued. Mrs Mason in contrast was apparently untouched by the ten years, and seeing the fine figure in the odd, untidy clothes, Claire recognized the best friend, apart from Shelley, she had ever known; as she wrote to Mary, 'with her I am as her child'.

Margaret Mason was now in her middle 40s, still the 'stern democrat' Godwin had respected, still devoted to 'free union' with her unmarried husband and their daughters. Claire, ignoring her friend's oddities, described her as 'very tall, of a lofty and calm presence. Her features were regular and delicate, her large blue eyes singularly well set, her complexion of a clear pale, but yet full of life and giving an idea of health.'[2] Mrs Mason's friendship in the past had shown her grasp of the entangled Shelley relationships; it was she who, seeing Mary's distress, had arranged for Claire to live in Florence with the Bojtis. She had also intercepted a letter from Godwin importuning Mary for money and sent it to Shelley instead.[3] Claire, who had spent ten years concealing the details of her past from curious employers, found it an intense relief to be herself. 'She understands me completely. I have no need to disguise my sentiments,' wrote Claire to Mary:

> From the merest trifle to the greatest object, she treats me as if her happiness depended on mine . . . Nothing can equal Mrs Mason's kindness to me; hers is

the only house except my Mother's, in which all my life I have always felt at home.[4]

Feeling at home, to Claire, did not imply being kept. She was determined to be independent in Italy as in Russia, and sought a position as non-resident governess among the English colony in Pisa, now somewhat reduced by the retirement of Dr Vaccà and the consequent reduction in the train of fashionable invalids. 'Quite given up to its native dullness', Claire told Jane. She lodged with the Masons, but found an appointment as daily governess which must have been satisfactory to both parties, since she remained with the Bennet family, apart from short intervals, for six years, both in Italy and England. Her pupils were Gertrude aged 10 and Charlotte aged 14, grand-daughters on both sides of the Whig aristocracy.[5]

After a year with the Bennets, Claire wrote an entertaining account of the family's progressive principles:

One thing is certain that Mr. B is a Malthusian. I never saw a man so frightened at the populating power inherent in the human race . . . to hear him, Italy, poor Italy is so crowded with human beings, there is not space left in it for one Rational creature. For nothing would he give a sou to a beggar though he is very humane, so much does he fear they might marry on it. He groans over the chestnut trees loaded with nourishing fruit and sighs over the fields of Indian corn and the hedges full of blackberries, thinking how easily the poor will get food and how that facility will set them on marrying. I believe he sees in every blossom that blows, in every blade of grass that sprouts, a new born babe.[6]

This was not prejudice, for Claire found just as much entertainment in the Masons. As she wrote to Jane, always interested in love affairs, 'Nerina is continually regretting that she knows three languages, is an accomplished musician and has a decided turn for literature, because she is afraid it will stand in the way of her marrying some black bear of an Italian.'[7] These letters represent Claire in high spirits; at other times she would grumble to Mary about the parties of young men who monopolized the fireside. Winters were especially hard: 'I must be out at 9 in the morning and not home before 10 at night. I inhabit at Mrs Mason's a room without a fire, so that when I get home there is no sitting in it without perishing with cold.'[8] To Jane, on the topic of clothes, Claire was positively perverse: 'I dress every day worse.' Jane, to whom dress was a matter of the highest importance, generously sent her a length of material, but in reply Claire, who resented any suggestion of charity, wrote instead of thanks, 'it is far too elegant for me, consequently I have put it by in the piece . . . you really would have done well to have kept it'.[9] This shows Claire in one of the moods her friends learnt to dread—sharp and disdainful until the fit passed. In fact she had spent both time and money in the elegant boutiques of Dresden, on the grounds that 'I dare not in my position dress shabbily; it would be a losing policy.'[10] Considering her fierce pride and independence, it is most unlikely that she would creep like a shabby mouse among grand families or fashionable resorts.

In March 1832 came news which made Claire 'nearly mad with fear' about her family. An international cholera epidemic had reached London; the first month of the outbreak saw a thousand cases and five hundred deaths.[11] Claire wrote imploring Mary not to leave her long without a letter,

> if it be only a line as often as you can to say you are well. I see it has crept into every part of the town, so in London there is no retreat; you may think how I fear for you all; for my mother, papa, William, Jane Jefferson and you and Percy.[12]

Claire usually took pride in her lonely, roving life—however hard it was. Always travelling alone, for instance, was a defiance of the society which had rejected her and Allegra. Now that her family and friends were in danger, she felt the pull of the past and did the one thing she could do. Mrs Mason, always generous, had given Claire as a present her own royalties from Longman on *Advice to Young Mothers on the Physical Education of Children* (1823). Claire had intended to give this money to her young brother William, but now she saw a more urgent need. Her letter to Mary continued:

> Should money be the thing that hinders you from leaving London, take it and use it directly with Percy if the sum be enough. Now do as I bid you and do not let any false scruples hinder you. I am in no want of this money for I have enough for my present needs . . . I would willingly pay thousands and thousands to be free of the fear I am in.[13]

Claire's gifts were always impulsive and reckless. She felt fully repaid to know Percy and Mary were safely in lodgings at Sandgate on the Kent coast, from June until September. Her pride and thankfulness were complete; she believed all danger past.

While they were in Sandgate, her adored Percy learned to swim, and when he returned to London, more robust but still stout, he completed his gentlemanly accomplishments with private riding lessons at the Cavalry Barracks. In September 1832, at 13 he entered Harrow as a boarder. His uncle John, next in succession to the family estates, visited him at school; contemplating the solid figure thoughtfully, he is said to have remarked, 'You *do* look damned well, Percy.'[14]

Yet the feeling that all was well with Claire's family was not to last long. William, the young brother whose intended gift of money she had so casually diverted to Percy, went out for an evening in the crowded streets of Bartholomew Fair, traditional treat of Londoners. Next day he collapsed at home. With vomiting and purging, fading pulse and chilling of the body, he showed the classic symptoms of cholera. For the rest of William's short illness, his young wife Emily and his parents stayed at his bedside. A letter told Claire that he was dead. The money given to Percy could hardly have saved William, yet Claire was shattered; 'he did not have medical assistance, which they say is of the highest importance—altogether I suppose his life was thrown away',[15] she wrote. William was buried in the churchyard of St John's, Waterloo Road, the nearest church to his home. Even the unemotional Percy remembered him as 'a very good fellow who used to take me to the play'.[16]

Claire's grief for William was as unbridled as her earlier fears for Percy: 'From the moment I heard of it until now I have been in a complete annihilation—how long it will last I am sure I cannot tell.' Memories of Pisa in 1822, year of Allegra's death, flowed back: 'A horrible and most inevitable future is the image that torments me just as it did ten years ago in this very city.'[17] The rekindling of her emotions perhaps stirred her sympathies for her mother, for early in 1833, she asked Jane Hogg to visit Mrs Godwin: 'My poor mother is very sad about her loss and if at any time you can spare an hour to visit her you will do a real charity.'[18] Claire recognized that in the Godwin family Mary, as Mary Wollstonecraft's daughter and herself a writer, was her father's favourite; yet she admitted a certain resentment on behalf of William that his parent thought little of him.

> I however was fond of him because I did not view his faults in that desponding light which his other relations did . . . In our family if you cannot write an epic poem or novel, that by its originality knocks all other novels on the head, you are a despicable creature.

Ultimately, however, Claire's mind reverted to herself and her future. Her legacy depended on Percy surviving his grandfather Sir

Timothy. To guarantee a portion of this legacy, Claire took out a life insurance policy on Percy Florence.

I have insured Percy's life for a thousand pounds and now all my end must be to keep up the payment on it . . . I feel my spirits greatly relieved for they were always looking towards the future and its unprovided state filled me with anxiety.[19]

Claire renewed and added to the insurance policy which by 1844 reached a total of £2,839 19*s*. 0*d*.

Percy's future was already problematic. His first term's account had arrived from Harrow and his mother was unable to pay his sixty-pound boarding fees in Mr Kennedy's House without being 'hampered for the whole year'. There was no hope from Sir Timothy, who had reasonably recommended day schooling, at St Paul's or Merchant Taylors', as suitable for Mary's station in life. Claire was opposed to boarding school for different reasons. Alarmed to think of her adored Percy as a boarder, she wrote to Mary in his first term:

I am very glad to hear that Percy likes Harrow, but I shudder from head to foot when I think of your boldness in sending him there. I think in certain things you are the most daring woman I ever knew. There are few mothers who depending upon the life of an only son, would venture to expose that life to the dangers of a public school.[20]

The nature of Harrow's dangers remains ambiguous. Were they to health or morals? In either case, Claire knew them only from Byron's memories of his school days. She saw with wonder and some alarm the depth of her stepsister's determination. Mary left London to live at 'odious' Harrow in lodgings, since 'I am too poor to furnish'. Percy attended the school as a day boy, though mortifyingly 'home-boarders' were looked down upon.[21]

For the next four years Percy plodded uncomplainingly through the school. He enjoyed games with a few friends, 'his boys', to whom he remained loyal, ignoring high society. Mary was forced to admit 'he has no talent for Latin verses—he makes sad work'. In the fifth form, as befitted a young gentleman, he achieved '*a tail coat and watch*', but unfortunately failed to qualify for the sixth form. Mary went on Sundays to church, passing a small anonymous mound of turf near the porch, but made no friends to tell her this was Allegra's grave.

Mary's misery and loneliness at Harrow ended in collapse. Her letters alarmed Claire, to the extent that she told Mary she found them full of the most melancholy predictions—that before another year comes round your fate will have been sealed and yourself no longer of this world and you speak of it with such a firm conviction that one must believe you and shudder.[22]

Claire made the usual well-meaning but futile attempts to cheer the melancholiac by blaming her distress on outward causes. 'Do you endeavour to avert the calamity by taking care of yourself . . . Make this sacrifice for a year, for this one terrible year and, when that is over, I will release you from your precautions.' It cannot have cheered Mary to learn that Claire, in the soft nights and cool dawns of Pisa, avoiding coffee and drinking lemonade, felt 'astonishingly well'.

The next year, 1833, brought hope of easier times for the Godwin household. In April, the prime minister, Lord Grey, appointed Godwin yeoman of the guard, with a small but regular salary and quarters in New Palace Yard, St James. Mary, loyally determined to forestall criticism, pointed out that his duty was to maintain the palace fire-fighting gear and his post therefore 'not a sinecure'. Events confirmed this all too thoroughly. On 16 October 1834, Godwin allowed wooden tally sticks to be burnt within the precincts while he left for the theatre. The Houses of Parliament caught fire and burned to the ground while Godwin was peacefully enjoying a performance of Shakespeare's *Richard III*. Not surprisingly, 'the jokes of the people were shocking'.[23]

Claire certainly fitted into the Mason household like a member of the family. She enjoyed the dramas of a household with two handsome daughters on the brink of marriage. She knew better than to take sides, yet she felt pity for the mother and the elder daughter, who disagreed on Lauretta's choice of husband, one Galloni—'the first time they were ever divided in opinion'. Mrs Mason disliked Galloni, who proved indeed a rogue, but Claire had seen too many love affairs to think him worth a family quarrel. She wrote:

Our friends live in solitude and have nursed themselves into a height of romance about everything—They both think their destinies annihilated because the union of their minds has suffered this interruption. However no violence mingles with their sentiment and excited displeasure—on the contrary I wish it did, for it would be easier to heal than the tragic immutable sorrow with which they take it.[24]

The younger sister, Nerina, flung herself into the drama, like Claire in her own young days at Skinner Street.

She forgets her own love affairs with all the sabre slashes and dagger stabs of her own poor heart, to fall into fainting fits and convulsions every time she sees Lauretta and her mother; then she talks and writes upon the subject incessantly even till three in the morning . . . she introduces into her lamentations observations on the faulty manner in which she and her sister have been educated, the nature of love, objurgations against the whole race of Man and appeals to the female sex to prefer patriotism to matrimony . . . I am sure she cannot complain of a dearth of sensation.

Nerina called Claire into her room to read aloud the outpourings in her journal, until the tide of emotion turned and they both broke down giggling like two schoolgirls. No one seems to have consulted the father of the bride, who prudently retreated to his vegetable love until the scenes were over. Early in 1834, Claire wrote that the Masons were hurrying to see their first grandson—'End of honeymoon for poor Lauretta.'

Nerina at 19 had married Bartolomeo Cini, one of the group of young evening visitors. She adored him and went gladly to live with his parents.[25] Cini was a thoughtful and tender partner, who extended his friendship to Claire too. He remained a lifelong friend to her and even at the age of 80 she was still thanking him for help. He was always her 'best and most delightful' support in business matters.

A year after the Cinis' marriage, Claire was on a visit to Florence with her employers when she heard from Bartolomeo Cini the news of Margaret Mason's sudden death. To lose this trusted older friend, source of comfort and good advice, left Claire desolate. Yet she knew the family's loss was greater than hers, and wrote:

So you are all well! It is a comfort to know that. I only wish I could see Nerina, you, and the dear little girl; but it is perhaps better to let a little time pass before I see Nerina; her bereavement is too recent and I could not help talking about it, which would renew her grief . . . I should like to say to our Nerina that she is not to write to me until she feels she can do it without upsetting herself, and further that I rejoice to know her with you dear Cini and in your care . . . Nerina is indeed happy to have found you, whilst she fully deserved to do so.[26]

Claire remembered to send messages to Lauretta, 'heartbroken' in her unhappy marriage, and to Signor Tighe, who had 'lost everything'. 'I should like to ask you both to think of me sometimes with the same very affectionate friendship which I bear towards you.' To lose her friend of Shelleyan days was like losing a mother. Mrs Mason had in fact been closer to Claire's real life than the possessive and domineering Mrs Godwin in London.

Another reminder of the old Shelley circle was Jane Williams, who now reappeared in Claire's life. For six years, since Jane had written of flaws in the Shelleys' marriage, Mary had felt 'cold as marble' towards her. Claire wrote urging her to forget what was in the wider world to her, a common experience.

> I rejoice in your friendship for Jane, who is sincerely attached to you: do not let the barrier the folly of a moment raised in you prevail. How can you expect, dear Mary, not to be traduced by your friends? What mortal can you point out alive or dead that was so privileged?[27]

Claire went on to relate a similar experience which she had endured 'with the greatest cheerfulness', having probably enjoyed the battle at the time. In her late 30s Jane gave birth to another little girl, and this perhaps stirred Mary's affections and enabled the women to draw closer.

At this time Claire, like thousands of others, was engaged in devouring Trelawny's best-seller, *Adventures of a Younger Son*. She wrote to Jane how strangely 'things so extraordinary have a perfect air of truth'. Yet she knew Trelawny well enough to penetrate the core of his endless fictions. Having been placed in the Navy at the age of 12 by his father, he had grown up at sea in wartime, wretched, often punished yet defiant, among fist fights, flogging, and the screams of the wounded. At 19 he was rejected for a lieutenant's commission and discharged as a failure. Claire wrote compassionately, 'Poor Trelawny, what a life he has had—how atrociously he was neglected and his good qualities overlooked by his parents.'

Meanwhile the author of this strange best-seller roamed from state to state of America in pursuit of vague schemes, all of which dissolved in failure. Late in 1833 he wrote to Claire:

> I have been in America nearly a twelvemonth—during which period I have circumnavigated the twenty-four states . . . Wandering over this country I see many spots that resemble my rural castle in the air—it is time I should begin to lay the foundations of them on earth.[28]

He went on to describe his imaginary feat of swimming across the river below Niagara Falls 'with high thoughts engendered by the sublime scene'.

There was, as so often with Trelawny, one puzzling omission. Mary had observed, 'You never mention Zella.' In fact, before leaving for America, Trelawny had sent Zella to board with a wealthy, childless Englishwoman in Lucca, Jane Bocella. Conveniently persuading himself his child was 'adopted', Trelawny dismissed the whole matter from his mind. Reminded of Zella he wrote vaguely, 'Let me see, she must be of nine years old?' But problems ignored do not cease to exist; when in the end they caught up with him, he wrote from Charleston, South Carolina, to pour out his troubles to Claire. Jane Bocella had found Zella's temper so violent that she was exhausted by the daily battles and asked to be relieved of her charge. 'Her acct. of Zella's temper has vexed me,' wrote Trelawny in the tone of one unjustly tried.

What can be done—can you not devise anything? you are on the spot—some remedy may be found . . . time with awakening reason be enough . . . I have ever found you loving and forgiving . . . you must not treat me according to my deserts—but after the emotions of your affectionate heart.[29]

His final instructions to Claire were 'Relieve Madam Bocella from the burthen of taking care of Zella—immediately!', adding the helpful information, 'Bye the bye, all the women of our family are devils.'

Claire was no paragon, but a small child, especially a small girl, abandoned, called out her deepest feelings. She applied to the kindly Bennets for leave of absence, suppressing Trelawny's shameless assumption of future thanks to Mrs Bennet 'for an anticipated kindness to the Greek orphan', and set out for Lucca. Trelawny had sent no money, nor could she afford to stay in Lucca on her own savings. Self-reliant of necessity, Claire took a temporary post as governess, and her next letter to Mary came from Villa Città di Lucca. She had met long-suffering Jane Bocella, whom she liked at once, though she noted with a trace of malice, that the trusting English lady cherished a portrait of Trelawny that made him appear 'too smooth and clean', indeed artificially 'handsome as the day'. Zella, by contrast, was real.

You want to hear of Zella. She is very like him without being nearly as handsome . . . She is impulsive in the highest degree in her feelings, her cheeks mounting to scarlet at the slightest word; her temper is tyrannical and it is odd to see such a little creature trying upon every occasion to beat down grown people and enforcing her own will by perpetual battles . . . abusing

Madame Bocella and the maids and company present and even God and her fate. Of course she looks anything but a child—her bold speech and looks when offended . . . are what you find in a robust man and make you forget those moments when she takes delight in a sugar plum or looks timidly upon a stranger. A good education will make a fine character of her, and that poor Madame B. sweats to give her. She abhors application of any kind. Notwithstanding her faults you cannot help liking her; even in her rages she looks so honest you pardon her, and when pacific she smiles, it is so sweet you adore her.[30]

Zella's youthful mother had married again, reverting to her wild origins; for most of Zella's life the child had been passed from one guardian to another, defending herself tooth and claw. Nor could Trelawny be blamed for his neglect; sent to sea at the age of 12, he had no idea of family affection. Claire, who had survived the young Galitzins, was probably the person best equipped to face Zella. She took the child to Florence and placed her in a homely, small school. Trelawny, of course, detested 'everything that has a resemblance to a school' and found Zella's 'antipathy to learning certainly natural',[31] but accepted the arrangement until he returned to London. Claire then firmly sent Zella home to him in the care of a returning traveller, and reminded Trelawny to meet his 11-year-old daughter at Dover.

Claire and Mary had one further exchange of letters during the Lucca stay, entirely characteristic of them both. They had once visited Lucca together, long ago in August 1820, exploring the little city and the tree-shaded walls for two days while Shelley was climbing Monte Pellegrino. Now Claire described the charm of Lucca in autumn, when the mornings and evenings were cool. The ancient villa where she stayed stood on a mountain side, hidden in its own woods. The spacious, lofty rooms were airy and the thick walls kept out midday's heat. Mary's reply lamented 'her dull life at Harrow', and Claire had the last word, 'Oh! Mary I want to commend you to try being a governess for a month or two.'[32] In ending her letter, Claire turned to her deepest concern, Percy, whom she vainly tried not to mention too often.

I do it upon principle as I think it right to like him much less than I do. Whenever I think of him I cannot help flattering myself he will become the greatest poet and the greatest philosopher England has ever produced and that he will follow the doctrines of his father.

Claire knew she was foolish, but could not overcome it. Minor problems were swept aside by the great disaster of 1835. The cholera epidemic which had swept through Britain in 1832 now raged in Western Europe. This international pandemic had appeared in Asia during the 1820s, claiming a thousand British soldiers in India. It spread overland through Russia, where troops surrounded stricken villages and shot down peasants who attempted to flee. By 1831 the infection had crossed the near East into Europe, carried by travellers. Trelawny, returning to England by way of France in 1835, found Paris 'like a city of the dead'. With inimitable perversity he wrote, 'So many people warned me not to come to Paris that I began to think of purchasing the lease of a house for life.'[33] During the hot summer months of 1835, the cholera was carried to Spain and to Italy. The fact that the disease spread through polluted water supplies was not known; seemingly a malignant mystery, it threw the Italian masses into panic. The devout feared a judgement from heaven or an invasion from hell; others attempted to murder the physician in revenge when a relation died. Italian cities slid into chaos.

Meanwhile the Bennet family was spending the hot weather peacefully by the seaside English fashion in Viareggio, then a small, quiet summer resort. Claire was with them to teach and chaperone her two pupils, perhaps also to enjoy her favourite outdoor sport of swimming.[34] While the girls, Gertrude and Charlotte, were enjoying themselves by the sea, Mr Bennet was forming his own plans. Like every self-respecting intellectual, he must show his family Florence; as Claire wrote to Mary from Florence in September, 'from the moment the Bennets were at Viareggio they must come here'. She had attempted to dissuade them, pointing out sixty deaths from cholera in Florence in the first few days and that half the city's population had decamped to the countryside,

> so certain are they that it is an instantaneous disaster . . . the dirt in the streets and the diet of the Italians makes it very much worse . . . A first rate Physician from Leghorn is in despair that he has tried every method and none succeeded.[35]

Claire's attempts at persuasion had no effect on Mr Bennet, who remained amiably implacable.

> I never expected the Bennets would for their own sakes go straight into a town where there was this frightful malady—but if I [had] money I could scarcely go—it is dishonourable to leave people who have been kind to you, in the midst of danger to leave them to shift for themselves just at the very

moment your services for their children are indispensable . . . the die is cast and I must abide by it.

The sight-seeing party settled at Casino Nerli, a hotel in the Via dell'Orto, Florence. Here Claire's thoughts turned, as so often, to the past and to the figures of her early life. Of Byron, whom she had no wish to meet after death, she said:

I am not revengeful and desire pain to no one, not even to him. But for me there could be no happiness, there could be nothing but misery in the presence of the person who so wantonly, wilfully destroyed my Allegra.

Shelley she still mourned across years of poverty and loneliness:

Of exile from all that is dear to us . . . this genius extinct, the greatest ever known, and the noble system he would have established therewith fallen for many ages to the dust.

These thoughts set down on paper, Claire considered the chances of death with the vigorous enthusiasm she brought to any dramatic prospect.

I can't eat, I can't sleep . . . I have suffered from cramps and pains in the stomach . . . I see they are the prelude to cholera. What makes me think this is that I never suffered before from these sort of pains—it must be the sickness that is in the air of Florence . . . I have made up my mind to die of it . . . I commend my life so far as anyone can to await it.[36]

Mrs Godwin, remembering her son William's sudden collapse, was 'uneasy' about her daughter. Mary read the long letters with amusement and a faint contempt: 'Claire is at Florence, expecting, poor dear, most firmly to die of cholera.'[37] Maria Gisborne wrung her hands over the alternatives. 'How much suffering she might have been spared if she had married Peacock,' a much belated thought, since Claire had refused his proposal fourteen years earlier. In fact, the whole party escaped infection, possibly because Mr Bennet had selected a hotel on the higher right bank, above flood level. Claire looked back with some regret; she would sometimes have liked to become a 'peaceful nothingness'. Instead she found herself an energetic guide to the Bennets. Her early stay in Florence had left profound memories of the city. 'This is a delightful town—for the beautiful crops up all around you and gives you pleasure and draws you out of the sphere of self.' Claire could walk her employers along the Lung'Arno and over the bridges, to churches when their Protestant prejudices allowed, past individual *palazzi*, each different, and to the statues under the Loggia dei Lanzi. Public galleries did not yet exist, but Claire knew where pictures might be viewed; *Cleopatra Applying the Asp to her Breast* by Guido Reni, Rubens's *Allegory of War*, Domenichino's *Magdalen*, 'clad in long and flowing hair', and Raphael's *Madonna della Sedia* were all in the collection at the Palazzo Pitti. Claire had visited the charming intimate theatres of Florence, having enjoyed farces at the Cocomero, ballets at the Teatro Goldoni, and Rossini's operas from the six tiers of curtained boxes at the largest house, the Pergola. She was able to introduce her pupils to Mozart operas: *La Clemenza di Tito, Don Giovanni*, and *Le Nozze di Figaro*, from which she played piano arrangements and sang arias transposed by herself. On a more frivolous plane, she could recommend music and dancing schools and a shop in the Mercato Nuovo for Gertrude and Charlotte to buy frocks. The streets of Florence grew crowded and noisy in the tourist season, but Claire knew a retreat in the cool woods of plane trees stretching along the Arno. Here Shelley, seeing the dead leaves driven before the west wind in autumn 1819, had written:

> Drive my dead thoughts over the universe
> Like withered leaves to quicken a new birth.

Claire had schooled herself to say nothing of the writer, but in this setting his words returned to haunt her.

Claire, speaking mostly French or Italian, began to feel her English deteriorating. It was true that she wrote endless letters, but their construction and style did not meet her literary standards. After her visit to London, she confided in Mary:

> Already I have lost the little I had gained in my English, and I can only write with an effort that is unpleasant to me; it precludes the possibility of finding any pleasure in composition. I pause a hundred times, and lean upon my hand to endeavour to find words to express the idea that is in my mind. It is a vain endeavour; the idea is there but no words, and I leave my task unfinished.[38]

In spite of these struggles, Claire managed to draft a short story that she hoped might meet the standards of a popular annual, and which she sent with an apologetic letter to Mary, whom she admired as a writer, out of her own sphere.

I have written a tale which I think will do for the *Keepsake*. I shall send it home for your perusal. Will you correct it? . . . Will you be angry with me if I ask you to write the last scene of it? . . . My only time for writing is after 10 at night; the rest of the tale was composed at that hour, after having been scolding and talking and giving lessons from 7 in the morning. It was very near its end when I got so ill I gave it up. If you cannot do anything with it you can at least make curl papers and that is always something . . . The truth is, I should never think of writing, knowing well my incapacity for it, but I want to earn money since it is the only key of freedom. One is even impudent enough to ask a great authoress to finish one's tale for one.[39]

The letter recalls Mrs Godwin's complaint that her daughter was thought and called stupid 'because she did not have Mary's first rate abilities'.

Mary placed this story, 'The Pole', as having been written by 'the author of Frankenstein' in *The English Annual* for 1836 and shared the customary outright payment with Claire. Claire's story was in the 'Gothick' style of her young days, already going out of fashion. The scene is set in Italy and the characters owe something to the Shelley household: handsome hero, romantic melancholy heroine, and rebel younger sister, whom Claire somewhat flatteringly presents as 'guardian angel' to the lovers. Claire's idea of literature, in spite of her wide reading, seems conventionally romantic. Yet when the action moves to Russia, Claire's experience of political repression under Nicholas I was real and leads her to foresee revolt to come: 'Through the strawberry picking and the mushroom expeditions, the sledge drives by moonlight and the rides to drink milk at the estate saw mills, those who had ears might have heard the clang of hammer and sickle.'[40] Shelley's early teaching had left Claire attuned for life to the underground stirring of revolution and alert for news. As though aware that she might be lost in a backwater, she begged Mary: 'In your next pray mention something about politics and how the London University is getting on.' In 1830, when starving field labourers of the southern counties rioted for a wage, three were hanged and more than four hundred transported to Australia, she wrote, 'The accounts of the distress in England are awful.'

Claire and Mary were close, but, as in all families, there were sometimes disagreements. Mary was by nature reserved, and knew that many people thought her cold: 'want of animal spirits of liveliness & strength to talk & amuse has been my great drawback in life'.[41] Claire's open declarations of feeling disturbed her, and Claire's attachment to a Bohemian past threatened Percy's gentlemanly future. Perhaps loneliness caused Claire to write so passionately of their old circle:

> You live—you are—that is enough for my happiness . . . Trelawny enchants me by some immense piece of unworldliness, Jane with her refined sentiments and graceful manner of uttering them; when I am away from you I recollect all these.[42]

Claire's doting on Percy was increasingly unsuited to that stolid youth. 'Percy has not written to me lately—I give him my love.' She wrote that she had 'set her heart upon seeing him'; 'Do not let Percy forget me—that is a very sore point.' When Mary wrote to Pisa, Claire devoured the letters.

> A treasure of a letter . . . wise opinions and thoughts which from their truth take a hold on one's mind . . . That you should write such letters I can well imagine; the flowers and fruit of a great writer's mind must necessarily be in his or her work . . . I embrace you all.[43]

Claire admired Mary's talents so passionately that she hoped to engage them in the cause of women writers.

> I am glad to hear you are writing again; I am always in a fright lest you should take it into your head to do what the warriors do after they have acquired great fame—retire and rest upon your laurels. That would be very comfortable for you, but very vexing to me, who am always wanting to see women distinguishing themselves in literature, and who believe there has not been nor ever will be one so calculated as yourself to raise our sex upon that point. If you would but know your value and exert your powers you could give the men a most immense drubbing![44]

Life has strengthened Claire's early feminism; here she speaks out.

Neither Claire's politics nor her passions suited Mary's increasingly Conservative temperament. Yet their affection seemed to hold steady, except under the strain of a family crisis. One of these was approaching, though still unseen, in the spring of 1836. Trelawny, who had returned to London, wrote cheerfully to Claire on 22 March that he had called on her 80-year-old stepfather and found him 'no more affected by time than the leaning tower of Pisa'. On 7 April, William Godwin died. He was buried with Mary Wollstonecraft in St Pancras churchyard. Mary and Mrs Godwin, rivals to the last, were both present at his deathbed.[45]

The stress of Godwin's last days and the burden of sorting his tumultuous papers made Mary feel 'an invalid'. At this unhappy time an emotional letter from Claire jarred on her and she poured out her vexation to Trelawny: 'Claire always harps on my desertion of her—as if I could desert one I never clung to—we were never friends . . . She poisoned my life when young . . . my idea of Heaven was a world without Claire.'[46] This was a passing mood: mutual trust and loyalty survived this declaration by many years. Yet in it, the seeds of their final parting were already sown.

13 *A Galley Life (1836–1841)*

Godwin's death presented an immediate problem, described by Trelawny to Claire as 'keeping your mother afloat'. After thirty-five years of marriage, of copying manuscripts, and attempting to publish books, of unpaid rent and household bills, of bankruptcies and loans spent before they were received, Godwin's widow was left with less than a hundred pounds.[1] She proposed that Claire should keep house for her and her son's widow Emily 'in some village about town', but Trelawny knew his old flame too well for this. It would be 'a galley life'. The widow was 'crony, rheumy—rheumatic and phtisicy . . . that will never do. Claire had better be housekeeper to my houseless self.'[2]

Neither prospect seemed hopeful. For the present Claire remained with her employers in Florence, while Trelawny, by his own account, and Mary, through Caroline Norton, petitioned the government on Mrs Godwin's behalf. Melbourne, as prime minister, declined to continue Godwin's annuity to his widow, but granted her three hundred pounds from the Royal Bounty. The Royal Literary Fund for authors in distress added fifty pounds, and the total remained Mrs Godwin's sole capital for the remainder of her life.[3]

Claire's conscience was evidently uneasy at living abroad while her widowed mother remained in London. She considered seeking a post in England as governess, or if necessary as housekeeper.[4] This problem was solved when in October 1836 Mr and Mrs Bennet made one of their sudden decisions to move. They planned to return from Florence to London, travelling by post-horses, thirty-five or sometimes fifty miles a day; Claire's 'head went round' as the trees flashed past the carriage windows, and she 'thought every minute my last'. Once arrived in Paris, the Bennets yielded to the charm of the city and changed their plans with no difficulty. They cashed drafts on their banker, Lafitte, and settled to enjoy themselves, with their governess as interpreter. Claire valiantly revived herself from the journey by 'drinking nearly a tumblerful of brandy'. After this she was ready to strike bargains with the French landlord, chef, and laundress, and to take Mrs Bennet, Charlotte, and Gertrude out to buy Paris hats. There was an atmosphere of holiday in the air. Claire wrote to Mary, who had planned to meet her in London, that she had no idea how long they would stay in France. 'Your health is the first thing—for God's sake go straight to the sea.'[5] Later events suggest that Claire may have found motives to linger in Paris on her own account, but she wrote nothing of this.

By New Year 1837, Claire was installed with the Bennets in their town house, 11 Queen Street, Mayfair, within walking distance of her mother. Mrs Godwin had settled in rooms at 3 Golden Square, between Regent Street and the Italian craftsmen: the carvers, gilders, music copyists, violin and piano makers of Soho. Only a handful of the William and Mary houses with tall windows and fanlit doors remain; a formal garden has replaced the grass and sweeping trees. Yet the square is still an oasis. Here Mrs Godwin found shelter and here she stayed until she died. Claire later shared her rooms and may have paid the rent, with further contributions when her mother's seven shillings a week failed to meet the cost of food or coals. No accounts survive to prove this so it remains a surmise, but Claire's board and lodging were provided by the Bennets and no other member of the family was in a position to help. Charles was hard driven to meet the expenses of his young family, and Mary's money troubles forced her to ask for a loan of twenty pounds from Trelawny.[6] She was determined at all costs to send Percy to university; since he had not reached the sixth form at school, he needed a year's private coaching from a country clergyman to meet the modest demands of the Cambridge Previous Examination.

The money troubles of the family stemmed from one source: the continuing life and health of old Sir Timothy Shelley. Nothing shows more clearly the contrasting temperaments of Mary and Claire than their response to this situation. Mary worried not only for Percy and herself, but sincerely on Claire's behalf. 'Poor Claire,' she wrote in July 1824, 'at least she will be independent one day.' In 1831 Mary was still anxious for Claire. 'When will her trials be over? When will independence be her lot?'[7] By contrast, Claire, for better or worse, was careless about money. In July 1823 she had lent Mary cash when her allowance was delayed and in 1829 had rented lodgings for herself in London, to be independent of the Godwin family. Whatever her private worries, from pride she treated Sir Timothy as a joke. In April 1832 she had written: 'I can never think of him without seeing his grey hair growing into fine clustering brown locks; his bent form assuming a manly straightness and strength and the most glowing pink creeping over his once aged, but now youthful cheek.[8] Two years later Sir Timothy had a severe attack of gout and was not expected to survive. When Claire heard from Mary of his recovery, her reaction was one of laughter; in her words, she 'laughed ready to kill myself'.

Oh! that undying . . . undyable Sir Tim! His jumps towards the grave and then his quick returns to life are too comical. Life and death are playing Bob Cherry with him poor man. You say he has lived long enough to ruin you. I am sure he has me and I give him permission now to live to all Eternity![9]

Obstinate herself, Claire almost admired the old man's stubborn survival.

During the years when they met so seldom, Claire and Mary had drifted apart in their political views. With one year's interval Claire had lived abroad from 1818 to 1837, from the age of 20 to nearly 39. Moving from country to country, from one aristocratic household to another, she had not experienced the growing seriousness and piety of everyday life among the middle class of Britain. Conversation, once airy as a syllabub, had now become as solid as cabinet pudding. Trelawny and Claire still shared Shelley's faith in the Promethean fire. Their contemporaries saw revolution as proof of the sinfulness of mankind and submission to God's will as the only remedy. Byron early felt the new atmosphere and put it tersely, '*cant* is so much stronger than *cunt* nowadays'.

Mary's dawning Conservatism began to show itself after her father's death, when his will directed her to select and edit his unpublished political papers. She wrote in 1836 of two octavo volumes, to include Godwin's autobiography,[10] but by 1837 confessed to Trelawny her 'fear of becoming an object of scurrility and attack'. Tacitly the Godwin project was abandoned. Even more painful was the task of 1838 when, 'torn to pieces by Memory', she worked on a definitive edition of Shelley's poems, dedicated by herself to Percy.[11] Her notes after each section of poems, replacing a memoir prohibited by Sir Timothy, are perhaps the zenith of her writing. As she described it, the canal near Pisa where Shelley wrote *Adonais* in 1821, was

sheltered by trees that dipped their boughs into the murmuring waters. By day multitudes of ephemera darted to and fro on the surface; at night the fireflies came out among the shrubs on the banks: the cicale at noonday kept up their hum.

Yet political problems intruded, and Mary found herself shrinking from her own early convictions. There was, for instance, the atheism of *Queen Mab*. 'I dislike Atheism, but I shrink from mutiliation.'[12] She deleted Canto VII and Shelley's dedication of the poem to Harriet, the wife of his youth, but restored both in the second edition, after protests by Peacock, Trelawny, and Hogg, with bitter self-reproach. 'Poor Harriet to whose sad fate I attribute too many of my own heavy sorrows as the atonement claimed by fate for her death.'[13] This sense of sin and punishment deserved is the keynote of a new age. A collapse followed and a 'nervous illness—driving me to the verge of insanity—often I felt the cord wd. snap'.[14] Mary was prescribed opium and seemed to recover, but the illness had been a turning-point. The headaches, pressure on the brain, weakness, and dizziness, were the beginning of the brain tumour which would eventually kill her.[15] For the present she felt that she had suffered enough in the cause of progress. When Trelawny requested her support for women's rights she wrote decisively, 'since I lost Shelley I have no wish to ally myself to the Radicals—they are full of repulsion to me . . . rude, envious & insolent—I wish to have nothing to do with them.'[16] She became and remained Conservative, not merely on Percy's behalf, but by her own conviction.

Claire, though never consciously atheistic as Trelawny was, had missed the religious awakening of English society. She was obliged to attend Sunday services with the Bennets in her professional role as tutor of the young, yet neither the seriousness of the Evangelicals nor the fervent reverence of the Oxford movement touched her. Week by week she had joined in the General Confession at the English Church in Pisa, with 'rage', as she repeated 'We have followed too much the devices and desires of our own hearts!—I, who am always forced to do everything my heart detests!'[17] Her secret creed was Shelley's faith in freedom:

> Lo, the sun floats up the sky
> Like thought-winged Liberty.

When Claire returned to England she no longer had to rely on Mary's regular letters as her source of political information and turned to Trelawny. He wasted no time before urging his latest enthusiasm, the Philosophic Radicals and their critical journal *The*

Westminster Review, in which Jeremy Bentham 'swept away the accumulated cobwebs of centuries'.[18] Claire had only been a few weeks at Queen Street when Trelawny wrote on 10 February 1837 asking her to write a review of Mary Shelley's novel *Falkner*.

> Assist me!! Lend me your hand!! Don't fob me off with excuses of its weakness, its engagements—an iron will can force a way anywhere. I must get written a review of Mary's new work—will you do it—or failing that will you write me one of your long flighty fanciful letters commenting on the peculiarities and individuality of the Godwin School in which Mary is saturated . . . for our new Radical Review the *Westminster*.[19]

Claire had no time to write, as her employers shortly moved their household to Windsor. What pleased her most was that Trelawny associated her with Shelley as a natural ally of reform. The radical party was pressing through its one MP, a barrister sergeant-at-law, Thomas Talfourd, a bill which became the Infants' Custody Act of 1839. This, for the first time, assured a separated mother legal right of access to her own children. In practice, the Act would not have given Claire access to Allegra, since the bill specified married women[20] and did not apply to illegitimate children. Nevertheless Trelawny assumed that she would support it on principle: 'The Godwins and the Shelleys are part and parcel of liberalism . . . are they and you not linked indissolubly together?'[21]

Mary, as she said, wished to have 'nothing to do' with Trelawny's party, and did not share Claire's radicalism. There is a note of reserve in her reply when Claire requested an autograph of Shelley for a friend. 'I hope the person to whom you give it will appreciate it as it deserves—or I should not like to part with it.'[22] Claire, in turn, had reservations when Mary thought of returning to her long-abandoned life of Shelley. 'Do not think of writing the memoirs—you must on no account use your mind—health is every thing.'[23] Her concern was genuine. Yet did she also realize how far Mary had moved from Shelley's revolutionary ideals?

Claire seemed unaware that her politics were odd or even unusual from the British point of view. When she went off with the Bennets to Windsor in summer 1837, grumbling to Trelawny about 'eternal want of time', she did not mention the fact which was exciting the whole nation: on 20 June King William IV had died and 17-year-old Victoria had succeeded him. Nor did she write a word about the coronation exactly one year later, although the Bennets—Whig aristocrats under a Whig government—were interested in court affairs. The nation might fall in love with its new monarch—Mary wrote spontaneously to Leigh Hunt of 'our pretty little Queen'—but Claire had learnt in Austria and Russia to judge monarchy by its government and not by appearances. As the 'hungry 40s' approached, she read of starvation wages, Corn Laws which prohibited the import of cheap foreign wheat and so maintained a high price of bread to the poor, and penal laws which condemned the hungry poacher to transportation or hanging. She wrote to Mary:

> The distress among the working classes in England is dreadful . . . I suppose it will end by a repeal of the Corn Laws and that measure will alleviate the misery of the poor—but some say it will only increase it. The Queen's offer of fifty pounds to all who convict others of fomenting rebellion, is a most immoral proclamation and a downright premium to calumny, malice and all uncharitableness.[24]

Claire lived forty-two years through the reign of Queen Victoria, yet she never became in belief or behaviour a Victorian.

In July 1837, Percy Shelley was entered on the rolls of Trinity College, Cambridge, as a pensioner.[25] At this, Crabbe Robinson the diarist wrote thoughtfully: 'If talent descended what ought he not to be who is the blood of Godwin, Mrs. Wollstonecraft, Shelley and Mrs. Shelley?'[26] Cambridge in fact revealed Percy's one unquestionable inheritance from his father: a passion for boats. Percy himself added an enthusiasm for amateur theatricals and popular music. In his second year he began to take flute lessons, soon abandoned because they cost too much, and voice coaching from an Italian teacher, 'Old Negri'. News of this suggested to his Aunt Claire, who pursued him with unrelenting adoration, a bond between them in the love of music. 'Does your passion for it still last?', she wrote eagerly. 'Mine does—I find it comes nearer my soul than poetry or philosophy or patriotism or even love.'[27] Percy's favourite pastime of the moment was to sing duets and glees, with Henry Leigh Hunt, as Keats had memorably described his father, 'at the music'. Claire's un-English rapture for classical music struck a false note.

Claire took Percy's undergraduate love affairs, never very ardent, with equal seriousness. In spring 1839 he 'engaged himself' to a girl whom his mother thought unworthy. Claire was quick to defend her favourite. 'Poor Boy, but I pity him and all young people of his age whose heart is just opening, who pine to expand themselves and find insurmountable barriers everywhere. Thank God I can never be young again.'[28] This picture of pining Percy is improbable, but Claire firmly believed in it.

Claire was determined that Percy should shine in university society, but he always preferred thc company of a few 'good fellows' whom he had known at Harrow. On learning that in his first year, like many young men of his age, he was shy in public, his aunt sent a rallying letter signed 'your Friend', to Trinity College.

> I hear *with dismay* that you are resolved upon making an Hermit of yourself and that you fly society as if drawing-rooms could only contain dragons and basilisks. Ah! dear me—great is my mortification—I had set my heart upon your being as high toned in your manners as was Sir Philip Sidney in his day . . . Of what use will your gifted mind and dispositions be if you shut yourself with one or two young men and bar out everybody you may not have known at nine years old.[29]

The idea of Percy as a glittering social figure was just as unreal as Claire's dreams of him as musician, philosopher, or poet in the tradition of his father. These delusions were totally at odds with Claire's usual clear-sighted scepticism. There seems no rational explanation for them. Perhaps her love for Shelley, confined during his lifetime within the bounds of brother and sisterhood even in her dreams, now broke free and spent itself upon the image of his son.

Towards the end of 1837, Claire needed a new post. Charlotte and Gertrude Bennet, whom she had taught for five years, were considered grown up, as Gertrude was now 17. Both girls were to marry within three months of each other, in 1839, feeling affection and gratitude for their carelessly generous, clever, and amusing governess, an opinion most of Claire's pupils shared.[30]

Claire was spared the anxieties of finding a post, for a new position awaited her almost immediately. This was usual in her experience, for sometimes she had found a new position before she had left the last. Abroad, English teachers were in demand so this was understandable, but this was the first time that Claire was seeking a post in England. Here the profession was so crowded (as the only resource of educated single women) that in 1841 a Governess's Benevolent Institution was founded to give discreet help to 'ladies in temporary distress'. For one modest annuity of twenty pounds, 150 elderly governesses applied, 83 of them without a penny in the world. By these standards Claire was fortunate. She left the Bennets at

Windsor in late autumn 1837 and by December had found a new post, five miles away at Winkfield Place,[31] to teach the daughter of Mr and Mrs Sanford.

The first days in a new family were always hard, especially at Christmas, when Claire had hoped to see Percy and his friends in London. Instead she found herself buried within the park of Winkfield Place, among strangers. 'Ah! happy Percy that you are—what I would give to be you.' The parish of Winkfield was large, scattered with hamlets and country seats. All around were woods—Ascot Heath, Cranborne Woods, Windsor Forest, and the fringes of the Royal Great Park. The pillars of the church nave were five stout trunks of oak trees from the forest, and the local gentry, many holding posts at Windsor Castle, were equally oaken. The Sanfords, judging by the parish registers, had no local connection and had rented Winkfield Place from its owner, abroad on military service. Mr Sanford was descended from a large county family of Nynehead Court, Wellington, Somerset.[32] He befriended Mary on a visit to Florence in 1842, and appears frequently in her letters of the 1840s. Mrs Sanford was a colourful, though less respectable, lady from Ireland. She had already been divorced for adultery, 'crim. con.', by Lord Cloncurry, and her daughter by this first marriage would later entangle Claire and Mary in her affairs.

Claire soon learnt why Mrs Sanford needed a governess so urgently. 'My pupil would make Iron or Steel nervous,'[33] she reported to Mary, and to Percy in graphic detail: 'Nothing loves she to do but eating, drinking and sleeping . . . even washing her face she must be quarreled with before she will do it—What a beast of a girl! I will talk no more of my Miss Sanford.'[34] This 10-year-old child might well become the Horatia Sanford whom Mary considered at 15 'really too silly to be let loose in society', though she improved when Claire eventually won her over, as she had done with Natalie Kaisaroff.

Winkfield Place had its own compensations. The Sanfords entertained lavishly, sometimes guests who were 'amiable and pleasant', even to the governess, and one man who 'sang divinely'. Claire, always a good pianist, was in demand to play accompaniments. Political house parties were less of a pleasure.

> Quantities of people in the house . . . half are Tories the other half Whigs; whatever opinion you mention, either in politics or morals, there is a party whom it displeases and they set on you . . . for the pleasure of abusing and quarreling with you.[35]

Claire claimed that she 'held her tongue', but this seems hardly in character. Another advantage of Winkfield was the chance to visit London. Claire's years there fell at one of the great landmarks of the century, the change from coach to railway travel. The Bath Mail coach, fast and frequent, changed horses at the inn in the village street of Slough. Soon however the journey to London would be unimaginably faster, for the railway to Windsor opened in January 1842, and the queen made her first excursion by train. Claire visited Peacock and his daughter at their riverside cottage, Lower Halliford, Chertsey. For one week she rented rooms from Mary's landlady at 4d Park Street, a week for which she planned visits and appointments: 'My mother, you, the Bennets—and my teeth . . . set my heart upon seeing Percy.'[36]

Lodging in the same house, Claire and Mary were able to exchange news of their old circle. Hogg still refused to marry Jane. Trelawny was having an affair with Augusta Goring. Their first child was born in 1839, and they married after her husband, whom Claire called 'a wretch—an english wretch', divorced her in 1841. For many years they vanished to farm at Usk.[37] This left the question of Zella—'poor dear little Zella—I hope she is well and happy'[38]—but Zella came of tough stock; she willingly left her father, married abroad, and survived till the age of 81. Claire's visit and the sisters' conversations continued when Mary moved to the Lower Richmond Road on the strand at Putney. This suited Percy, who kept a boat on the Thames. In the long vacation of 1839 he rowed with two friends to Oxford and made a leisurely return 'fishing by the way'. 'I wish he would study more', sighed his mother, but Claire insisted Percy was perfect.

One member of the old circle who still had friendly feelings towards Claire was Leigh Hunt. His affairs, since they had parted in 1822, had slid into a chaos of failed journals, debts, a family lawsuit, and ill health. Publishing *Lord Byron and some of his Contemporaries* had shocked British ideas of what was decent and confirmed Hunt's ruin. Yet in the winter of 1839–40 his affairs at last were looking up, for his play *A Legend of Florence* was coming on at Covent Garden. He wanted to meet Claire at Mary's house, but between them the three Romantics characteristically could not fix a day.[39] So Hunt, (most generously considering his finances), sent Claire an order for the first night, 3 February 1840. She was in the audience for the successful opening of *Legend*, which continued to play to good houses, and could afford a night at the Lansdowne Hotel, Dover Street. Trips to London always included a duty visit to her mother at Golden Square, within easy walking distance.

This particular visit, made almost by chance, was decisive. Claire chose not to write an account of the state of affairs in the lodgings, yet it apparently convinced her that her mother could not survive alone. By 10 March she had left Winkfield and was living at 3 Golden Square with Mrs Godwin. 'I never see Claire',[40] wrote Mary, rather plaintively. Although their homes were now closer, Claire was engaged in juggling time and tasks. Mrs Godwin had at last achieved the aim she had been pursuing since at least 1828, in a manner Mary thought 'artful'. Where art had failed, her own weakness succeeded, and her own flesh and blood daughter lived with her. Mary had forecast this dependence as 'l'inferno stesso',[41] hell itself, an exaggeration of her lifelong resentment of her stepmother; yet in sober fact it cannot have been easy. By her generous impulse, Claire had given up a post with considerable advantages to undertake the care of a fractious, elderly parent, for whom she must also earn a living. Daily companions were very cheap, or possibly William's widow came in. Mary wrote that Mrs Godwin was 'better and more tractable . . . not well enough yet to rebel'.[42] Somebody must have watched the old lady, for Claire was out at all hours earning enough to keep the household above water. 'I am so worried I fear I shall go out of my mind,' she wrote hurriedly to Mary in 1840,

> Thus is now my life—I go by nine to Mrs. Kitchener's house where I give lessons till one—then I rush to the top of Wilton Place and get a Richmond omnibus and go to Richmond to give a lesson to the Cohens—their daughter is going to be married to a Genoese and must have an Italian lesson every day . . . that vile omnibus takes two hours to go to Richmond and the same to come back, and so with giving my lesson I am never back before seven.

The omnibus was a vast closed box drawn by three horses and carrying twenty-two people, their feet in straw during cold weather. It was the cheapest and slowest form of transport in London.

Claire's was the life of the poor and overworked in any time or place, without colour or variety beyond heat and dust in summer or muddy streets and fog on winter mornings. Did Claire sleep on the sofa, as she had when Mrs Mason's house was crowded? Did she find cheap food in Soho street markets? Were her Sundays spent in starching and ironing? Pride closed her mouth on every humble detail. Jane recognized her own mother's symptoms in Mrs Godwin:

wandering in the street, giving a cheque to a passing stranger, hiding objects and forgetting where, unfit to be left for a moment.[43] What, in the end, was the feeling between this mother and the daughter who had left home so young to follow the Shelleys? They had never been close, yet a family loyalty remained. There were secrets on both sides, long and stubbornly guarded. In their last months together, were these ever shared? Did Mrs Godwin hear of the life and death of her grandchild Allegra? Or did Claire begin to solve the mystery of her unknown father? Was there some last tenderness between these two? We do know that her mother persisted, after twenty years, in calling Claire 'Jane'.

A single fact is clear. Without sentimentality or protestations of love, Claire came to respect her mother. As she wrote in the end, 'Her affection and devotion to Godwin were admirable and remained unalterable from the day of their marriage till his death.'[44]

Claire's chief or perhaps only distraction during 1840 was to read letters from Mary. For the first time in their long correspondence, Claire was forced to stay at home, while Mary could at last afford to travel.[45] She took Percy to Italy during the long vacation of 1840 with a reading companion, Alexander Knox, a former Scholar of Trinity reading for the Bar. Mary paid Knox's expenses, and also took her own maid for comfort. Knox's ill health, talents, and poverty play a large part in the letters to Claire. For Mary herself the journey was both sweet and sad, a pilgrimage, which she nevertheless thriftily recorded and published in a travel book.[46]

Claire followed the stages of the journey as the English party travelled down the Moselle, through the Black Forest, and into Italy, perhaps sharing Mary's thought of 'long, long ago'. They stayed for two months at Cadenabbia, a fashionable resort on Lake Como. Here Claire certainly shared Mary's fears when Percy bought a small sailing boat—'I look at it and shudder.' The most secret and piercing memories stirred in their hiding place when Mary returned to France by boat through Lac Leman, seeing 'Diodati . . . [Byron's villa] our humble dwelling Maison Chapuis, the terraces, the vineyards, the little port where our boat lay moored'. Claire's well-tried defence against memory was to be practical. She replied 'in great haste' to Mary, now staying in Paris, 'If you want more money pray let us know that we may send you some.'[47] That was all.

The following year Percy graduated from Cambridge. He came down, having passed examinations in classics, mathematics, and one unspecified subject, with a pass degree, devoid of class-mark, distinction, or honour.[48] Mary decided he should read for the Bar. Claire, usually ready to greet the smallest news of Percy with enthusiasm, was silent. This is a measure of how hard-pressed she was in the last months of her mother's life.

Claire taught by day and nursed at night, since there was no one else to do so. She was out at work when on 17 June 1841 Mrs Godwin died of an illness certified as Nervous Fever, a current term for 'irritable excess of functions in nerve centres',[49] a ceaseless, restless agitation, which might now be considered one form of senile dementia. Present at her death was a stranger, another tenant in the house. There was no one to make funeral arrangements as Trelawny had done for Mary at her father's death. Claire herself arranged her mother's burial, beside Godwin and his great love Mary Wollstonecraft. Here, by the same tombstone in St Pancras churchyard, Shelley and Mary had held their secret meetings, while Claire stood out of earshot and watched. It is not known who attended Mrs Godwin's funeral. Her sons were dead or abroad, and this tough, irritable woman had few friends. A small tablet recorded her presence.[50]

Claire apparently spent July at Golden Square, clearing and sorting their shabby possessions. Godwin's desk, which Mrs Godwin had seized upon after his death, went by request to Mary. Nothing else was mentioned, perhaps because there was nothing worth a mention. In autumn 1841, apparently without explanation, Claire vanished.

PART III

Claire's Independence (1842–1879)

14 *In Paris (1842–1845)*

Claire once wrote to Jane that she felt herself like a weathercock, veering about to every point of life, because she had no 'attachment'. She certainly knew flirtations, which amused her, perhaps brief love affairs which left no regrets, but nothing to match her early worship of Byron.

A happy passion like death has *finis* written in such large characters in its face, there is no hoping for any possibility of change . . . I am unhappily the victim of a *happy passion*. I had one—like all things perfect in its kind it was fleeting and mine only lasted ten minutes but those ten minutes have discomposed the rest of my life. The passion, God knows for what cause . . . disappeared, leaving no trace whatever behind it, except my heart wasted and ruined as if it had been scorched by a thousand lightnings.[1]

After all that followed—the loss of Allegra, the bitterness which outlasted Byron's death—Claire still wrote of those ten minutes without regret. After 40, by conventional standards, she had nothing to hope for but memories. Yet after her mother's death, her life took a new turn.

This new life was set in Paris. The first account of it, written at the end of 1841, records 'perpetual scruples' of some long standing. The tentative beginnings of a relationship may have been five years in the past, during the autumn of 1836, when Claire went about Paris by herself as French-speaking courier for the Bennet family.[2] Tied to London by Mrs Godwin's illness she had not visited Paris for some years, but now she was again free. When Claire left London in 1841, all Mary knew was that she had gone to Paris. Mary sent letters poste restante but received no reply. It was the last week in November 1841 before a letter came from lodgings at 41 rue Caumartin. The hasty note announced a new Claire: no longer the worldly-wise traveller, but a woman confused, anxious, even apologetic. Claire apologized for not answering Mary's letters in a long while:

I wished to consider well before I came to a decision. It is a most difficult thing to come to a resolution when you are . . . diffident to an extreme of your own judgment. At last, after a wretched state of doubt and dismay, I have decided; that is to say I have allowed my feelings to decide for me, my understanding, poor thing, being literally in the last stage of feebleness from the tortures inflicted on it by perpetual scruples. I am happy in Paris; I never was happy before in my life and think therefore it is madness to go from here . . . and I will stay here.[3]

This is most unlike Claire's usual style. Even more improbably, she seems to be pleading for Mary's understanding and forgiveness.

If only one dared to be frank in this world and tell all one feels—and all that rarely, so rarely, but yet sometimes *is*, how clear and comprehensible would one become both in action and thought to others . . . yet one is often obliged to conceal one's affairs or feelings from the person one would most like to disclose them to. More I cannot say, but I am sure *your* . . . intuition will guess my meaning and be glad that I am happy and think that I am right.

The reason for Claire's happiness in Paris is hidden from first to last in complete secrecy. She, who kept letters and journals, kept none from these years, and her own intimate correspondence was apparently destroyed. Claire had gone to Paris immediately after her mother's funeral, as though sure of a welcome there. She wrote no letters that survive to answer an invitation or discuss travel arrangements, from what Claire called a need to 'conceal one's affairs'. The source of her new happiness is never mentioned by name, but the allusions to 'you know' suggest he was not a new acquaintance. Perhaps Mary may have known of him, but she sympathetically promised to be 'as secret as the grave', and offered 'on a marriage or any event of equal importance' to come to Paris.[4] Nothing as respectable as marriage was in question. Yet Claire did not intend to live, like her mother in the early days, as a kept woman. Unwilling to leave Paris even for a few days, she wrote to her attorney in London to borrow money against her expectations under Shelley's will, something she had refused to consider for almost twenty years. He purchased annuities, which in pre-inflation days were a sound investment,[5] and Claire, for the first time in her life, was financially independent.

In March 1842, after long years in other people's houses, Claire bought the lease of her own apartment, on the upper storey of 3 rue Neuve de Clichy,[6] on the borders of Montmartre. (Mary wrote to her for the sake of privacy under cover to the Russian vice-consul Alexei Ivanoff, whose mother was a friend.) It was not a good address, but the district had a raffish charm. Low rents attracted artists, musicians, and political exiles. Two rowdy and disreputable inns, Le

Perroquet Gris at the north end of the street and Les Porcherons at the south, were later demolished in the interests of respectability. The cottage gardens and windmills of old Montmartre offered a miniature countryside in the city. In the Cimetière Montmartre writers, painters, and musicians shared the impartial retirement of death with ladies whose scented visiting cards offered 'tout confort' to the passing traveller. Claire was childishly delighted with her first home. 'I am quite an altered creature . . . I am comfortable in my apartment and more than ever charmed with it.'[7] Mary encouraged her—'Make your home snug—& all will gather cheerful and pleasant about you.' This was a fortunate time to furnish. The severe Empire style was yielding to comfort, but classical elegance was not yet smothered in upholstery; cabinet makers offered writing desks, scroll-ended beds, and fireside chairs of inlaid mahogany. Claire kept such household possessions as she purchased for the rest of her life; a visitor in 1879 recorded them as 'old fashioned'.[8]

Playing house, however delightfully, is not enough to fill a lifetime, and secret relationships involve long days of lonely waiting. Claire swung between joy and depression, when she lay on the sofa reading endless French novels. Her changing moods are reflected in her many letters to Mary—at least fifty-five. Yet after three years in Paris she could still write about her unnamed bringer of happiness:

> I saw you know, who looks well and was in excellent spirits. He calls on me every now and then and I take it as a sign of extreme good-heartedness in him—he sees how painful is my position in life, how many difficulties . . . I have to struggle against and fight with and he gives me what support he can by his society and small attentions.[9]

The earlier, imperious, Claire would never have been grateful for so little. She considered buying a house in Paris to live near him indefinitely.

Mary, feeling Claire would welcome English acquaintances, suggested she should visit Mrs Boinville, in whose house Shelley had stayed during his first marriage. The lady was ardently progressive, with a penchant for vegetarian diet and atheism. Claire did not enjoy the family's company. She wrote:

> I count the Boinvilles and Turners as nothing in that respect . . . The circle that frequents their house is ever the same . . . no new face ever penetrates . . .

another defect is, the want of young people in it—there is no romance, no legerté, no wit, no animal spirits, nothing that belongs to Youth and is so refreshing.

Claire, released from employment, lacked the patience to fit into this stressful family. She admitted frankly that intellectual discussion led to open conflict.

I thought when I came to Paris and lived idly, my understanding would have recovered a little strength, and my character the fun and gaiety which is so natural to it . . . at Madame de Boinville's the people are clever and I go there and I like the conversation, but I am never allowed to speak myself . . . I like very much to hear others talk especially if they are clever, but certainly I wish also to talk myself and especially after being fifteen years silent. I want to talk a good deal to make up for lost times as may be imagined to clear out my mind of all the ideas that have been accumulating and literally rotting there for so many years—but they won't allow me this.[10]

Claire looked forward to visits from English friends, delighted to see the sights and shops of Paris. Yet the first visitor, Dina Williams, a favourite of Claire from childhood, was a most unhappy guest. Her family in London had received continual visits from Leigh Hunt's son Henry, the sociable, musical friend of Percy Shelley. Everyone who saw Henry remarked on his good looks, charm, and cheerfulness—he appeared content even with his poorly paid job as clerk at Somerset House. Jane Hogg, accustomed to admiration, encouraged his visits and 'betrayed a degree of interest' in the firm belief that he was courting her. This delusion ended in March 1842 when Dina confessed to her mother that she was pregnant by Henry. She was banished to lodgings south of the river in Brixton, where on 11 June she gave birth to a baby boy.[11] Jane, set on concealment, refused to register the birth, hurried on 'the weaning job', and sent Dina as fast as possible, without her baby—'it would be the height of imprudence for her to go in company with the child'—to Claire in Paris. Claire, who had welcomed the prospect of a young mother and baby with delight, went to meet Dina at the offices of the Messageries and found an exhausted girl who had embarked at two in the morning, her only luggage a change of linen in a carpet bag.[12] She wept for her lover, from whom she had been torn, and soon even more bitterly at the news that her baby had died; perhaps as a result of the forced weaning, it had 'death in its face'. Claire was convinced by Dina's grief that she and Henry were sincerely devoted and should marry, ending Jane's need for concealment.[13] She revealed to Dina her mother's wish to 'marry her to someone else', which Jane had intended to keep secret, and declined Jane's plan to let Dina stay with her to see if she could forget Henry. 'I have a great objection when an attachment has once taken place to being a party to thwarting its course; I think lovers should be left to themselves.'[14] Dina, with Claire's affectionate support, returned to London in September, and the couple married from Leigh Hunt's house on 21 October. Jane took this as a personal insult: 'They are both determined to murder me,' she wrote. She never forgave Henry and it was some years before she forgave Claire's part in the affair. 'I thought I was doing such a prudent thing,' wrote Claire ruefully, 'such a wise thing, that I could not only not be offensive to any party but on the contrary be pleasant to all parties in attaching myself to Dina, and—I ran to my ruin.'[15] Once again, she had leapt before she looked.

Claire, although usually eager for guests, refused to have her brother Charles's two growing daughters to stay with her in Paris on the pretext that 'leisure and a certain degree of luxury' would unsettle girls who had to earn their own living. The true reason was probably her own equivocal position, and the fear that they might report it to their parents. She attempted to make up for this failure by sending Charles's family money which she earned from tutoring or posts as temporary companion.[16]

She also expended time and skill on shopping in Paris for family and friends. Mary's letters include a string of miscellaneous requests—'don't forget the things I asked you to do for me in my last letter'—with appeals to make a good bargain, for 'I am quite ruined'.[17] On a visit to Italy in 1843 with Percy and Knox, Mary needed, unromantically, corn plasters, a new pair of black boots (since 'martyrdom in mind and body' followed long walks), a warm, dark winter cloak, a sixpenny foreign railway guide, and two hundred visiting cards. Nor were Claire's former employers forgotten: 'Mrs. Sanford says you must send her stays by the first opportunity'.[18] One item stands out from this mundane list. In May 1846 Claire bought as a gift for Mary a black lace mantilla from Maison Vallin, which she sent to London by a returning traveller. Mary wore this when sitting for a miniature portrait by Richard Easton, the soft, dark folds framing her grave beauty.[19]

All these activities—letter writing and errands for old friends, housekeeping or teaching—still left Claire with time for Paris society. Outwardly she was well equipped for social life—lively, amusing, sophisticated, able to negotiate the pitfalls of the French language for foreigners. Yet inwardly she found the alternations of the social season stressful:

It is not only impossible to lead a quiet life in Paris, but also impossible to have one day in which you have not twice as much to do as you can possibly get through . . . you find acquaintances swarming in on you like locusts, and society forces itself in an overwhelming torrent into your solitude.[20]

Then came August, the general exodus from the city, and 'solitary confinement'. 'I hear no music, go scarcely anywhere . . . no ideas or sentiment in my own mind.'[21] Later she added, 'I have not attained what I so much desired to get, two or three people of my own way of thinking.'

Mary begged Claire to join her in Florence in order to visit Laura and Nerina, whom she said 'would have been too delighted to see you'.[22] Claire declined; her ties in Paris were too strong. In this situation, isolated or wearied by formal society, Claire found an unexpected resource; she felt at home with Russians. The passionate emotions, the uncontrolled scenes of which she had complained in Russia now seemed nearer to her than cool French civility. The first arrival from Russia, to Claire's joy, was 'my old pupil Betsy Zotoff' with her family of children. The aunt of another pupil followed, and they fell into the old, easy routine of casual visits and gossip. The dark side of Russian life, too, was present in a Russian lady

who turned out to be a most desperate character, her conduct is so extraordinary, I think she is a spy placed by the Russian government. There are a quantity of such people everywhere in the guise of travelling ladies and gentlemen.

This woman copied a key, entered Claire's apartment when she was out, opened the bureau, purloined papers and copied letters. 'She is a complete Gorgon upon earth,'[23] wrote Claire.

Her heart went out to a neighbour, Mme Ivanoff, who was a widow. 'I bid her have hope and try to seek consolation. She said how can I do you remember what a noble character he was, my companion for thirty years never apart from my side and I lost him and cannot be consoled.'[24] These depths of feeling commanded Claire's respect. The Russian circle was completed by the arrival of Claire's old employer, Mme Kaisaroff, released by the death of the general from his reign of terror. She was bringing Natalie, now in her 20s, healthy and affectionate, to Paris to find a suitable husband. 'Madame K had already written to me on the subject,' announced Claire to Mary, 'she is now free and can marry whom she pleases and says she shall not look for money in a husband. She is rich and it would be an excellent establishment.'[25] Claire entered enthusiastically into the enquiries, speculations, and arguments over Natalie's engagement, including the essential Russian question: would the papers with the Czar's permission arrive from St Petersburg? In the mood of the moment she wrote to Mary, with conspiratorial gusto, 'Do not mention anything about Natalie's marriage . . . These sort of things never succeed unless they are kept secret . . . Pray burn this letter directly.'[26] Involved as always in her correspondent's world, her mind had followed Mary's party on its journey with lively imagination and humour.

> I am glad Knox and Percy lost their money, because petty troubles preserve from great ones . . . so I hope every now and then they will lose their shirts and their braces and trousers and coats, not so excessively as not to have enough to cover them because that would be an offence to public morality, but lose enough to keep their own lives and yours in safety.

She compared them with Polycrates to whom 'a beast of a fish' brought back his lost ring, causing him to lose his throne.

No friends, Russian or French, could take the place of Mary, whom Claire longed to receive for the first time in her own home. The chance came in July 1843, when Mary was returning via Paris from a winter in Italy with Percy, intended as his Grand Tour. Claire dreamed of inviting Percy too, but he had already had a surfeit of culture. In Florence during the winter of 1842–3 he had been bored and ill, 'the effect of indolence and inactivity'. As Mary wrote, he 'takes no interest in pictures or antiquities and scenes that speak of past ages . . . he goes out a good deal here but does not enjoy it!' Perhaps Percy foresaw weary, improving excursions to the Louvre, for he sent a message to his aunt that he would not come. 'Percy hates Paris & won't stay there. He will go to England and leave me at Paris . . . I shall be very glad to see you and stay with you.'[27] The young man thus escaped the dreaded improvement, and the stepsisters remained together for the last two weeks of July 1843.[28]

There were small, inevitable tensions. Claire felt it 'a sore point' that Percy did not write to her; 'he is very lazy', answered his mother curtly. Mary was shocked by Claire's worldliness when she offered to introduce Alexander Knox—talented and handsome but poor—to the rich Kaisaroffs. 'I think if he pleased Natalie she would marry him . . . he had better come and try. I will give him all my help.'[29] Yet these differences did no lasting harm. Mary was genuinely happy in Claire's kind welcome and the rest from responsibility in her 'pretty house'. She had lived more among books than among people, and the equivocal nature of the neighbourhood seemed to pass her by. But Claire ought to have given more thought to Mary's innocence before taking her on a July evening to a party given by Lady Sussex.

Mary was clearly delighted to go. Lady Sussex, a courtesy title, was the wife of Sussex Lennox, a younger son of the fourth Duke of Richmond.[30] Mary had written pathetically to Claire, 'I am entirely exiled from the good society of my own country on account of the outset of my life.' Now, at 45, she hoped to enter abroad the circles closed to her at home. Lady Sussex, however, was not the paragon of virtue Mary imagined. She was born into a large, rollicking Anglo-Irish family, grew up at Cloncurry, Kildare, and had been married and divorced from Baron de Robeck before marrying Sussex Lennox. Her mother, also divorced, was Claire's former employer, Mrs Sanford. Her lively Paris salon included passing travellers, English debtors, political exiles of all nations, and a sprinkling of rogues. During the party, among the trays of punch, the piano playing, and the gossip, Claire and Mary were introduced to two Italian guests. One, Sig. Guitera, was middle-aged and married; the other, Gatteschi, was young, a bachelor of dazzling good looks.

The two Italians explained that they were members of the Carbonari, a political secret society named after the charcoal burners who lived in the thick woods of the Abruzzi. Their aim was to drive out foreign rulers from Italy, especially the Austrian military occupation of the north, and to establish free political life for the whole country. A rebellion in 1830 had failed, and they fled abroad to continue the struggle by agitation in foreign cities. Claire, who had heard the Carbonari praised by her trusted friends the Masons, was won over.

She accepted the exiles as 'respectable and distinguished people'; it was a year before she noticed that their claims to earn a living by teaching Italian were somewhat spurious. 'They have neither of them had a lesson for more than a year . . . yet they never try either of them to get lessons—nor do they seek situations—I will tell you frankly I do not understand the character of either of them.'[31]

Many tears would have been saved if Claire's suspicions had awoken earlier. For Mary, emerging from twenty years of drudgery and self-sacrifice on Percy's behalf, was swept off her feet by handsome Gatteschi. Reading her with practised skill, he dwelt on his own high birth and fallen fortunes, which he bore 'so nobly' that Mary exclaimed, 'Would I were rich to free this poor devoted struggler.'[32] It emerged that Gatteschi might accept help 'delicately' offered. This should surely have warned Claire, yet with her usual careless generosity she lent Mary two hundred francs to pay the Italian's debts, as well as another two hundred for her travelling expenses the day she left, 30 August 1843.

After Mary's departure the two Italians 'never put foot' in Claire's house for six months. A call at their lodgings revealed a stirring domestic scene. The men had gone to dine with Lady Sussex, unknown to Guitera's wife: 'When they reached home Madame Guitera beat her head, poor woman, on the floor and wanted to throw herself out of the window—the servants all assisting to hinder her.'[33] Claire, a seasoned observer of other peoples' families, dismissed them from her mind. Gatteschi was coaxed by Mary to visit England in summer 1844, but Claire poured cold water on schemes for giving him money. A hundred francs to a governess to take Italian lessons in Paris—'make her pay 4 or 5 francs a lesson if you can'—would cause scandal. The idea that Gatteschi 'might make £200 a year as Italian master' in England Claire dismissed because she considered him 'too handsome'. 'Do me the favour therefore not to introduce him to the Sanfords as Mr. S has a peculiar contempt for Italians and as Gatteschi is so handsome he would not let him frequent the house on account of his daughters.'[34] She also asked that rich, unmarried Natalie Kaisaroff should not be mentioned in Gatteschi's hearing when he visited London. Two years passed, filled with family and business affairs, from the time of the first meeting with the two Italians. Gatteschi talked of going to Ireland,[35] but drifted back to Paris.

In the last week of 1844, Claire wrote casually, to entertain Mary, with the latest Paris gossip. Lady Sussex had fallen in love with Gatteschi and was 'half intoxicated with happiness: she called Gatteschi her beloved Ferdinand and said she intended to carry him . . . to filer le parfait amour with him in an obscure cottage . . . she was trying to borrow money in England for that purpose'.[36] Claire had been to see Lady Sussex and found her 'full of despair and exclamations . . . the details are sometimes a little comical and provoke a smile in spite of my better self'. Yet Claire had experienced her own illicit love affairs, and her final feeling was compassion: 'She is so frank and bold in her love one cannot despise her, so firmly convinced of Gatteschi's devotion and so ready to encounter direct misery for him, it is impossible not to sympathize and pity her.' Throughout the spring, Lady Sussex was 'driven half crazy' and in July she abandoned home and children to travel with Gatteschi to a remote chalet on Mount Rigi, above the Lake of Lucerne. Claire related this news, which was common gossip, in the same calm and casual manner: 'I trust the bracing air of Mount Rigi will give him that independent spirit he has talked so much about and performed so little.'[37]

Suddenly, on 16 September 1846, Claire received an anguished letter from Mary: 'I will only write a few words—for I am too agitated—I am indeed humbled—& feel all my vanity and folly and pride.' Three weeks later came another letter: 'I meant no ill—I thought I was doing so kind so good an action—comforting an angel—till I found he was not one . . . till his affair with Lady S.'[38] Claire now learned what she might perhaps have discovered earlier. Believing Gatteschi had 'the materials of greatness', and declaring, 'I am never afraid of loving a man who does not love me,' Mary had poured out her adoration in a series of letters, which the young man prudently filed. Now, hurt and jealous, she reproached him bitterly for his desertion and his affair with Lady Sussex. He had planned long and patiently for this moment. His reply was bold. Mary could buy back her letters, or he would publish them.[39] In her anguish and shame, Mary clung to one thought. Percy must never know her folly.

Claire's reply was instant; no money must be offered to Gatteschi or 'that unhappy woman', Lady Sussex. She herself was away on a visit near the Bois de Boulogne, but returned instantly to Clichy to meet Alexander Knox, who as a barrister had agreed to act for Mary. Claire served in her usual way as agent and interpreter, finding quarters for Knox, making appointments, and translating documents.

Inquiries revealed that Gatteschi had fled from Italy after joining riots in the streets of Bologna. Knox persuaded M. Delessert, the Paris Prefect of Police, that this dangerous terrorist should be investigated, and followed the suggestion with a fairly large bribe from Mary. 'She says would she were dead for robbing Percy her son of money', reported Claire. The Paris police entered Gatteschi's lodgings and seized all his papers; by 10 October, Mary's unhappy letters were at the Préfecture.[40] Here Knox extracted and destroyed them. Claire received 'a very violent letter from Lady Sussex', saying she had betrayed her secret. 'I have not answered and she has not written again.'[41]

Mary was out of danger, though also out of pocket. Knox's living expenses in Paris, apart from the bribe, were a hundred pounds, which Mary sent to Claire to 'settle his affairs'. It seems a remarkable achievement for a young and unknown foreign lawyer who had only been called to the Bar[42] in 1844 to extract his client so swiftly from the clutches of a blackmailer. How did Knox discover the details of Gatteschi's political past? How did he learn that the Prefect was open to bribery? How did he secure a meeting with this senior official? How was the bribe—so odious to any good lawyer—transmitted? Judging by Mary's replies, Claire wrote some twenty letters which might answer these questions, but all were destroyed to conceal the sordid affair. Mary's gratitude to Claire—'you who have ever shown me so much kindness'—was pathetic. As the end of this terrifying year came in sight, she wrote on 1 December 1845: 'Indeed, dearest Claire, I can never sufficiently repay you for your exceeding kindness during my late unhappiness—& I rejoice very much in the prospect of having you among us this winter.'[43] Percy, the source of his mother's deepest fears, presented no problem. He could never imagine his middle-aged mother falling in love, and his easy-going eye found no deficit in the accounts. He never knew what had happened or how near disgrace his family had been.

To establish truths, they eradicate a hundred superior ones. Eradicate is a gentle word, murder, assassination is the just one. Liberalism is a spirit . . . they consider it to be a mere material fact, which they apply like a dissecting knife and destroy all they touch. I have never seen either people or characters or circumstances flourish under their protection.[44]

Not for the first time, Claire resolved to be more cautious, though not for the first time she later forgot.

15 *Inheritance (1844–1846)*

During the years of the Italian intrigue, Claire had learnt to follow the Parisian custom and leave the city each summer during the hot weather. She did not travel far, but explored the villages of the Seine with their waterside cafés and holiday fishermen or the royal parks of the Île de France. At Versailles 'the air was like heaven'. In spring 1844 she went to stay in 'a miserable lodging' at St Germain-en-Laye because 'economy for my brother is uppermost in my intentions'. The lodgings mattered little, since she wanted to be out of doors, walking in the forest or on the Terrace with its famous view over the valley, the winding Seine, and the woods. Here a letter from Mary was redirected to her. Claire opened it and was overwhelmed by

> a strange inexplicable feeling to receive a letter saying Sir Tim is dead, it is but a common bit of news and analagous to what happens every day, yet my first emotion was disbelief; the most hardy, unyielding disbelief. The idea of that man has been so long my companion, that it seems tearing half my mind out to convince me I have not occasion to think of him any longer.[1]

Sir Timothy Shelley had died 'quietly, without a sigh' at the age of 90 in his family home at Field Place on 23 April 1844. The *Annual Register* remembered his benefactions: 'in him the agricultural labourer has lost a kind friend'. His long life had shown 'the best qualities of the English country gentleman'. It would have been hypocritical to pretend sorrow at his death, and Claire wrote frankly to Mary, 'I am glad for you and very glad to call my dear Percy Sir Percy.' She admitted this was 'a vulgar pleasure', but excused it by the malice of the Shelley family towards him. For herself Claire felt the old gentleman's death 'no occasion to rejoice', since she had already raised money against her legacy[2] to settle in Paris and did not expect his death to 'add a penny' to her income. Nor was Mary relieved of care by the inheritance so long and wearily awaited. Percy at 24 had come into an estate burdened with debts: to Sir Timothy's widow, to his half-sister Ianthe, daughter of Shelley and his first wife, Harriet, to the providers of his own college fees. His father Percy Bysshe had estimated his own debts two months before his death in 1822 as between £2,000 and £2,500. They included: a loan from a plumber in High Street, Oxford, when he was an undergraduate; debts to a coachmaker when he was with Harriet in Edinburgh; to a surgeon in Wales who saved him from imprisonment for debt; and to the suppliers of the piano Claire had played at Marlow. Six months after Sir Timothy's death, Mary was writing with habitual pessimism: 'For Percy to live as a gentleman on £2,000 a year is barely possible.'[3] Mary, who had said she could 'never sufficiently repay' Claire's kindness, was shaken by the reality of the provisions for Claire in Shelley's will. When this will was proved in 1844, after Sir Timothy's death, she wrote to Leigh Hunt that the bequest to Claire was 'by a mistake of the Solicitor just double what he intended it to be'.[4] There is, however, no evidence of any mistake by this unknown solicitor. The will of February 1817 which, apart from provision for Harriet, corresponds with the draft of 1816, makes it plain that Shelley intended Claire to receive two bequests of £6,000 each. One of these was specifically for herself, and the other for herself or for another 'if she should be pleased to name one'. This second £6,000 was certainly intended for Claire's child by Byron, but, as the will stood, it legally belonged to Claire, just as the first £6,000 did.[5]

Mary urged Claire to 'come over very soon' and settle her legal affairs. But Claire could not bring herself to leave Paris. Three months after the news of her legacy, she wrote with frivolous fatalism: 'With regard to my money I expect only to lose it—I am so unfortunate!' As the lawyers proved the will, she grew impatient at the delay: 'Gregson is a very slow man—I know the dear phlegmatic creature of old . . . Dear Mr. Gregson what a fund of angelic patience you must have in your breast.'[6]

As her temper rose, Claire sought consolation by imagining Percy as a lawyer.

> I know so little about my dear Percy and all he is doing . . . I should so much like to see him on his law transactions—he will at last understand why, with my irritable temperament, I chafed and fumed and was driven almost wild by Gregson's eternal prorogations. And he makes you dance attendance upon him day after day, as if he were a prime minister, and when you come, your heart beating, your pulses in a commotion, expecting your fate from his lips, he begs you will read the Times and goes away.[7]

This was not of great interest to Percy, who had already wearied of the law's delays as a career and planned to devote himself to his inheritance. Claire's limited supply of patience was at an end, and she scribbled a postscript to Mary: 'If you come to Paris . . . can't you pin up my money in a bit of paper and put it in your stays?'

Claire's original instinct was to invest her capital where she was happy. 'I mean to place it in France,' she wrote from Paris, later 'I much incline to buying a house here.'[8] First, with her inheritance, she took a seaside holiday at Dieppe. This showed her full of youthful abandon. She swam two or three times a day from the steeply shelving pebble beach, surrendering to the sea with deep pleasure:

We can scarce keep our legs against the waves—but when they beat against my breast and dash wildly over my head I feel well and strong . . . Tall white cliffs rise out of the sea covered with the greenest sward . . . there the air is so boundless and you are so far from Earth, from noise, from trouble, so alone with wind, sky, water and grass, with the elements and nature, in a new and joyful life.[9]

Mary marked her stepsister's new riches by addressing letters to Mlle *de* Clairmont for some weeks, until discouraged: Claire and Clairmont were both assumed names, but their bearer had no wish to assume the particule claiming nobility.

Mary pressed Claire to visit her in London to sign the essential papers for receiving her legacy. It was spring 1845 before Claire could bring herself to leave Paris for London. She found Mary in a furnished house, White Cottage, on the Lower Richmond Road at Putney. Mary had described it, in her deprecating manner, as shabby, but to Claire it was 'the dear Cottage' on the Thames, with Percy's dogs in the garden, a gate to the tow-path, and Percy's boat tied up alongside. She stayed with Mary at White Cottage for several weeks. 'I was so truly happy there,'[10] she wrote after her return to Paris. The two women had discussed investments, and in a subsequent letter as casual as the first fatal introduction to the Italians, Mary asked Claire whether she would go shares with her in an Opera Box. To her surprise, a letter of acceptance came from Paris within a month. 'I am convinced it would be a most excellent thing for me if I could buy a whole box.'[11] Percy advised his mother against the speculation, but Claire was afire at the idea. By June 1845 she wrote that she would give £4,000, a third of her capital, for Box 23 on the Grand Tier of the Italian Opera at Her Majesty's Theatre in the Haymarket. She directed her bank to sell out £4,000 worth of securities to invest and was irritated that they made only £3,782, 'a great hole in my capital'.[12] Totally unaccustomed to business, she had expected shares to stand always at par. This first experience, which might have suggested caution, made Claire more obstinate. 'Directly I hear from you . . . I shall set seriously to work to place my money permanently.' She had been generous when poor, but now she was rich, the desire to help Charles, her nearest kin, became an obsession. 'I shall have enough for myself and a hundred a year to give to my poor Brother, which is the dearest wish of my heart.'[13]

The only immediate luxury Claire allowed herself was to engage a lady's maid, Stephanie, who added to the comforts of the Paris apartment and the elegance of Claire's dress. She gossiped in the traditional style with Lady Sussex's maid, who related 'all the most extraordinary tales' of that irregular household. Who is to tell what Stephanie and the maid said together? Curiously, Claire failed to see that her own domestic secrets might be revealed, and return to haunt her.

The holiday at Dieppe in August 1844 had been shared with the Kaisaroffs. The two elder women passed their evenings discussing candidates for the position of husband to Natalie. As always, Claire's first impressions were hopeful. 'Who pleases Natalie will also please Mme K. She is such a good mother—all she asks is to see Natasha happy and smiling.'[14] Yet by the end of six months, various young men had been rejected. One seemed to Claire 'the very thing', but held 'violent anti-religious opinions' which would not do in Russia. Another broke down and became 'a confirmed lunatic'—to Claire's regret, since he was a 'thorough-paced Liberal'. In spring 1845 Natalie appeared at Claire's house with 'a strait-forward, good-looking and very clever' young man. She had solved her problem by falling in love with Gustave de Romand, son of the French ambassador at St Petersburg; she hoped the Czar would permit their marriage though 'the Russian coterie say the Emperor will refuse his consent . . . I hope it is a false alarm'.[15] For three months the papers did not arrive from Russia and Mme Kaisaroff's true feelings were revealed. She could not bear to part with Natalie. As Claire observed to Mary:

A small civil war rages . . . such things are said, such things are thought and done, they set one's hair on end . . . She is a good woman and kind-hearted. She suffers so very much. She said the other day—My child is torn from me—this marriage is for me as if I buried her and I have but one child. Then de Romand . . . ranges round the house like artillery round a beseiged town . . . Then Madame K asks how he dare command in her house . . . Then Natalie weeps and asks him if he doubts her constancy . . . then he hates the Mother doubly . . . And so they go on and they all look and are so dreadfully ill—all three as thin as sticks, as pale as ghosts . . . so dreadfully haggard—their eyes sunk in their heads emitting every now and then terrible flashes.

On reading this, Mary was scandalized: 'What a terrible picture you give of Casa Kaisaroff.' Claire seemed for the first time to see the Russian household, where she felt quite at home, through Mary's eyes. 'I advised Madame Kaisaroff to read Shakespeare and then she would not feel such horror of Natalia and Gustave, but she would not listen nor do it.'[16]

In the end, reason prevailed and on the last day of July 1845 Natalie was married. Claire hoped her 'dear Natalie' would be happy, and predicted that in time Mme Kaisaroff would be fond of her son-in-law; 'what is odd is that their two characters resemble each other extremely'. After weathering the stormy courtship, Claire could not attend the marriage ceremony; her brother Charles, whom she had not seen for sixteen and a half years, came to visit.[17] 'Charles has come to Paris to see me . . . He arrived yesterday and you may imagine how happy I was,' wrote Claire to Mary. Charles had planned a London visit, 'to bid an eternal farewell to England', but soon found he could not afford it. 'It cuts him very much, but he is like me, immensely *prudent* as regards money,' explained Claire, without a trace of irony. Instead, Charles spent the extra week with her. She ruled out Paris sight-seeing in the heat of August, and instead took him every day into the countryside of the Île de France—riverside terraces, old châteaux, and shady parks—where they talked, reviving Shelleyan ideals.

No passer-by would have recognized the Clairmonts as brother and sister. Charles was short and well-knit, with fair, clean-cut features and clear eyes. Claire, by contrast, suggested the exotic: sleek black hair, eyes 'of an almost oppressive brilliancy' yet so black the iris could hardly be distinguished from the pupil, and complexion which had darkened in middle age to an 'almost African' brown.[18] Yet this incongruous pair felt no doubt of their relationship; in the baffling confusion of their origins they clung to each other. Childless Claire was touched by her brother's account of his six children—'really a more happy father or more devoted to his children I never saw . . . very sentimental and very quiet—no vanity and altogether careless of himself thinking only of his children'.[19] Yet she was distressed by the treadmill existence to which the needs of Charles's large family condemned him. He visited private pupils to give English lessons every day from seven in the morning until half-past three, then swallowed a hasty dinner before classes at home, which continued until half-past nine every evening. Claire imagined him 'cramming the occupations of two hours into one, rushing from one street to the other, the fear of being too late following at your heels'. On 15 August 1846 Charles's leave of absence was up. Claire gave him the ten pounds generously sent by Mary to buy presents for his brood, from 20-year-old Paula to Sidonie, who was only 7. Parting was a wrench, but the prospect of helping Charles took the worst from it. She even promised to provide for his family in her will. By the end of the year, after 'eight months of my own affairs', Claire was becoming bored with the subject of finance. She advised Mary 'not to fret about money difficulties', and appeared all too ready to take her own advice. Trustees had placed Claire's six thousand pound investment among various industrial enterprises, but this did not appeal to her. 'There is a quantity of money in the world but no one has got a penny at his disposal. Our capitals are all in the clouds, or in smoke and boiling water, or bursting their way through tunnels or mining down into the centre.'[20] This confused statement seems to reflect the unwelcome discovery that when money is invested in industrial shares, one cannot touch the principal. Claire admitted her impatience with professional advice to Mary: 'I am dying to see whether by chancery I cannot get rid of trustees and trustee-ships and be my own mistress.'[21] Absurdly, she argued that she could not afford an attorney, since 'it is not prudent for me to begin by reducing my capital by a thousand pounds'. She would come to London and manage the opera box lettings herself.

Claire arrived in June 1846 at 24 Chester Square, Belgravia, the Shelley town house, now Mary's first permanent address since her elopement in 1814. It was a dignified terrace with classical porticoes. For Claire its chief attraction was that Percy lived there. She hoarded scraps of news about him—'Pray let me hear what he thought of his presentation at Court—what he felt when he was there and what he said when he came back. Every little trifle belonging to him interests me.'[22] She studied *The Morning Herald* to find Percy's name at Almack's or the Opera. She enquired hopefully after his abortive attempt at various careers: 'I am glad he is in the militia and glad he is in the law and now if he goes into Parliament . . . as he is a musician and a metaphysician and a jolly boater, in a little while he will be a universe of a man, comprehending all things.'[23] None of these prospects was achieved, but the usually realistic Claire liked to dream over them as she worked a rose-patterned hearth rug for Percy's study, 'to be an emblem of my love past and future'. During the weeks of July and August 1846 which she spent at Chester Square, she began to 'meditate' settling in London.

This was a change of heart. During 1844, with money available, Claire had called in painters and carpenters to refurbish 3 *bis*, which meant 'living a year from room to room with one box for one's clothes like a travelling tinker'. When the workmen, with their powerful aura of garlic and *eau de vie*, had tramped downstairs for the last time, she wrote 'I find my little apartment so quiet and so comfortable';[24] she sounded both happy and settled. During the summer she had two women friends to stay, one from Vienna whom she had not seen since 1823, and took pleasure in their enjoyment. Yet later, Claire grew restless. 'I felt dying when in the house, so I drove every day and the air kept me alive.'[25] It became necessary to dislodge Claire from Chester Square. This Mary did with tender apologies. 'I am the last person who ought to inflict the smallest pain on you—I to whom you have ever been so kind.'[26] Yet Mary wrote that she must go to Baden-Baden to relieve her 'nervous sciatica'. Claire, 'not being mistress & not going downstairs' for the daily interview with the cook in her basement kingdom, could not stay alone at Chester Place; the house must be shut up. Claire tried to resist, but was worsted; 'if I hurt you,' wrote Mary, 'you must attribute it to the suffering of an invalid'.[27]

Claire had to return to Paris, where she found herself out of love with the French—'Heaven help anyone who trusts to them doing anything without sending a police officer after them.' Her feelings swung wildly towards England. By New Year 1847 she planned to come to London 'the instant I can', staying in lodgings if Mary could not receive her. By summer 1847 Claire had bought a crown lease and was installed at 26 Osnaburgh Street, Regent's Park. The transport of furniture, forte piano, books, music, and personal effects across the channel was expensive. Moreover, Claire's income was lower than she had hoped.

Her financial problems had begun with her decision to invest in the opera box at Her Majesty's Theatre in the Haymarket. In 1845 this looked a good choice. Mr Sanford had taken a lease for himself. An Irish peer ruined by the potato famine was believed to live on the rent of his family's box. Claire wrote to Mary: 'I have thought over the purchase of the Opera Box and I am convinced . . . my affairs would then be settled most happily.'[28] Her Majesty's had long been the sole home of Italian Opera in London when Benjamin Lumley took over the management in 1842. His early success was brilliant: he reorganized orchestra and chorus, paid arrears of wages, and redecorated the shabby front of house. He introduced new works, which still hold their place in the opera repertoire, from Donizetti's *Don Pasquale* in 1843 to Verdi's *La Traviata* in 1856. His famous ballet led by Taglioni appears in romantic lithographs of the *Pas de Quatre*. But in 1847 when Claire returned to London she heard rumours of battles backstage. Lumley had quarrelled with his conductor and the leading singers called The Old Guard. When a rival Royal Italian Opera House opened at Covent Garden, conductor, singers, and the fine orchestra deserted to it in a body. Claire at first felt no alarm at this. As she wrote to Dina, she had visited countless small resorts in Germany and Italy where the opera house was the citizens' pride. Surely London, so large and so rich, could support at least two houses? Claire had forgotten, if she ever knew, how marginal the arts were in English society. Lumley fended off failure for a time by engaging Jenny Lind, the 'Swedish Nightingale', to sing at the Haymarket. From her first appearance she cast a spell over British audiences, and 'Jenny Lind fever' kept his theatre open. Claire found it difficult to let her box in the usual manner, through libraries because Lumley charged such high prices, but she remained hopeful because 'Jenny Lind is coming back'.

The 1849 season brought a hazard no investor could have foreseen. 'There is a story about that the Bishop of Norwich had been persuading Jenny Lind that it was sinful to sing on the stage & that she was only to sing at concerts.'[29] This strange story, so utterly in tune with the times, was true. Jenny Lind sang for the last time on any stage at Her Majesty's on 10 March 1849; she was only 29 when she sacrificed her stage career. For Claire and other box-holders this was the end of their hopes. She attempted to sell her box but found no buyers, and received a dwindling income until the theatre closed finally in 1858. By this series of hazards—a backstage feud, a rival theatre, the influence of a zealous bishop on a ravishing singer—Claire had in five years fulfilled her prophecy of being 'unlucky' and lost one-third of her capital from Shelley's will.

Claire's new house in Osnaburgh Street was, like the opera box, an attractive but risky investment. Regent's Park included not only the sumptuous buildings around the parkland, but also streets of smaller houses on the east side. Osnaburgh Street, built in 1823, was the most modest of these, yet it formed part of Nash's grand design. Number 26 was one of a terrace, a narrow town house with basement kitchen and yard and four storeys each of two window bays. The entrance floor was rusticated in cream plaster, the doors topped by fanlights, the windows scaled in classical proportion.[30] Claire could walk round the lake in the park or on the tow-path of the Regent's Canal, where the trees of Hampstead Heath and the spire of Highgate marked the northern skyline. Primrose Hill offered a southward view over London and the river to the Surrey Hills.[31] Claire welcomed the house and its surroundings with her usual impulsive delight.

Yet only half a mile to the east, along the New Marylebone Road, the Doric arch of Euston Station gave warning of changes to come. Claire's arrival in Osnaburgh Street had coincided with a peak in private railway development. During the years 1844–7, nine thousand miles of new lines were authorized by Parliament. At the same time, terminus stations for the north were planned in open fields north of the New Road.[32] Before long, the scenes of railway building were visible as Dickens described them in *Dombey and Son*. Somewhere beneath the seamed and scarred landscape lay the scene of Claire's earliest memories, the Polygon, (where her mother had first met Godwin), now demolished for ever. The steam trains, when they came, brought soot that blackened the houses. Everything in their reach 'went down', the social verdict without hope of reprieve. The house in Osnaburgh Street would lose value as surely as the opera box.

At the back of a journal appears a passage without date. 'All is love in the universe—the silver showers of the fountain, the quiet life of the leaves, the flowery path in May even the deep night of Heaven is strewn with golden blossoms.'[33] Claire was seeking comfort in Nature, for the happiness which took her so unexpectedly to Paris had run its course and come to an end. The ending coincided with the climacteric of which she wrote frankly to Mary:

> This nervousness which teazes you so—I had it dreadfully for three or four years—it wore me to a shadow—I could neither eat, drink nor sleep for it was so bad—but it is all gone . . . and had I only been happy how well I should have been.[34]

She could not deny her faults in this time of stress. She had left letters unanswered for weeks or sent 'dismal little notes'. The air of the house was intolerable, so she had spent hours out of doors, walking or driving in the Bois de Boulogne. Sudden fits of giddiness left her anxious and irritable. She was grateful to her Russian neighbour, Mme Ivanoff, who visited her most kindly; yet, alone in her pretty apartment, she felt her spirits sink lower than in all her years of hardship. The fount of vitality, which had survived the griefs and follies of so many years, was drying up. How could she face a future without its mysterious powers? She concluded: 'It is long ago I ought to have put an end to my own life.'[35] Time passed and health returned, but somewhere in the years between Claire had lost the source of her mysterious happiness in Paris.

16 *Conflict at Field Place (1847–1850)*

Whatever Claire's financial misjudgements, she was safe in London, where she took up her new life during 1847, before the year of revolutions on the Continent. The riots, which began in Sicily during January 1848, spread to the streets of Paris during February. In March the poet Lamartine issued a revolutionary declaration to the nations of Europe which threw Mary Shelley into trembling alarm. France, she wrote to Claire, was spreading 'wicked and desolating principles among the nations'. The Days of June in Paris, 23–25 June 1848, brought the bloodiest fighting its streets had ever seen, as the army fought its way from the west through barricades to the headquarters of the revolutionary forces in the Place de la Bastille. Had Claire remained in Clichy, she might have been trapped between the two. Revolution kindled in Central Europe. The emperor of Austria abdicated, Metternich's government fell and with it his repressive system. Charles was at risk, since he went three times a week to the Schönbrunn Palace to give English lessons to the two younger brothers of the emperor.

Yet when Charles wrote to Claire on 7 June 1848, he showed no fear for himself, and a Shelleyan enthusiasm for Venice and Milan rebelling against Austrian rule:

> Have they not suffered enough under their kings, under their popes, under their republics, under their own native princes? and are they now to writhe and groan under the iron hand of the foreigner . . . I wish them complete success from the bottom of my heart.[1]

Yet the 'full and complete change' in Austria for which Charles hoped was doomed. On 2 December 1848 Franz Josef was crowned emperor in place of his uncle, and the year of revolutions ended.

Throughout 1848 Claire remained in London apparently undisturbed by the prospect of a Working Men's Charter, to be carried in procession to Parliament on 10 April. This prospect threw the London middle classes into such alarm that some 170,000 enrolled as special constables. 'How much I wish you were nearer to us,'[2] wrote

Mary in Belgravia on 8 April 1848 to Claire in Osnaburgh Street, evidently expecting riots. In the event the mass procession of 10 April dispersed, and the charter was trundled ignominiously to Parliament by cab. Claire, accustomed to the revolutionary tradition of the Paris mob, was confirmed in her belief that there was little to fear from the British working man.

The events of 1848 and the Clairmonts' Shelleyan response to them showed how far the England of Victoria and Albert had moved from the spirit of Claire's youth. Religion and its handmaid respectability had defeated Shelley's revolutionary hopes. During her decades in Italy, Russia, Germany, and France, Claire had become a foreigner in the now decorous land of her birth. Thus, while she respected Mary's religious beliefs—'I believe in her attendance at Church she follows the impulse of her convictions and feelings'[3]—she did not pretend to share them. The outward observances of piety—family prayers, bowdlerized Shakespeare, the blank and silent Sabbath, the religious tracts which replaced the stories of Miss Edgeworth that her pupils had loved—all had passed her by. In some ways this was fortunate, for she remembered her adored Allegra without shame. Nor was she tempted to denounce zealously the minor faults of others. She could not share the general movement by which the English middle classes became the respectful allies of the landed gentry.

The price of Claire's freedom was high. She was independent, but also lonely. There were few among her relations to whom she could talk of her innermost thoughts. Superficially she was popular in society, considered amusing and elegant.[4] Yet these were passing acquaintances, from whom the names of Byron and Shelley must be hidden and who must not learn that she had borne and lost a child. Claire's one link with her past was love for Mary and Percy, but soon this would be at risk. To provide for Percy, Claire in her deplorably continental manner had suggested 'an orphaned young lady of 16, elegant, well-educated and agreable with £30,000 and £30,000 more to come',[5] but Mary shrank from this.

In the autumn of 1847 a young widow, Jane St John, arrived to stay with her sister at Chester Square. She had been married to a son of Viscount Bolingbroke who died after three years, leaving her well off. The Hon Mrs C. R. St John took a romantic interest in the poet's widow opposite, but was prevented from calling by tales of her 'cleverness'. Meanwhile Mary heard of her rich neighbour from a friend, Rosa Robinson, and decided to call. Jane St John's memory of their meeting set the tone for the rest of both their lives. She entered her sister's drawing-room one afternoon and saw someone sitting there:

> I said to myself, 'Who are you—you lovely being?' . . . rising gently from the sofa she came towards me and said very softly, 'I am Mary Shelley'. You ask what she was like. Well, she was tall and slim and had the most beautiful deep-set eyes I have ever seen.[6]

Though undoubtedly beautiful, Mary was neither tall nor slim, but this is beside the point. Jane St John had fallen in love and found her life's work. Mary had found the provider and protector for whom she had prayed.

There is no record of a meeting or courtship with Percy, who was reported to be 'an awfully nice fellow', caring only for sailing and boats, with amateur theatricals in winter. Yet by March 1848 Mary wrote of Jane as 'a prize indeed in the lottery, being the best and sweetest thing in the world'. Percy had always been 'biddable', and now he was engaged. On 22 June 1848, without demur, he married Jane at St George's, Hanover Square.[7] Henceforward Jane spoke of Mary as 'Madre'. Characteristically, Mary had one worry; Jane was 'not however nearly as rich as Rosa has been told'.[8]

Mary, though increasingly dependent on Jane, remained affectionate to Claire, whom she had invited for 'a LONG visit to Field Place' in summer 1848.[9] In late October or early November Claire took rooms at 11 Waterloo Street, Brunswick Square, in Brighton, where she stayed until New Year 1849,[10] delighting in the sea, the chalk downs, and the crisp winter air. In November she persuaded Mary to join her, promising relief from the perpetual dizziness and debility of which her stepsister complained. It was not a success. 'You were so good', wrote Mary after her visit, 'but the least exertion brings on a renewal of my illness . . . and I had a violent nervous attack . . . perhaps Brighton air is too much for me.'[11] Yet Field Place was no better, for in March 1849 she still suffered 'a trembling alarm which they call nervous'. All that devotion could do was done for Mary by her daughter-in-law.

Sir Timothy's death, so long awaited, had left problems. Cash was short, in part because of Percy Bysshe's unexpectedly large bequest to Claire. It was mortifying to think, as Percy Florence later put it, that 'Miss Clairmont, being a stranger in the Shelley family, received

£12,000 from money raised upon the Shelley estate'.[12] Field Place was heavily mortgaged. The 1678 front across the old farm buildings proved damp and cold; neglected by Percy's aged grandfather, it now needed expensive repairs. Claire wrote cheeringly:

> I am so grieved to hear such a bad account of your money concerns. Farming and rents are in a detrimental state, but it will only last a year or two and then they will rise to great prosperity—so some old farmers tell me . . . Your estate must be an improvable one and now with a Scotch Bailiff he will improve it.[13]

Jane, the new Lady Shelley, could not accept this airy Miss Clairmont as a connection of the Shelley family. From the start, their meetings were riven with mistrust and rivalry for Mary's affections. Jane, described by a niece as 'short and stout, with features large and rather masculine', habitually wore a dark jacket and skirt, and looked coldly on Claire's French frocks and manner. Claire congratulated Mary ironically on her economical daughter-in-law, who had told her that 'she did not care for the Luxuries of Life and wanted only Bread and Cheese',[14] and other sarcastic jibes. From this time forward, Jane emphasized that Percy's adoring stepaunt was 'no relation'.

Claire's own relations, Charles and his family, were very dear to her. She promised a thousand francs regular allowance to help Charles, sent the first instalment in June 1845, and found herself with only four pounds for the rest of the month. Claire's house in London, unlike the house in Paris, held no secrets, and she could have young relatives to visit without fear of scandal. Her first visitor at Osnaburgh Street was Charles's eldest daughter, Paula. Paula taught English in a school for the daughters of the aristocracy, and her manner at 20 was still deceptively demure. The way Charles described her looks—'a very pretty face, brown hair, dark eyes, neat pretty round little figure'—gave warning of a livelier future. She played the piano well and was 'Beethoven mad'.[15] Claire took pride and pleasure in this attractive niece, and learnt to know the rest of the family: two brothers at school in the great Benedictine Abbey of Melk; sister Clara, called Cläri, shy and timid, who gave lessons 'to keep poor papa from working so hard';[16] Hermine; and two young sisters, Emily and Sidonie. All lived in the English Language School at 267 Wallnerstrasse, and their mother kept house for the large brood on her husband's modest earnings.[17]

The family had one grief. Gentle and affectionate Hermine was tubercular. Charles had bought a country cottage at Weidling for the pure air. Here the 15-year-old girl 'crept slowly about the charming garden with her mother, resting for hours in the warm shade'. If asked how she felt, Hermine would smile and reply, 'You will see how quickly I shall get better.' In fact she was dying. When death finally came, in 1847, Charles's letter to Claire described her death in Shelleyan terms.

> Up to the very moment of dissolution she had not the smallest idea of her danger, and I am glad it was so. I would not allow a priest to come near her; can such a spotless being be better prepared for her passage into eternity in the pure state of her own unconscious innocense? Why contaminate her last moments by the vulgar whisperings of those low polluted creatures.[18]

Charles's trust that his sister would understand and share his Shelleyan principles drew her closer to the Clairmont family. Paula's stay in London was followed by invitations in 1849 to Cläri and Willi to visit their aunt and further their education. In March Willi arrived at Osnaburgh Street, followed on about 25 April by Cläri.

Claire's plans began with one of her wilder impulses, that Willi should go to California and join the 1849 gold rush.[19] Mary pointed out the legend of the Wild West with some alarm—'Americans—savages, lawless, brutal—how could gentle Willy fight with them?'—and suggested that Claire should bring Willi and Cläri to stay at Field Place instead. This kindly and simple invitation alarmed Claire. She who had sailed through social life abroad took fright at the thought of English upper class society. 'Write me one line—say if you are alone . . . believe me it would be a great inducement to me to come, if I thought you would have few people with you.'[20]

Jane Shelley, who frankly disliked Claire, proposed to go abroad with Percy during her visit, but reported later that Mary exclaimed: 'Don't go! Don't leave me alone with her, dear! She has been the bane of my life since I was three years old!'[21] This may be true, since Mary had complained to Trelawny about Claire's over-emotional tone. Yet now as then, the irritation seemed only momentary, for she wrote to Claire:

> When I think of your life—how left unexpectedly to your own resources you courageously took your fate on yourself—supported yourself for so many years—refusing to be a burthen to anyone—making dear and valued friends

wherever you went through your own merit—I feel sure you ought to meet with some reward.[22]

Mary wrote almost wistfully of Claire's social success, compared with her own reserve. 'You have talents—you have brilliant powers to make yourself agreable & are generous & kind hearted & true.' This generous verdict suggests the usual ebb and flow of love within a family. Claire, who had faced her own poverty bravely, was worried by her relations' needs: Willi's farming apprenticeship, a school for Cläri, new clothes for both, hung over her like storm clouds. 'This year I lost fifty pounds on my box . . . I am always so unfortunate that I have no heart to set about anything.'[23] She was impatient with her cautious banker. 'Robinson promised to send me a draft of £160 on the fifteenth of April—it was all I could do by the most rigid economy to wait till the fifteenth—when it came—no draft. So here we are without money.'[24] Aware of the poverty of her young Clairmont relations, Claire saw them lost in the imaginary splendours of Field Place:

poor dears they have to earn their livelihood . . . it would be a pity too turn them from the right path and make them miserable for life, which often happens when poor people frequent the society of the rich.

I cannot imagine what you want to see these two children for and I am so afraid of them not pleasing and incurring the criticism of your *savoir faire*.[25]

Claire warned the Shelleys that Wilhelm's head was 'a sleeping volcano' of revolutionary politics. As a finishing touch she scribbled defiantly across the letter head 'our clothes are shabby, that I warn you of'.[26] Anyone familiar with the English Home Counties may well sympathize with Jane Shelley, awaiting these shabby, foreign, revolutionary, and penniless visitors.

Meanwhile Claire took lodgings for herself and Willi at West Malling in Kent, where she found a farmer who would train him as a daily pupil. Responsibility for his health weighed upon her, for he was short of breath, 'like a child with the croup'—'he must have sea bathing . . . it is imperative—he suffers too much from the glands of his throat swelling—they are terribly enlarged'.[27]

Cläri was due to arrive from Vienna about 25 April and the day for the Field Place visit approached, but Claire was still anxious about Willi. Concerned about the forthcoming visit, she wrote to Mary: 'He is far from well and I am so anxious about him . . . I think it best to propose that Cläri should come alone with the proviso that [when] I can come I will . . . Perhaps you will allow her to come without me.'[28] She assumed that Cläri, like any girl of her age on the Continent, would be closely chaperoned. So casual and thoughtless was the suggestion which would darken the rest of Claire's life.

Cläri arrived alone at Field Place, her first impressions the long avenue of beech trees and panelled hall. She was nervous and timid, as her father had said, and more so when she found she was not the only guest. There was a thoughtful, bookish young man, with a disconsolate air. This was the Shelleys' travelling companion, Alexander Knox, whose engagement had just been broken off because the bride's mother objected to it. His misery, wrote Mary, was most painful to witness.[29] In this distress, his feelings were touched by the pale little foreigner who crept so shyly around the house and grounds. Both were unhappy and both lonely. The park of Field Place in spring offered retreat to these troubled spirits. Tall plantations shut out the world, and the scent of flowering may hung on the air. Beyond wide lawns, a footpath led through fields to a chain of heron-haunted ponds reflecting sky and trees in their clear water. This sanctuary, invisible from the house or farm, bewitched the girl from a crowded city apartment. In the privacy of the park, Alexander and Cläri shared their overwrought emotions, finding what seemed a miraculous sympathy. After a few days' acquaintance they agreed to marry without telling parents or relations. Claire arrived full of plans for her brother's family, expecting love and happiness in return, to learn of Cläri's secret engagement. Her happiness turned to misery and mounting fury at her niece; 'her duplicity, her ingratitude broke my heart'.[30] Her grief at the deception was natural, but her anger became one of the blinding rages she had shown since her girlhood.

Claire, beyond all reason, held Mary Shelley responsible for the engagement, since she had failed to chaperon Cläri. She angrily persuaded herself that the Shelleys, at worst negligent, had urged Cläri to treat her parents 'as if they were the dirt under her feet' and to plunge 'a dagger in all our hearts'.[31] This threat to Mary's peace of mind alerted Percy's wife Jane, her chosen protector, who described the scenes which followed.

> She had not been long in the house when Clairey[32] came rushing up to my room, flung herself on the floor at my feet, clasped my hands and said 'Save me! Save me from my aunt; she is kneeling on the floor of the drawing-room cursing me' . . . She was sobbing hysterically.[33]

Lady Shelley, judging Mary too delicate for such scenes, locked her mother-in-law firmly into her bedroom and said with authority:

'You must stay here until I come back'. I went down and found Claire, I said 'You are very ill, come to bed at once' . . . She began in a wild half-mad manner to say all sorts of horrid things. In a loud voice I told the groom to go instantly for the doctor, as Miss Clairmont was very ill and excited and he must bring some drug to her. I meant her to hear, and understanding the meaning of it she instantly called out she was better. After that we had peace for a while.[34]

Some allowance must be made for Lady Shelley's narrative verve, but her mind was made up about Claire. 'It was deemed by those who cared for Mrs. Shelley desirable that she should go and return no more.'[35] Whether Claire broke with the Shelleys of her own free will or whether she was evicted by Jane and Percy, the result was the same: she never saw Mary again. Though the details of this conflict are obscure, the outcome is certain, and remained so.

It seems likely that Claire did not see the Knox couple either, since she asked for news of Mary Shelley's health through Willi, who could not get it from his sister.[36] She knew nothing of the Knoxs' wedding on 12 June 1849, about four weeks after the proposal at Field Place. They were married by a curate at St George's, Hanover Square, well known for minimal residence qualifications.[37] By an irony, Percy Shelley and Jane had married at St George's the previous year. Apparently no member of the Knox, Clairmont, or Shelley families was present at Cläri's wedding, not even Willi to 'give' his sister in marriage as the liturgy required. In the absence of kindred, the signatures of bride and groom in the Register of Marriages were witnessed by two total strangers. The wedding, though not strictly clandestine, was furtive enough to escape the *Alumni Cantabrigienses*.[38] A dark cloud hung over the whole occasion.

The circumstances of the couple were precarious. Knox had no home, but lived in rooms in Pimlico. His father, described by Mary Shelley as 'landowner', was in fact a merchant and apparently not well off, since Mary paid his son's travelling expenses on their continental tour. Though he had been admitted to the Bar, Alexander Knox had failed to make a living from the law and in fact worked as leader writer on the staff of *The Times* from 1846 to 1860. Cläri's home address was correctly entered in the register as Osnaburgh Street, St Pancras, but not in care of her aunt, the householder.

This raises the question of where the bride lived in the month before her marriage. Possibly the young woman without home or money took shelter with her future husband, a disgrace which would account for the universal boycott of their wedding. A daguerrotype of Cläri in 1850, pale anxious little face huddled within the shelter of a hood, pleads forgiveness from the world.

Claire, exiled from Field Place, was defiant. She wrote to Wilhelm, blaming the disaster on 'the confusion reigning in her [Mary's] house where the young dictate'.[39] She could not imagine how Cläri could have fallen in love with Alexander when her own idolized Percy was in the house; surely, she speculated, 'the now-married wife feels far deeper interest in her husband's male friend than in her husband himself'. At first, Claire seemed not to realize that her exile would be permanent for what in her own experience was a normal momentary loss of temper. To Antonie, Charles's widow, Claire blamed Percy's wife for her banishment. Lady Shelley had 'torn the old friend of my youth from me after five and forty years that we had stood together'.[40] She could as soon forget the guillotine that 'had destroyed someone nearest to one's heart'.[41] Blame or punishment were soon beside the point. Time was a destroyer as infallible as the guillotine.

17 *The Shelleys and the Clairmonts (1850–1868)*

Mary continued to suffer from weakness and lassitude, while Jane Shelley complained of an obstinate infection in chest and throat. In the new year of 1850 Percy patiently escorted his ladies to the French Riviera, where the company of two invalids was hardly cheerful. Mary wrote from Nice to Trelawny's wife:

I should have written to you before, but I have suffered so much anxiety and ill health all the winter, that I ever deferred writing . . . and I only wish I could look forward to a stationary abode at Field Place—but it is so low and damp . . . being in a hole in the clay soil.[1]

When the Shelley family returned to England, Percy and Jane went down to Field Place, but judged Mary too weak to be moved again. She stayed at 24 Chester Place, latterly in her room, increasingly an invalid. Jane believed 'she had no definite illness; she was just exhausted', and described her lying 'for ten days without a word . . . She could not speak, but she turned her beautiful grey eyes on us and towards her desk[2] . . . apparently not suffering thank God and on the first of February with those she had dearly loved and who idolized her standing by her side, her sweet gentle spirit passed away without even a sigh.'[3] Percy, though as he admitted 'mournful and wretched', described his mother's illness less romantically: 'a succession of fits, which ended in a sort of stupor—without any sign of life but her breathing which gradually ceased'.[4] Mary's physician attested the cause of her death as 'Disease of the Brain, Supposed Tumour in left hemisphere of long standing.'[5] This seems the cause of twelve years' distress which neither drugs nor the search for a mild climate, nor her daughter-in-law's devotion had relieved.

There is no record that friends or relatives visited Mary during her illness, nor that her oldest associates were told of her end. Jane Hogg wrote to Dina, 'announcing the death of my beloved friend Mrs. Shelley . . . I implore you not to mention the circumstances, as I have had no instruction of the event from the family.'[6]

Like Jane Williams, Claire had no news of Mary's death from the Shelley family, which led her to write bitterly to Percy two or three days later: 'I have heard today that your Mother is dead. I have no wish to add anything to your affliction, but indeed it was most unkind in you never to let me know she was ill. Most unkind. Now I can never see her more!' Claire described how she had asked through Willi of Mary's health, in vain:

> After the contemptuous way in which I had been treated in your house, I could not apply personally. Though I am no toady and resent insult, though I am poor and will not put up with indignity from the rich—yet I have as much feeling as others and the loss of an old friend has afflicted me most sensibly.

Much that followed was in Claire's vein of eccentric fantasy: her brother's despair at the 'hard girl's conduct', Percy's lack of feeling 'when you gave a ball for her wedding and she went to it', and her own conviction that she was herself dying.[7] Yet self-delusion could not cloud her continuing love for Percy.

> You were a good son to her and she felt it and it made her happy and that you will find an ineffable consolation in the present moment. She always said—she always wrote—My Percy is the best and dearest of Beings! . . . I saw you born—I nursed you as my own Child—I ever loved you as my Child—and I ever shall.[8]

Yet this adored being had given her 'a deadly blow' from which she would 'never recover'. But talk of past love and present grief was useless; by her own anger Claire had lost her link with the visionary being of the poet.

The years of loneliness and regret were further darkened by a series of deaths in her own family. Early in 1850 came a letter from Vienna with the news that her brother Charles had died suddenly of a cerebral haemorrhage on 3 February 1850. He collapsed at home and was rushed to the general hospital but died on the way. His royal pupils were only less shocked than the Clairmont family, by the loss of 'pauvre Clairmont, le maître anglais'; when they went to pay their respects to his corpse, 'Maxi', the youngest, was in tears.[9] Tonie buried her English husband in the great cemetery at Währing; when this was closed, his descendants removed the coffin to her family's tomb at Matzleinsdorf.[10]

Charles's death was followed by a settlement of his estate which shows that he left no provision, other than British nationality, for his wife or their six surviving children, four of whom were still under 20. There is evidence that for the rest of Tonie's life, Claire kept her promise to help her brother's family. She was already supporting Willi's training as a farmer, had maintained Cläri until her marriage, and later offered a home to Paula.

Claire's correspondence with her sister-in-law continued for the next eighteen years, but from consideration for the wishes of the Clairmont descendants, the texts will become available only when her collected correspondence is published. A letter from Tonie in June 1851 thanks her for a gift of money,[11] the first, as we can now establish, of many subsidies at Claire's expense. These letters also record a series of family tragedies which fell upon Antonie Clairmont. She had already lost her husband and one daughter. Cläri died, less than five years after her wedding, on 5 March 1855, at her married home in East Sheen, Mortlake. The cause was the disease of which her sister Hermine had died, 'Pulmonary Consumption'.[12] Her family mourned her, though Willi reminded them that Knox suffered even more from his young wife's death. Claire wrote to Tonie on 12 July 1856: 'Our family is consumptive and very delicate; our vivacity, our readiness to oblige, our energy, gives us an appearance of strength which we do not possess.'[13] There is no sign that Claire attended her niece's sickbed or her funeral.

A larger family disaster followed. In 1856, a third great outbreak of Asiatic cholera entered Europe through the battlefields of the Crimean War and spread across the continent. Three young Clairmonts—Emily aged 23, Charles aged 21, and Sidonie aged 19—died in Vienna. By these six deaths, Antonie had lost the greater part of her family within ten years. One son and one daughter remained to her, because they had been in Australia during the epidemic, Wilhelm working as a farmer, and Paula, like her aunt, as a governess. These two survived to play their parts in Claire's old age.

The 1850s, darkened for Claire by estrangement and death, were lit by an unexpected reunion. During the summer of her 55th year, a letter came from Jane Hogg, who had blamed Claire for encouraging Dina's love affair. 'I regret our personal estrangement, which is for many reasons unavoidable at present—but believe me, my heart clings to the memory of the long past and from that it will never be estranged.'[14] This reconciliation was on Dina's behalf; Dina and Henry had begotten seven children in their ten years of marriage. The family's plight grew worse with each new birth, and Jane now appealed to Claire 'in the confident belief that nothing stands between ruin to . . . poor Dina and her family, save the kindness of your heart'. She asked for a 'loan' of two hundred pounds, to be repaid by Henry Hunt over five years. In addition to his normal difficulties, Dina's husband was in danger of losing his job, yet with her usual careless generosity and without demanding any form of legal security, Claire advanced Dina the two hundred pounds. Presumably the money sank in the whirlpool of the Hunts' housekeeping, for it was never heard of again.

Claire was amply repaid over the next decade, though not in money. Dina, whom she had loved as a baby, became in part the daughter for whom she hungered. In 1852, Claire moved from London to the Kent coast. Her choice of home had its roots in her childhood, when Mary had been sent to Ramsgate, on the Kentish foreland, for her health. Charles had visited her there and came home with glowing descriptions of the little port sheltered by its stone pier.[15] Inspired by these early memories, Claire found a house, 11 Arklow Square on the East Cliff, where sea winds scoured the house fronts.[16] Within a few weeks, Dina arrived at Claire's invitation and expense for a holiday, leaving Henry in London. She settled with her tribe of undisciplined children in 27 Albion Street, Broadstairs, a few miles to the north. These holidays were repeated frequently, and Claire wrote reports of the family's health and well-being to Jane.

In 1854 Claire invited Jane to stay with her at Ramsgate, where the Ramsgate Packet sailed from port to port along the coast, including Broadstairs. Jane was delighted to see Broadstairs and her grandchildren, but, like Mary visiting Brighton, she fell ill. Claire put Jane to bed and nursed her devotedly, running from room to room in her nightclothes to make up the fire or bring hot possets. 'I sincerely hope you took no cold from leaving your room half dressed,' wrote Jane, with 'a thousand thanks for all kindnesses.'[17] Their old affectionate relationship was restored, and Claire continued to help Dina. As an independent woman, she had a useful part to play in the days before the first Married Women's Property Act of 1870: any sum saved by Jane or given to Dina belonged legally to their husbands; as Jane lamented, Henry was 'at liberty to pounce on his unhappy wife and may see fit to appropriate whatever comes her way'. Claire acted as banker to the struggling housewives, receiving the sums of perhaps three pounds or five pounds which Jane had managed to scrape together and dispensing them in even smaller sums to Dina.

After five years on the coast, Claire began to hanker for London society and moved to the Thames-side district of Surbiton. Here the

Southampton Railway had built in 1838 its stop for Kingston, Surrey. Nineteen years later, when Claire arrived, tree-lined avenues of early Victorian houses had spread over the Surrey hills and around the common. Claire wrote that she 'flourished' there, with access to the pleasures of London,[18] theatres, concerts, shops, and invitations from old pupils. She settled her much-travelled French furniture in 3 Milford Place, and by mid-August 1857 her surviving niece arrived to live with her.

It was their first meeting since Pauline, whom Claire called Paula, had come to stay with her aunt in Regent's Park. The pretty 20-year-old who had visited Osnaburgh Street—how far away it seemed—had since lived a life crammed with high spirits, travel, horseback riding, drinking, smoking, and sexual adventures with one man after another, all recorded in the sixteen manuscript volumes of her *Lebensbuch.* She earned a living by free-lance teaching. As a governess in Australia, near Sydney, New South Wales, she had met the great love of her life, a man nine years younger than herself; he finally left her for her pupil. Claire, with her own memories of an early passion, sympathized. The two women shared vivacity, energy of body and mind, a love of freedom and adventure. They found they could talk to each other more readily than to their own nearer relations. Paula stayed for two years, but left England in 1859 to become governess to a noble Hungarian family, leaving Claire alone.[19]

Percy and Jane Shelley were beginning a new existence. Field Place had been a Shelley house since the reign of Charles II,[20] and to leave it uprooted tradition. Yet the damp and Jane's throat were grounds for their move to Bournemouth, shortly before Mary's death. Mary was buried there in the churchyard of St Peter's, and the coffins of her parents were removed from St Pancras to lie beside her. Percy had bought four hundred acres to the east, where a handful of thatched cottages and an inn, The Ragged Cat, made up the hamlet of Boscombe.[21] The pinewoods, the sand, and the sea pleased him; he built an amateur theatre, produced pantomimes, and sailed boats with unaffected pleasure.[22] His wife had more serious activities to attend to. Having protected her husband's mother as long as life lasted, she now took on a further duty as guardian of Shelley's and Mary's joint reputation. This was urgent, for letters by the forger, Major Byron, who claimed to be Byron's son, and the uninhibited gossip of the old Shelley circle, exposed the poet to 'false aspersions'. Lady Shelley, with the consent of Percy, legal owner of the Shelley papers, determined to find a biographer who would refute all criticism. It is beside the point to blame Jane Shelley for her determination to direct and control research: she was attempting to meet the demands which her generation made of literary biography. When religion was challenged by science, readers turned to the poet as moral teacher, exemplar, and object of worship. The writer's personal life must conform to the highest ethical standards. The wayward, footloose wanderers of 1814–22 must somehow embody the domestic ideals of the mid-century, and for this she must find a biographer equal to the task.

Lady Shelley's first choice fell on Jefferson Hogg, who arrived at Boscombe Manor in 1854 to collect the Shelley documents, bringing his Jane with him. Claire, of course, was never invited to Boscombe, and feared that she might be disparaged there. Jane Hogg wrote firmly to Claire:

> The chief object of my writing is to set you right on a point about which you are in error . . . you may believe me when I tell you that in all my visits to Boscombe neither you nor your nieces are ever the subject of discussion, nor do I ever speak of Dina, her husband and family, or of your relations with others.[23]

Jane described what Claire would never see: the Shelley Shrine where a red lamp burned perpetually before a curtained corner of the drawing-room. Here the 'Boscombe relics' were ranged, from Shelley's baby rattle to the copy of Keats's poems found with his skeleton. Most sacred was the urn which Lady Shelley insisted contained the ashes of the poet's heart salvaged from Mary's writing desk.[24] The neighbouring clergy found these objects of worship embarrassing; the vicar of St Peter's, Bournemouth, apologetically declined the offer of a life-size marble Mary supporting Shelley's naked corpse like a Pietà. Jane Hogg's admission to the Boscombe circle of Shelley-worshippers did not last long, for Lady Shelley, reading Mary's journals, arrived at the year 1827 and her frenzied distress at 'my Janey's' revelations of flaws in the Shelleys' marriage. After this, Jane Hogg, like Claire, was banished from the house for ever.[25]

In 1858 two memoirs of Shelley, by Trelawny and by Hogg, were published; both caused extreme resentment at Boscombe as unworthy of the poet and his wife. After criticism by Leigh Hunt in the *Spectator*, and a defence of Harriet by T. L. Peacock in *Fraser's Magazine*, Jane Shelley reached a decision: she would keep the Shelley papers in her own hands. Trelawny described the result to W. M. Rossetti:

> The writers who knew nothing of Shelley, under the dictation of the present Lady Shelley, are endeavouring to show that the Poet's wife was endowed with every talent and every virtue . . . It is impossible to describe the Poet as he was without describing his wife as she was.[26]

The decision also drastically affected Claire. Lady Shelley's *Shelley Memorials from Authentic Sources*, 1859, claimed to clear 'all mists of false aspersions and misconceptions' from the poet's name. His desertion of Harriet, the most damaging charge, was firmly denied. According to Lady Shelley, 'estrangements' between the couple grew during 1813 and 'separation ensued'. At some unspecified date in the next chapter, Shelley met Mary romantically 'by her mother's grave'. To blame them for Harriet's death is 'entirely false'.[27] Lady Shelley's account of Harriet's end angered Peacock, who had seen Shelley's 'deep agony of mind' at her untimely fate.[28]

After this opening to the *Memorials*, Claire was prepared to find herself misrepresented. In fact she did not find herself at all: in Lady Shelley's eyes she had apparently never existed. Experiences Claire had shared with Shelley and Mary were recounted in order, with their stepsister absent. Thus, in 1814 'they went abroad',[29] with no French-speaking interpreter. In 1816 they 'again visited Switzerland and made the acquaintance of Lord Byron for the first time',[30] with no introduction from Claire. In 1817 they 'resided at Marlow with their children and a little daughter of Lord Byron called Allegra'. An emphatic footnote insists, '*The mother of Allegra was no relation whatever to either Shelley or Mrs. Shelley*, as some have asserted,'[31] a statement equally true and false. The death of Clara Shelley in 1817 called for equal ingenuity. Little Allegra, apparently motherless, 'was sent . . . to her father in Venice'. When Clara fell ill, 'the parents hastened to Venice for the best advice . . . unhappily it was too late'.[32] A reader would infer that Shelley travelled to Venice with his wife and child; in fact he had already travelled there with Claire. The moves of the joint household, later including Edward and Jane Williams, were simplified to the statement 'Mr. & Mrs. Shelley were devoted lovers of travelling',[33] which implies they enjoyed it alone. Claire's presence is again suppressed in April 1822 when she went with Shelley and Williams house-hunting on the Gulf of Spezia. Her arrival at Casa Magni to the news of Allegra's death is omitted.[34] Shelley's vision of the child rising from the waves is identified in parentheses as '[Allegra who had lately died]' without reference to her mother.[35] After the wreck of the *Don Juan*, 'Mrs. Shelley and Mrs. Williams remained in miserable suspense',[36] while Claire's care for their small children is passed over in silence, to maintain the fiction that she was not one of the household. Last as first, the name of Claire is not allowed to sully the *Shelley Memorials*. Understandably, she felt her life had been 'lost in oblivion'.[37]

That year, 1859, with the publication of *Shelley Memorials* and the loss of Paula's lively company, was a desolating year for Claire. The links with the past—Mary, Percy, Charles, William, Fanny, even her own demanding and aggressive mother—had been broken, one by one. Paula's going confirmed that Claire belonged nowhere. Moreover, Tonie's needs reduced her income for housekeeping; lodgings would be cheaper. Claire therefore decided to give up the house she had taken so enthusiastically two years before and return to the pattern of her early years: visits, strange places, strange houses, and strange faces, once feared but now a distraction from loneliness. She spent 1859 in lodgings at West Croydon, Wimbledon Common, and Cambridge Street, Hyde Park, for the London season. If she hoped for a glimpse of Percy at social functions, she was disappointed.

Claire's alienation from England increased in the 1860s. For this decade, also the 60s of her own life, saw the old Shelley circle dwindle. The first to go, in August 1859, was Leigh Hunt. He had spent a lifetime on good causes and progressive journals. Knowing that Claire shared his enthusiasm for music and drama, he had sent her first-night tickets; whenever she was in London he wanted to meet her, remembering 'agreeable evenings' when she was 20.[38] Claire knew the drawbacks of Hunt's friendship, the importunities to support his enterprises and his large family, yet his going left a gap in her life.

The next link to break in the Shelley chain was Jefferson Hogg, who died in August 1862. He had hoped for a place as Shelley's confidant in his 'rambling and egotistical' biography of the poet.[39] Hogg's career at the Bar had been respectable rather than distinguished; to his mortification, he was listed among the 'obscure' members of the Municipal Corporations Commission. Claire had never hidden her opinion that Blue Bag, as she had called him, was an unromantic partner for Jane.[40] When Hogg died, Jane, who had often complained of his parsimony, missed his solid presence.[41] Claire was anxious for this widow who had never known financial freedom, and wrote urgently to Dina on the last day of 1862 asking if Jane was 'comfortable in her money affairs'. In fact, Jefferson Hogg's will had contained a disagreeable surprise for his widow. Jane received £160 a year, while their daughter Prudentia inherited an income of £360 with £1,500 capital. At first Claire was indignant on her friend's behalf.

I never thought Jefferson would have behaved so shabbily to her—she was the good genius of his life for more than thirty-five years. I thought he was close in his expenses, but that at bottom he was just, and also his self-respect which was immense would cause him to make a handsome provision for the partner of his days.[42]

Claire had never pretended to like Jefferson, but experience had taught her the nature of family quarrels, and she advised Dina:

I think her generosity to you may have injured her with him; he may have thought all I leave her will be spent on Dina and she whom I wish to benefit will never be a bit the better for it—so my dear Child you never can sufficiently repay her by your gratitude and affection.

Experience also warned against expectations from the Hogg family—'Men always ponder so long and shuffle about so much before they will part with money—at least the generality of them do.' All Claire could do was ask for news, although in doing so she remembered that Dina's poverty made letters a luxury.

Pray write as soon as you can and do not stamp the letter and that will save you expense you can ill afford . . . I often think of you, and what troubles you have gone thro' and should be glad to hear your prospects and situations were bettering.

Claire continued to write to Dina, but not till a postscript would she admit her hunger for news.

Do tell me if Percy Shelley is well—if you ever see him and if he lives ever at Boscombe. I saw some friends of his here two years ago and they said he never thought or felt for himself but only through his wife. His Mother always said his character would depend entirely on the wife he took.

With this excuse, Claire faced the unendurable fact; she had no place in the life of Shelley's son.

Jane, in fact, survived Jefferson Hogg by twenty-two years, losing hearing and memory but retaining some confused image of her own beauty. Dowden saw her at a dinner party when she was in her 80s, infinitely pathetic, with one cheek unpowdered and a meagre tress of false hair. She outlived Claire and died in her sleep at the age of 86.

The next death after Hogg's in the shrinking Shelley circle struck another companion of Claire's youth. Thomas Love Peacock had entered their lives during the months of lyrical happiness at Marlow in 1817, when Allegra's cradle lay near Willmouse on the grass, the kittens slept peacefully under the sofa, and Claire's voice filled the twilit garden with music.[43] Early in 1818 Peacock had proposed marriage to Claire, 'knowing her whole history', but she refused, tactfully staying in her bedroom to read while he dined below with the Shelleys.[44] She was not only absorbed in Allegra, but still attached to Byron, 'my dearest friend'.[45] 'How often I regret her not having married Mr. P.', wrote Mrs Mason from Pisa later, seeing Claire's struggle to earn a living, and Maria Gisborne echoed, 'How much suffering she might have been spared had she married Peacock.'[46]

Peacock entered the East India Company as an examiner, married 'the most innocent, the most amiable, the most beautiful girl', Jane Griffiths, whose death was to leave him desolate. Claire visited him and his beautiful daughter, Mary Ellen, in his riverside cottage at Lower Halliford. She thought highly of Peacock, especially when he corrected the errors in Hogg's biography of Shelley, including the unjust account of Harriet.[47] Claire wrote to Dina, 'I have a great admiration and esteem for Peacock—he is a rare specimen of humanity—so generous and unselfish—May he flourish many years!'[48] Yet Peacock, so witty, courageous and loyal to old friends, had not many years left. By the time he died in January 1866, Claire had already been out of England, where she felt a stranger, for seven years.

When Claire had given up the struggle to live in England, she first chose Baden-Baden, an elegant spa in the Black Forest with hot springs famous since Roman times. It was where Mary had stayed independently in 1846, relying on Claire in Paris for homely errands of walking boots, plasters, and railway guides. It was as though being here could restore their old sisterly relationship. From Baden-Baden, Claire went on 2 February 1860 to Florence, drawn by a path beyond Mary's widowhood and Allegra's death to the world of Shelley's living presence. Yet by an irony it was not Shelley's ghost she met in the Pensione Scarpa, but a more solid figure from the past, the now elderly Lady Sussex. This old acquaintance invited Claire to visit her villa—Poppi la Toscana, Borgo alla Collina—in the upper valley of the Arno. There is nothing to show their friendship was close or what subjects their gossip covered, but they were amicable enough to share a summer visit to Venice in 1863. Otherwise Claire moved restlessly with her shabby luggage between a series of lodgings in different quarters of the city. From the addresses on the letters from Tonie and Willi to this bird of passage, we learn that she moved at least ten times in the years 1861–8.

Claire's enjoyment of life in Florence, where she felt essentially at home, was not spoilt by her poverty, and her health was very much better at all seasons of the year than in England.

> We have had six weeks of winter—dry bright and sunny but very cold—now it is breaking up and spring days beginning. This is a delightful town—you can be happy here without any happiness in your own personal fate—for the beautiful crops up all round you and gives you pleasure, and draws you out of the sphere of self and prevents you brooding over personal sorrows.

Florence gave her the best she could hope for, to be 'happy without happiness'. By contrast, she felt alienated from the triumphant society of England in the early 1860s.

> In England there is no escape—the streets and buildings are all modern—all like one another, when you have seen one you have seen all—it is the same with the people, they have all the same character and the same costume and this dreary monotony throws one completely back upon oneself and makes one the complete captive of one's fate.

Even in Florence, though, Claire could not escape the overpowering British tourist. 'There are so many of them here,' she wrote. She clearly thought of her fellow-countrymen as 'them', not 'us'.

Claire moved so often because she lived 'out of trunks' in lodgings bargaining with rival landladies for the sake of cheapness. As she told Dina,

> I let things run and live on a pittance of bread, cheese and fire in the winter and sun in the summer. If the fashion of Diogenes only came in, of living in a tub on the market place, I should like it very much as it would quadruple my income.[49]

Claire's explanation of this poverty was noncommittal: 'I have so many cares for my relations which prey upon my mind.' In 1868 news came from Vienna of Tonie's death. Within months, Claire moved from lodgings into a comfortable apartment in central Florence; this seems to confirm that she had used part of her own income to maintain her brother's widow, and now was free to spend it on herself.

In October 1868 Claire settled in a wing of Palazzo Orsini, Via Valfonda, the street where the Shelley household had stayed in 1819 and she had seen Percy Florence born. Here she lived in comfort with a resident housekeeper and a series of young English companions who came to her house as though to a finishing school. Laura and Nerina, the little Tighe girls of 1832, were married women. Laura's husband had proved a rogue, as her parents feared, and Nerina, though happily married for some years, died after a lingering illness. Her husband, Bartolomeo Cini, survived her and opened many doors to the Tighes' old friend. In summer Claire took holidays following in the footsteps of Shelley at Bagni di Lucca, where they had escaped in the hot summer of 1818 and he had taught her to ride among the forests and torrents. She even found courage to visit Pisa, where she had opened a letter in 1822 and dreaded telling Mary of two bodies washed up on the shore. The rest of her life belonged to Florence.

18 *New Generations (1868–1872)*

Florence, in the forty-eight years since Claire had boarded with the Bojti family opposite the Court of Grand Duke Ferdinand III, had played its part in the creation of Italy. Leopold II succeeded as ruler and was driven out in 1848 by Liberal revolutionaries, only to be restored a year later by an armed Austrian escort. In 1859, when the kingdom of Savoy led a campaign to break the Austrian occupation of north Italy, Tuscans again rose against their prince and voted to join Savoy's constitutional kingdom, with civil and religious freedom on the model of Britain. Florence served as capital of Italy from 1865 to the liberation of Rome in 1870. The enthusiasm of British Liberals for unified Italy was overwhelming.

Claire took her place among the foreign population of the city, which numbered thousands. They cherished the broad fertile valley of the Arno, between spurs of the Appenines, the ilex and poplar groves, the vines, the olives, and the wild flowers from which the city took its name. Poverty was transformed by a low cost of living and smiling Italian servants, eager for employment. On New Year's Eve 1869, Wilhelm Clairmont, now a 38-year-old husband and father, came to Florence to visit the aunt he called without formality 'Claire'. She was now 70 but had 'hardly altered at all' since he saw her last. 'She looks well and is well.' An amateur but affectionate hand sketched her in watercolour; Claire sits, composed and upright, beside a window looking over garden trees; her small table holds a Majolica vase of fresh flowers and an ink-pot with two quills, ready for impulsive letter writing. Her taste is still fastidious; she has chosen to be painted in black satin cape with goffered lace cap and collar. The dark eyes sparkle, the brows arch ironically, and the lips are set in a small, private smile. In one side of the cap she has tucked a flower.[1] There were ten years of life in Claire yet.

Claire rented a wing of the Palazzo Orsini—'a narrow winding staircase leads up to it from a small courtyard and out into the garden'. The apartment soon developed Claire's atmosphere of *amitié amoureuse*. All the doors were concealed by tapestry, making secret entrances to the palace, 'for admission of servants, but also I think of the lovers of ladies', speculated Wilhelm. Since Claire housed 'two young ladies' in her spare bedrooms he slept in the large drawing room, and like Mary Shelley in the winter of 1819/20 suffered from the cold which Italian folklore denies. Even when the fire was lit he could see his breath, and privately wore his coat in his bedroom. He could hardly have guessed that in still colder weather fifty years before, his aunt had played at snowballs. Yet despite the cold he enjoyed a sociable visit, for Claire was popular and had many friends, both Italian and foreigners who lived in Florence.[2]

The next family visitor was Alma, younger sister of Wilhelm's wife, with her mother. They came in the month of Claire's 71st birthday. Claire's scandalous past had been concealed from her, as from the Clairmont children, so Alma's interest in 'Aunt Claire' was simple and spontaneous. The aunt who in London had seemed disturbingly exotic was to Alma 'a small, distinguished, very English lady with white curls',[3] who blew up the fire in her sitting-room, 'simply but nicely furnished with small chintz-covered furniture', and asked anxiously after Willi's health. The housekeeper, Mrs Jones, appeared with a friendly welcome; she ate, sat, and walked with Claire, evidently as much friend as employee. A young student boarder from England, May Moulson, was also part of the family. 'At half-past one we had our lunch . . . seated in the following order: Aunt Claire between Mrs. Jones and Miss Moulson and we facing her. We had rice soup, chicken with cauliflower, potatoes and pork, pastry, stewed fruit and biscuits, oranges and apples.'[4] This artless account sounds comfortable. Claire had come to speak dismissively of 'that idiotic Opera House affair', having discovered that in Italy one pound sterling bought twice as much in goods and services as in Britain. After lunch the elder ladies retired discreetly to rest, while the young women went out to explore the Giardino Pubblico with its beautiful views. Another visit was spent 'playing on the piano and singing . . . Alma sang *Voi che sapete* by Mozart, *Der Wanderer* by Schubert and *Altösterreich* by Handl . . . Home at 10 o'clock.'[5] Though she still loved music, it seems Claire's singing days were done.

In Claire's 70s came the experience all elderly people know: later years fade, while distant youth rises sharp and brilliant in the memory. Claire wrote to Trelawny about the question of Allegra's final rites who replied as casually as if he had strolled out of the room for ten minutes:

What a gap in our correspondence—nearly half a century . . . we wandered by different paths—people never alter—we are still the same . . . Now for your questions [about Allegra] . . . the body was inclosed in lead and sent to England . . . she was, that is her remains, interred in the Harrow Churchyard with the usual burial service—you can't be buried in consecrated ground without.[6]

The question which had troubled Claire for forty-eight years was answered at last. Trelawny also put an end to the nightmare which had haunted her in times of illness or loneliness and now became habitual; perhaps Byron had merely feigned Allegra's death and her child was still alive as an enclosed nun in the Bagnacavallo convent? Her old friend wrote bluntly: 'You may be well in body; but you have a bee in your bonnet—an insane idea has got into your brain regarding Allegra.' Trelawny was struck by another obsession of Claire, incomprehensible to him. 'Another thing in your letter amazed me—I asked you to write me some recollections of Percy Shelley—of course meaning our drowned Poet—and you write me an account of his son.'[7] This, so irritating to Trelawny, suggests that twenty years after their bitter parting at Field Place, Percy Florence still held the place in Claire's heart which had been his since birth. Her enmity was reserved for his wife.

Trelawny's interest in Shelley had revived since his own life took one of its unexpected turns. For twenty years he had farmed with Augusta and three children at Usk, in the nearest to family life he had ever known. This ended suddenly when at 66 he introduced a young servant as mistress into the household, and moved away announcing to his nautical friend Captain Roberts his intention to 'ride at single anchor awhile'.[8] Trelawny settled alone at 7 Pelham Crescent, Brompton but spent much time at a seaside cottage at Sompting, near Worthing, Sussex. Here he prepared to write the book which appeared in 1878 as *Records of Shelley, Byron and the Author*.[9] Seeking information for his draft, Trelawny turned naturally to Claire in Florence: 'our lives are far behind us . . . you, Jane and I are the only survivors—and we shall soon follow . . . you are of the few left that knew and could appreciate him'.[10] Trelawny asked for 'your memories of the Poet, his way of life from day to day, his talk, his acts, his opinions; any and everything regarding him is to me deeply interesting'.

These questions strengthened the pull of early memories on Claire. At the end of 1870 she sent what Trelawny called a 'missel'. She wrote of Shelley as truthful, 'womanly' in tenderness, adoring Genius and so able to think no ill of Byron, inconstant in Love. 'The poet should have had his fifty wives—five would have done for me,' noted Trelawny. In June 1871 Claire sent him copies of Shelley's letters to Godwin; to Trelawny, they proved Godwin 'a sly, mercenary, unprincipled man', and Shelley 'a simple dupe'.[11]

Godwin led to Mary, whom Trelawny dismissed with contempt: 'her aim and object was fashionable society; she was conventional in everything'.[12] More damning still in his eyes, Mary 'affected the pious dodge'. Claire, even after their separation, defended Mary's beliefs: 'I never saw the smallest appearance of hypocrisy in her on this point.' Claire herself speculated:

> We do not belong entirely to this world . . . My own firm conviction after years and years of reflection is that our Home is beyond the Stars, not beneath them. Life is only the prologue to an Eternal Drama as a Cathedral is the Vestibule of Heaven.[13]

When Claire's young companion returned to England, Trelawny's darkest suspicions were confirmed. Unwilling to live alone, she closed her apartment, and made a normal Italian arrangement—having freed herself, it would seem, from her old prejudices—to live for some months as a lady boarder in a pension run by nuns. Trelawny, like Claire, heaped up wild speculations, either that Claire had become a nun and entered a convent, or more colourfully still that she had become a lunatic enclosed in an asylum. Nevertheless, he still welcomed her letters about Shelley.

Inevitably, questions about the past led Claire back to Byron and Allegra. She wrote with fellow-feeling of Augusta Leigh, whose letters to Byron Claire had seen while copying *Childe Harold* in the Villa Diodati in 1816. 'Poor Mrs. Leigh! What with her Brother, and what with her two daughters, she must have undergone torture.' Claire could not quite bring herself to believe the common sexual scandal of incest. 'There is no positive proof that the connexion between L.B. and Mrs. Leigh existed.' But that was the limit of Claire's tolerance. 'Never, never, neither here nor in Eternity can I, nor will I, forgive the injuries he inflicted upon my defenceless child.'[14] Like Shelley watching the waves at Lerici, Claire saw Allegra rising from the sea of time. 'The only thing I had to love—the only object in the world I could call my very own . . . for fifty years I have kept a profound silence with every one on the subject of her wrongs.'

By long brooding, Claire had convinced herself that the children in the convent school, Allegra among them, shared the austerities of the enclosed nuns.

> The order of the Capuchins renounce every comfort and devote themselves to the practise of the most terrible austerities . . . they never touch meat, the winters in Romagna are extremely severe, but no fire is ever allowed in that Convent . . . the building is of course in keeping with the severity of the order, and is dark as a prison, gloomy damp walls and almost bare of furniture. You may think what pangs of anguish I suffered in the winter of '21 when I saw a bright fire, and people and children warming themselves by it, and knew my darling never saw or felt a cheerful blaze and was more starved with cold than an English pauper child in our Unions.[15]

Claire remembered herself in Pisa at the age of 24, going from one person to another, 'imploring them to help me get her out . . . In this life, one dies of anguish many times before one really dies.' Recalling the past also revived her dread of Byron, 'so dreadfully had he made me suffer, the chill of Death fell upon my heart if anything recalled him to my mind'.[16]

Claire was fortunately not left alone with her old sorrows. She was able to move back to her own apartment. Alma, in 1870, was shown the 'friendly little room' reserved for Paula's visits.[17] Wilhelm and his wife hoped she would live permanently with their aunt, but Paula had her own life to lead. She confided an edited version of her adventures to Claire, who received them with sympathetic interest, remembering her own years travelling as governess from house to house, country to country, and changing the language of everyday life. At Christmas Claire heard that Paula might find a settled home by accepting 'an elderly Austrian retired Major [who] wishes to marry her . . . I have told Paula to do exactly what she thinks will be best for her happiness.'[18]

In spring 1870 Paula arrived, radiant, and told Claire the secret of her happiness. It owed nothing to marriage or respectability. Seven years earlier, Paula, sheltered by her brother Wilhelm, had given birth out of wedlock to a little girl whom she adored, as Claire had adored Allegra. The baby, Georgina Hanghegyi,[19] was begotten by an unknown American—perhaps later transformed into the elderly Major by her mother's fertile imagination?—and handed over to the Hungarian Countess Karoly to rear. Paula made regular trips to Pest to visit Georgina, but was worried to see her 'so primly dressed with neat little stays & cuffs & little buttons . . . She speaks in almost a whisper . . . How unlike my wild gypsy nature!' As Paula now learnt, Claire was equipped by experience to understand the situation, and she confided in her aunt. Claire, at 72, was overwhelmed by yearning for this homeless little girl. She said, in a voice Paula never forgot, 'You will bring the child here and I will adopt her.'[20] Paula refused utterly to part with her daughter: 'a powerful voice within me cried No'.

Paula's refusal led Claire to a rash choice. For some time she had thought of buying land near her nephew's farm; in a letter of 25 January 1871, Willi urged her to come to a decision about it.[21] By 5 August she had bought, with a substantial part of her remaining Shelley bequest, a farm in the Austrian empire.[22] This was the real cause of her final poverty. She did so, she said, because she wanted to be near Wilhelm's young family—a reason of which Wilhelm himself was dismissive: 'on this I throw cold water', wrote her worried nephew to his wife. He knew Claire was happy in the cosmopolitan society of Florence: the gallant elderly French scholar, unnamed, the learned ladies apparently German, writing a Kunstgeschichte, the opera, the *conversazioni*, the evening promenades. Further, he rightly judged that she had no realistic idea of farming. 'I know Aunt would be very much disappointed . . . and would find it nasty and get ill and be discontented',[23] wrote Wilhelm with equal accuracy and gloom.

None the less, Claire arrived about mid-September 1871 and met her young relations. She was affectionate to Caroline and delighted with the children, Walter who was 5 and 2-year-old Alma Pauline. Walter, who grew up to be Dr Walter Clairmont and lived to the age of 90, remembered his Aunt Claire even when he was a very old gentleman. She had given him a ball, and when it fell into a pond rescued it with surprising agility. She was nimble and lively; though he knew she was both old and small, to the little boy she seemed a commanding figure. Claire moved in to her new estate, called Nikolaihof, inhabited by Croatian peasants in the valley of the river Drau between Marburg and Pettau, in the Imperial Province of Carniola.[24] The river falls from a height in the wooded mountain district between the Drau and the Mar and rushes through narrow gorges to the fertile lower valley. In late autumn, the climate and aspect of Nikolaihof became cold and increasingly damp. In the years since 1828 when illness had driven her from Russia, Claire had forgotten the effect of northern and central European winters on her health. She was quickly reminded by a painful attack of arthritis, which drove her south to take refuge in Trieste for the winter. The city had no English church, but the Anglican chaplain and his wife, Mr and Mrs Tucker, took this elderly, crippled English lady into their house and made sure she kept warm. Their kindness marked a new stage in Claire's gradual turning towards religion.

By March 1872, Claire had returned to Florence, tacitly admitting that her too-hasty experiment had failed. One friend who had no doubt of it was Trelawny, who wrote under Reform Club letterhead: 'You have added to your experience the knowledge that farming in Austria won't do',[25] and added that he hoped Claire's senses were now restored. Realizing that she must have lost a considerable sum, he offered to 'remit you £50', though he was later shocked to learn that from her original £12,000 she now drew only £120 a year. 'You must have managed badly.'[26] Claire's usual response to any mention of a mistake about money was obstinacy. True to form, in spring 1872 she gave up her modest flat near the Central Station, and moved to an apartment in the Palazzo Cruciato at 43 [now 73] Via Romana, where the front windows looked over the large walled garden of the Viviani della Robbia, relatives of Shelley's Emilia. The back windows opened over the Boboli Gardens, behind the Pitti Palace Claire had known as a girl.[27] The gardens rose from the palace in a series of terraces, shady walks of cypress and oleander set with statues, to a basin where fountains played. From the summit a view of Brunelleschi's Dome floated above the old city.

The apartment was large enough to offer a home to Paula and Georgina, whom Claire in her own mind adopted as the daughter she had lost. Paula believed Claire was re-enacting Byron's part and trying to rob her of her child. The two women, old friends, drew apart in a tug of war which lasted as long as Claire lived. Visitors could not understand Claire's concern with this small stranger. Ironically, Georgina was an unappealing child, snobbish, interested only in clothes and jewels, speaking German with a Hungarian accent which grated on Claire's linguist's ear. Paula attempted to inspire her, at the age of 8, by a romantic pilgrimage to Shelley's house at Lerici, but the unfortunate Georgina was frightened and seasick, provoking her mother's scorn.[28] Just when Claire had squandered most of her remaining capital, she saw that Georgina needed education. She was reduced to attempts to raise money on Shelley's letters, until now sacred relics carried through all the light and shade of life.

It was a time for old friends. Trelawny wrote that he would do his best to sell her papers 'to the greatest advantage . . . so cheer up'.[29] He sent an Anglo-Italian acquaintance to examine her papers, with a letter of introduction: 'Please SEE him.' Claire, unwilling to disappoint a friend, received William Michael Rossetti on 14–15 June 1873, although it was an unfortunate time for a visit; a few weeks earlier, she had suffered a fall, which left her jolted, bruised, and apparently with a sprained ankle. She could not walk around the house to bring out her papers. Nevertheless, the elderly lady gamely received Rossetti in her bedroom, lying on her bed outside the covers and talking with lively courtesy. She spoke freely and affectionately of Shelley, but did not mention Byron. She also admitted to being somewhat deaf.

Rossetti was invited to take lunch with 'Miss Paula and a relative of hers, a prepossessing little girl aged ten or eleven'.[30] Evidently Georgina, if not acknowledged as a daughter of the house, was benefiting from her education. After lunch Rossetti returned for 'a further little colloquy' in the bedroom. Claire at 75 was 'a slender and pallid old lady with hair that had once been dark and with dark and still expressive eyes . . . Her face was such as one could easily suppose to have been handsome and charming in youth—her voice was clear, even-toned and agreeable.' Yet so soon after her fall, she seemed far gone in old age. Rossetti, who did not know her volatile temperament, could not imagine that in lively company she might seem younger.[31]

Old as she was, Claire had not lost her shrewdness. When Rossetti received through Richard Garnett a number of unpublished scraps from Boscombe and published them with a memoir presenting Shelley as faultless, she wrote: 'To me it appears that Mr. Rossetti has written his memoir to suit Lady Shelley's predilections—she is a warm partisan of Shelley and Mary, and like all warm partisans does not care much about Truth.'[32] Claire's own thoughts on the events of sixty years ago admitted facts she could never have faced in her youth. She remembered Shelley's deep grief at Harriet's suicide and his slow admission that he had been its cause; 'he became much less confident in himself and not so wild as before'.[33] Trelawny admitted the justice of this implied criticism of Shelley and asserted that in another edition Rossetti would 'gladly correct' the errors in his book.[34]

W. M. Rossetti did not bid for any of Claire's Shelley documents. Nor did Trelawny's next candidate, Mrs Elliott, wife of the Dean of Bristol, who had collected Byron papers; as Trelawny later complained to Claire, 'she would have dealt with you for the Shelley papers, but from the enormous price you set upon them she thought you mad'.[35]

Claire was untroubled by this rebuff; the papers of a poet who had been fifty years dead were a magnet to draw the living to her house.

19 *The Shelley Papers (1872–1879)*

In October 1872, a weatherbeaten man in his 40s called at Palazzo Cruciato and introduced himself in a New England accent as Edward Silsbee, sea captain, of Massachusetts.[1] He had been a seafaring man since boyhood, at home with trade winds and distant ports. He spoke of himself as 'an ardent Shelleyite', though many acquaintances called him 'Shelley mad'.[2] Alone in night watches he had learnt Shelley's poems by heart, and on the New England coast or in the drawing-rooms of the Florence expatriates would quote his favourites 'with a trumpet-like twang, without reference to the conversation'. Richard Garnett, however, considered this maritime eccentric the best critic of Shelley he had heard.

Silsbee had come to the house in search of the Shelley papers Miss Clairmont was known to possess, and was enthralled to find this woman of 74 who had lived *en famille* with his idol.[3] Claire soon discovered that her American visitor could not give the high prices she needed to restore her fortune after the folly of buying the farm, which proved hard to sell. Yet he was glad to settle as a lodger in her apartment,[4] thus solving the problem of household expenses. The attraction, as Paula tartly remarked, was Claire's conversation. 'Mr. Silsbee is with Aunt,' she wrote to Wilhelm on 27 February 1873, '& she is quite happy & delighted I am not there to watch her funny ways with men—when she plays the Gürli, or the imbecile . . . which she does to perfection.'

By the summer of 1875 Silsbee had become part of the Clairmont family, reading Shelley's poems, talking of literature and art with Claire, and flirting in Florentine society. Paula found this vigorous and virile man disturbingly attractive and grew jealous, ironically transferring her feelings to Claire. 'There is Aunt at 77 so jealous that no man dare come into the house, but what must be exclusively occupied with her—This morning Mr. Silsbee came at 11½ she talked with him till dinner time, as soon as that was over she talked again till 4.'

Paula's sexual demands had always been frank, and according to her journal she did not often meet with a refusal. Silsbee became her lover for a time but showed no intention of marrying. Paula complained he was of 'a cold nation', yet decided that he was the one man she wished to marry. To Claire he proved a disappointment, since he could not afford her price for the major Shelley manuscripts, though he bought a Shelley fair-copy notebook that he cherished with religious devotion like a holy relic.[5] He went home to America, leaving Paula to mourn him like a widow. Yet Silsbee had not given up hope of the papers, and after Claire's death in 1879 he at once returned to Florence hoping to buy them from Paula. Paula put her own price on the Shelley papers, but Silsbee would not give it; gossip said that it was marriage.[6]

Claire had offered her life to English literature when young; fate returned the gesture in her old age. Henry James, at Florence in 1887, spent many evenings visiting an American invalid at Maiano, Eugene Lee-Hamilton, who passed his days on a wheeled bed yet was observant and devoted to gossip. For a writer he was a heaven-sent source. Lee-Hamilton repeated the story of Silsbee's quest for the Shelley papers and the price which Paula had put on them. He related with malicious glee how Silsbee, faced with marriage to this daredevil, had panicked, fled, and like the wolf in La Fontaine's fable 'court encore'.

Eight years had passed since these events before Lee-Hamilton related them to Henry James, and another year was to pass while James transmuted them into his brilliant novella, *The Aspern Papers*. James recorded Silsbee's plan as he first heard it.

> This gentleman, an American of long ago, an ardent Shelleyite, a singularly marked figure and himself in the highest degree a subject for a free sketch . . . was named to me as having made interest with Miss Clairmont to be accepted as a lodger on the calculation that she would have Shelley documents for which, in the possibly not remote event of her death, he would thus enjoy priority of chance to treat with her representatives. He had at any rate . . . become on earnest Shelley grounds, her yearning, though also her highly diplomatic *pensionnaire*—but without gathering, as was to befall, the fruit of his design.[7]

James also noted 'a younger female relative of the ancient woman as a person who for a clear climax had to be dealt with'.

A reader of *The Aspern Papers* experiences surrender which outlasts the discovery that plot, setting, and characters seem deliberately removed from their source. Yet disguised scenes and characters cannot conceal the inner truth of *The Aspern Papers*. Aunt and niece are adrift in life; 'they had long ago shed and unlearned all native marks and notes'. The niece fears her aunt—'I'm afraid! She was terrible when she was angry'—yet had courage to burn the papers 'one by one in the kitchen'. Miss Bordereau, like Claire, used her papers with 'the humour to test me and practise on me'. She awaited death calmly. 'I'm not afraid to wait till I'm called.' Of the poet she said 'He was a god!' Henry James had penetrated the inner life of these two women he had never met and why luckless Silsbee 'couldn't pay the price' for the Shelley papers. Claire, like Miss Bordereau in the novel, knew the value of her documents and sent them to Trelawny, who replied in March 1875:

> You alone could have made these disconnected details regarding Shelley intelligible by connecting them with a clear narrative: you can write very well—omitting sickly German sentiment and exaggeration and eulogy . . . you might have made a very readable book—you have had fifty years to do it—even now it's not too late—it's impossible for anyone else . . . There is time to do it but not time to shilly shally.[8]

Then, remembering that Claire was by now almost 77 years old, he relented and added 'I must end my sermon'. Claire worried over the delay in returning her copies but by June 1876 they had arrived. 'They are in Florence at last and you will sleep the sounder for it,'[9] wrote her old friend indulgently. He continued to work himself on a revision of his 1858 *Recollections of the Last Days of Shelley and Byron*, under the eyes of Amelia Curran's two romantic portraits on his study wall: Mary fair and meditative, Claire brunette and glowing with vitality.[10]

Trelawny's suggestion that Claire should write a memoir of Shelley drew no response. She was too old, and knew too well how odious the idea would be to Percy and his wife; she would never be allowed to see their Shelley papers. At various times Claire had tried to approach Percy Florence through intermediaries, always without success.[11] Her last attempt was through a member of the former Browning circle. This lover of literature undertook in 1872 to write to Sir Percy Shelley on Claire's behalf, offering to sell Shelley documents to the Boscombe collection.[12] The reply was a courteous, but frigid refusal. 'Since nearly 26 years ago by reason of circumstances which I will not trouble you with detailing, I have not seen Miss

Clairmont.'[13] Percy emphasized the point made in his wife's *Memorials* that Allegra's mother was no relation but 'a stranger in the Shelley family'. Claire could not reasonably have expected a warmer reply. Nor did it seriously affect her decision not to write, which had been made long before. Claire had spent her youth in the company of great writers; she never claimed to be a writer of professional standard, worthy to present Shelley to the world. By conscious choice, she wrote, for fifty years 'I have kept a profound silence with everyone'.[14] This silence blanketed Allegra, Byron, Shelley's marriage, and her own inner life.

By August 1876, at the age of 78, Claire had to admit that the summers of Florence, described by Dostoevsky as 'scorching as a stove pipe . . . a hell heat', overcame her. She wrote to her adviser Bartolomeo Cini:

> I was confined to my Bed by the heat and so weak I could think of nothing. Parigi [her physician] was at Poretta—another doctor came and bid me go without delay to Fiesole. I was put in a carriage and threw myself on the kindness of two old maiden ladies, whom I knew at Fiesole. I am very happy with them and am recovering some strength—the air here is so fresh and pure.[15]

Fiesole was a favourite island in the archipelago of Florence's foreign residents, each nation with its own church, library, and tea-room. Fiesole, a thousand feet above the Arno valley, the towers and domes of Florence, the terraced gardens and ilex woods, the cool quiet nights and the view which Shelley had loved, refreshed Claire.

From autumn to spring, Claire took up her life at Via Romana. Although Silsbee had left the house, he continued to help her with money until 1878,[16] and she remained at home to her circle of friends. In sociable Florence, one might meet anybody. After dinner one evening an unexpected caller arrived. He was an old Italian gentleman, rather deaf and with a paunch, though even Paula found him 'clever—amiable and cultivated'. She had in fact met him once before, three years earlier, when he had called at the house during Claire's absence, but left no message. Now he asked to be announced to Miss Clairmont as her old acquaintance Luigi Gatteschi, adding, as though at random, that he possessed an *excellent* memory. This plump, elderly beau was the handsome blackmailer who had entrapped Mary so skilfully in Paris during the 1840s. He would certainly remember Claire, who had played a part in seizing Mary's letters and frustrating his plans. Since he now lived near Florence, he was well placed to take his revenge and through the gossiping lady's maids of long ago he possibly knew the identity, so carefully concealed, of Claire's Paris companion. He was well capable of extorting money by threats to reveal her secret. As this danger from the past returned to haunt her, Claire exploded into the last of her great rages, Shelley's 'fiery comet'. 'She grew livid with anger,' Paula wrote. 'It is all a plot to entrap you,' she cried, 'I won't have it . . . if you go to their house you shall never enter mine again.' Paula, baffled by this sudden rage, asked questions among Claire's friends. 'Somebody observed that most likely G[atteschi] knew secrets of Aunt's that she would dread to have revealed.'[17] Paula took Claire's warning seriously, for she avoided any further meetings with Gatteschi. Claire was left to brood over her indestructible past.

By the impulsive decision to buy her uninhabitable farm, Claire had become poor during the last years of her life, when she wanted money for Georgina. This, rather than unwise investments or the drain of allowances to Dina and the Clairmonts, caused the final penury in which she asked Cini to offer her papers to Panizzi, librarian of the British Museum.

> I want if I can get it, an addition to my Income; it is enough for me as it is—but I want so much to give a tolerable education to dear Georgina and this I cannot do on my present resources . . . for myself I would not sell my letters—but to benefit dear Georgina . . . you can scarcely tell how grateful I am to you for your kind friendship to me.[18]

Bartolomeo Cini remained in Claire's eyes the visitor to the Masons' house at Pisa in the 1830s, 'la Crème de la Crème of young men, in instruction in beautiful feelings and delightful manners', and she turned to him, now an elderly widower, for help in drafting her will.[19] As a mark of her gratitude, she gave him Shelley's inkstand, 'in memory of one of the most exalted minds that ever breathed'. This inkstand formed part of a lifetime's collection of small Shelley treasures. The object of the will was to provide income for Paula while preserving the capital, which produced only £120 per annum, intact for Claire's ultimate heir, 'my dear Georgina Hanghegyi who is living with me'.

Claire's letters connected with the Shelleys were an important part of the estate. Moreover, she was concerned to preserve them, feeling that in the *Memorials* truth was sacrificed to partisanship. A second edition of the *Shelley Memorials* in 1875 had confirmed Lady Shelley's determination to present a blameless version of her husband's parents to the world. Claire therefore carefully listed the contents of her deed box, specifying letters to herself from Trelawny, Mary, and Shelley and asking Paula to make copies of the originals in case of 'destruction'.[20]

Claire's will shows her at 78 clearly competent to handle her own money, yet liable as ever to erratic ideas. The 'sufferings' of her own varied life aroused transitory moods. Desire to adopt and endow Georgina was of long standing. By Claire's determination, the remains of the Shelley legacy passed to a stranger of mingled Hungarian, Austrian, and English descent, and, like Claire herself, of unknown parentage.[21] Wilhelm and his family do not appear in the will, although Claire was writing to him intimately within three months of her death. He is known to have managed her farm, Nikolaihof, which was within reach of his own property, but was unable to make a living from it. In June 1873 he wrote to Claire that this ill-fated property was being sold.[22] On 6 September 1877, by mutual agreement, Paula became 'housekeeper without pay' to her aunt, in return for board and lodging for herself and 13-year-old Georgina. Their relations were no longer confiding and affectionate as in earlier days; jealousy over Georgina divided them and they lived separate lives under the same roof.[23] But life's experience had taught them realism. Paula needed shelter, and Claire at 79 needed care. Without false sentiment, both honoured their agreement to the end.

The following year, 1878, brought two memorials of Shelley for Claire to read, among writings by Jefferson Hogg, Charles Middleton, Medwin, Peacock, and Richard Garnett, which showed a rising tide of interest in the poet. Trelawny, at 86, brought out *Records of Shelley, Byron and the Author*, his account of events now fifty-five years in the past. It was a harsher book than his *Recollections* of 1858, dismissing the Pisan circle as 'a base crew' who 'used the poor Poet as their purse'.[24] An appendix was devoted to a bitter and sustained attack on Mary, her jealousy, her 'yearning for society', the 'commonplace and conventional' novels she wrote after Shelley's death.

These publications convinced Jane Shelley that official lives, based on the documents of her collection *Shelley and Mary*,[25] must be written to establish the blameless purity of the poetic couple in the public eye. Earlier disappointment with Hogg led her to avoid personal acquaintances of the poet, who were beyond her control. The biographers must be writers to whom she could reveal or withhold sources at her own discretion. It seems clear that this decision was prompted not by any conscious will to deceive, but by Jane Shelley's vision of filial duty. The biographer chosen for Shelley was Professor Edward Dowden of Trinity College, Dublin, in his own words a 'fanatical worshipper' of the poet.

Three years after 1886 when his more important biography of Shelley came out, a life of Mary Shelley followed: F. A. Marshall's *Life and Letters of Mary Wollstonecraft Shelley*. The writer, known in society as Mrs Julian Marshall, was a friend of Richard Garnett, and it was he who recommended her to the Shelleys. She was the author of 'Tonic Sol-fa in the Classroom', somewhat distant as a field of scholarship from English literature. Without disrespect, one can trace in her *Life and Letters* Jane Shelley's own belief that Claire made Mary's life a martyrdom: 'Her father's remarriage proved a source of lifelong unhappiness to Mary.' In their shared childhood, Jane was 'wilful, rebellious, witty, probably a good deal spoilt'. 'Jane's presence added to their unsettlement [Shelley and Mary], with that dash of charlatanism which characterised the Clairmonts.' Jane in 1814 was 'excitable and enthusiastic, demonstrative and capricious, clever but silly; with a mind in which a smattering of speculative philosophy, picked up in Godwin's study, contended for the mastery with such social wisdom as she had picked up in a boarding school'. Claire in 1825, 'after her one miserable adventure', had 'from first to last an innate affinity for anything in the shape of social gossip or scandal; her really generous impulses were combined with the worldliest of worldly wisdom'. In later years she appears only in fragments of quotations. Her years of struggle to achieve independence as a governess abroad are dismissed as 'entire oblivion . . . Allegra no more . . . [Claire] at present absent and forgotten'. Her appearance 'seemed unmistakably to indicate an admixture of Portuguese if not African blood in her descent'.

Claire's position in the Shelley household is redefined by omissions. Nothing is mentioned in Marshall's *Life and Letters* of her love for Percy as a child, of the affection and practical help between the stepsisters, still less of the vivid, spontaneous friendship which inspired Shelley and Claire. Mary Shelley's biographer sums up Claire Clairmont's life in terms of the information she received from Lady Shelley: 'a stumbling block first, then a bugbear to Byron, a curse, which he persistently treated as a blessing to Shelley, a thorn in the side of Mary and of everyone who was ever responsible for her'.[26] Claire, at best a nuisance, at worst a curse, became the lay figure reproduced without question in book after book—until the mid-twentieth century, when research began to reveal a living being, rash, hasty, but of deep and generous feelings, a true Romantic.[27]

While Lady Shelley planned her official biography, unauthorized writers pursued their researches, hunting out survivors of Shelley's circle. In spring 1878, near the date of Claire's eightieth birthday, an enterprising young journalist planned articles on *Last Links with Byron, Shelley and Keats*, to be published in *The Nineteenth Century*, where they aroused considerable controversy.[28] William Graham, who artlessly described himself as a good-looking boy of 20 with dark curling locks, made an appointment to call on the 'once brilliant and espiègle Miss Clermont [for Clairmont]' at eleven a.m.

Graham began his article with determination to create a romantic atmosphere: the golden light of spring in the Arno valley and the old, dark Italian palazzo—nothing was left to chance. He told how he was shown into a room of carved Renaissance panelling with 'old-fashioned furniture'. This, which suggests Renaissance court cup-boards and chests, was the Paris furniture, scarred by Claire's travels over the last fifty years. Without a trace of irony, Graham admired a portrait of Shelley the atheist and a carved crucifix, close neighbours on the wall.[29] Various copies of Shelley portraits were known to exist and Claire probably had one of these,[30] although it is not identified in her will.[31]

This carefully described scenery set the stage for the entrance of the leading lady. 'She was a lovely old lady: the eyes were still bright and sparkled with irony and fun; the complexion clear as at eighteen, the lovely white hair, the slender willowy figure remained unaltered . . . and she laughed with a very silvery laugh.'[32]

At 80, Claire could still appreciate a visit from a handsome young man. This suggests itself in the luncheon arrangements—a 'light collation perfectly served' by Paula, who withdrew to the kitchen and her own thoughts about 'Aunt's ways with men', as Graham and Claire ate tête-à-tête by an open window surrounded with flowers. The young journalist was having the time of his life. 'The Chianti was a dream',[33] he noted, probably unaware that it was among the cheapest wines his impoverished hostess could find in the market. After lunch they sat talking, while Graham's commonsense deserted him in the manner of such interviews; 'there was in the lady herself a charm which old age could not kill—a charm that must once have been all-powerful'.[34] Perhaps Claire enjoyed leading him by the nose, for he believed he had seen the guitar given by Shelley to 'Jane', who of course was not Jane Clairmont but Jane Williams. The guitar was nowhere in Florence, but prosaically stored in Mrs Hogg's London house. Claire consented to sing for him, standing by the open window, her voice a thread of its old splendour ringing across the Marlow lawns.

By this time Graham felt bold enough to ask personal questions. She denied that Trelawny had been her 'friend', in the sense of a lover. Graham then pressed in another direction: 'You must surely have some Italian blood in your veins.' This touched on her unknown father, the question which had troubled Claire all her life. Yet she answered coolly enough. 'Not that I am aware of; but one never knows.'[35] She would never know her father now, and perhaps it had ceased to matter. Claire maintained the same calm even when Graham questioned her about Byron. The old lady paused, as though considering the past, and finally answered:

> In 1815, when I was a very young girl, Byron was the rage . . . I was young, and vain and poor. He was so famous that people, and especially young people, hardly considered him as a man at all, but rather as a god. The result you know. I am too old now to play with any mock repentance.[36]

This seems to be the last word Claire spoke on the subject. It was worth the whole romantic farrago of Graham's interview to win this truthful reply. The loves, the sorrows, the quarrels, the constant moves from place to place, had not been wasted, since in the end Claire had learnt to see her life whole and with honesty.

In Claire's last years the major change, after a lifetime of agnosticism, was her reception into the Roman Catholic Church. This is usually dated by a remark of Trelawny about 'your Pope' to the age of 77, but he had warned Rossetti two years earlier that Claire was 'a somewhat bigoted Roman Catholic', so the date is uncertain. Paula may have spread the alarming news that as a convert Claire considered 'writing a book to illustrate from the lives of Shelley and Byron the dangers and evils resulting from erroneous opinions on the relations of the sexes'.[37] The project, if begun, was abandoned, surely to the general relief of Claire's relations and friends.

The circumstances of Claire's conversion remain mysterious. Most of her life's decisions—joining the Shelley household, the determined seduction of Byron, entrusting Allegra to him, the pursuit of independence after Shelley's death, the flight to Paris and the return, the devotion to Mary and Percy, the fatal conflict with Percy's wife—had been occasions of drama and much letter-writing. Claire's religious instruction and baptism, by contrast, seemed calm, almost matter-of-fact, as though she were reverting in due time to the faith of unknown ancestors. Paula apparently played no part in it, although she was a cradle Catholic and the daughter of a pious mother. Her journal frequently records that she went to confession and communion, but never that her aunt accompanied her.[38] It would be edifying to report that Claire after conversion became an improved character, but she was too set in a lifetime of free thought to change. Father Edward Weld, of the great Catholic family of Lulworth Castle, Dorset, who was chaplain to the English-speaking Catholics in Florence, had acquired an obstinate parishioner. He visited her conscientiously, but by her 80th birthday his reception was unpredictable. 'Father Weld came', wrote Paula on the last day of 1878, 'and wants Aunt to take Holy Communion and she wont.'[39] Claire had reason enough for scruples of conscience, but was just as likely to refuse from sheer obstinacy. Yet this wilful survivor of the Romantic Age received the gift of feeling. As she wrote to Cini:

> I find a great consolation in how many distinguished and virtuous friends I have had. *Nudrirme de memoria piu che di speme* is my daily occupation. And in this way I banish from old age that stupid Melancholy which generally accompanies that stage of life.[40]

As she looked back on the past, Claire had one regret: 'I have trodden life alone without a guide and without a companion and before I depart for ever I would willingly leave with another what my tongue has never yet ventured to tell.' In fact, her journals and letters are an eloquent witness of joy and sorrow, of genius and the common round. Looking beyond death to the future, Claire allowed herself one hope: 'I would willingly think that my memory may not be lost in oblivion as my life has been.'[41]

Claire felt convinced that her end would be calm. The weeks passed quietly at Via Romana. She no longer wished to receive visitors, nor even to write letters, the harvest of her lifetime. She showed only one anxiety in the early spring of 1879: would Paula promise that the shawl Shelley had given her nearly sixty years ago would be buried in her grave? The promise received, Claire confidently awaited her 81st birthday on 27 April. Yet she did not live to celebrate it, for on 19 March Paula wrote in her journal:

> This morning my Aunt died at about 10, calmly, without agony, without consciousness—as she had predicted herself, she went out like a candle . . . She was buried, as she desired, with Shelley's little shawl at the Cemetery of the Antella.[42]

In old age Claire had considered her burial with the realism of experience. She had no hope of lying near those she had loved in her lifetime. There was no place for her with Allegra in the churchyard at Harrow, with Mary in state at Bournemouth, or in the place of which Shelley had written, 'It might make one in love with death', among the cypresses and wild violets of the cemetery at Rome. She had died in Florence and she would be buried there, in the public Camposanto della Misericordia di Santa Maria, Antella. She had even opened a savings bank account, setting aside twelve hundred lire for 'my funeral expenses which shall on no account exceed this sum'. Her one extravagance was provision for an epitaph, of her own composition, to be chiselled on her tombstone.

> She passed her life in sufferings,
> expiating not only her faults
> but also her virtues.[43]

This was Claire's final self-justification and her considered verdict on her life.

True or false, it did not last. Early in the twentieth century the cemetery was replanned as an open space enclosed by porticoes. Claire had no family to protest or bribe officialdom on her behalf. Her tomb was destroyed and her bones reburied, among many others, under the black and white pavement of the arcades. The feet of passing strangers tread now upon the bare record:

> Jane Clairmont
> Clara Mary
> Di Anni 81
> m. il 19 Marzio 1879[44]

Appendix

Will of Claire Clairmont in an English Translation[1]

I Claire Maria Constantia Jane Clairmont spinster now residing at Florence 43 Via Romana and being of sound mind and memory declare this to be my last will and testament. I elect my dear friend Bartolomeo Cini, who for so long a time has enjoyed the esteem of all his friends to be the executor of my will entreating him to undertake this office, feeling well assured that otherwise no respect would be paid to my last will. As a token of my gratitude for all the sympathy which he and his dear departed wife have shown me for more than forty years, I bequeath to him the inkstand with which I always write and which is the same with which Shelley the poet wrote many of his poems, begging him to have it preserved in his family as an heirloom in memory of one of the most exalted minds that ever breathed. I further leave to the care of the said B. Cini a tin box containing letters directed by Shelley the poet partly to Godwin the philosopher, partly to me, and letters from Trelawny to me, two letters from Sir Percy the poet's son, written at the time when he was young, two small and first poetical trials and some doggerel verses by the dowager Lady Mountcashall Cini's mother-in-law, describing in a humorous manner the qualities of Shelley the poet which made him appear in the eyes of the world as His Satanic Majesty. And in short I leave all my papers to the care of B. Cini and beg him to sell all the letters from Shelley to Godwin or to me as well as all Shelley's letters or Mrs. Shelley's letters to me or others as well as the letters from Trelawny to me and to invest the proceeds in 5 per cent Italian national rent in such a manner that only the interest of these stock shall be paid to my niece Paula Clairmont and after her death the whole amount shall go to my dear Georgina Hanghegyi who is living with me. The copies of all letters from Shelley or Mrs. Shelley to me I bequeath to my niece Paula begging her to preserve these copies with great care as they would prove of great value in case of the distruction of the originals. All my other papers I leave to Cini that these may be preserved by his family. All my furniture, plate, linen and books I bequeath to my niece Paula Clairmont, begging her to leave them after her death to Georgina Hanghegyi. In a secret shelf of my press will be found 25 bons [share certificates] of the municipality of Trieste, these I leave to the care of B. Cini and destin them for my niece Paula C. the interest amounting to about L.15 shall be paid to her every year, but she shall not have any right to touch the capital which is to go after her death to Georgina Hanghegyi.

In the savings bank will be found after my death the sum of 1200 lire this shall pay my funeral expenses which shall on no account exceed this sum. The savings bank book bearing the number 186 B 12 will be found in my strong box. Any amount above the said 1200 lire I leave for the private use of my niece Paula.

I wish to be interred at Antella in a coffin of oak and the following words in English to be inscribed on my tomb:

She passed her life in sufferings,
expiating not only her faults
but also her virtues.

Notes

Abbreviations used in Notes

Abinger	MSS formerly in the possession of Lord Abinger, now on deposit in the Bodleian Library.
Ashley	Library of the late T. J. Wine, now in the British Library.
Ashley 4088	*Shelley and Mary*, ed. Jane Shelley and Richard Garnett, with MS notes by E. Dowden, British Library.
Ashley 5119	Letters of E. J. Trelawny to Claire Clairmont, British Library.
GG	R. Glynn Grylls, *Claire Clairmont, Mother of Byron's Allegra*, London, 1939.
HRC	Harry Ransom Humanities Research Center, University of Texas at Austin.
J	*Journals of Claire Clairmont*, ed. M. K. and D. M. Stocking, Cambridge, Mass., 1968.
Kegan Paul	C. Kegan Paul, *William Godwin, His Friends and Contemporaries*, 2 vols., London, 1876.
KSMB	*Keats–Shelley Memorial Bulletin*, 1948–85.
LLB	*Lord Byron's Letters and Journals*. ed. L. A. Marchand, 12 vols., London, 1973–82.
Marshall	Peter H. Marshall, *William Godwin*, New Haven, 1984.
MSJ	*Journals of Mary Shelley*, ed. P. R. Feldman and D. Scott-Kilvert, 2 vols., Oxford, 1987.
MSL	*The Letters of Mary Wollstonecraft Shelley*, ed. B. T. Bennett, 3 vols., Baltimore, 1980–8.
NIW	Newman Ivey White, *Shelley*, 2 vols., London, 1947.
PBSL	*Letters of P. B. Shelley*, ed. F. L. Jones, 2 vols., Oxford, 1964.
PBSW	*The Poetical Works of Percy Bysshe Shelley*, ed. Mrs Shelley, London, 1839.
Pforzheimer	*Shelley and his Circle, 1773–1822* [an edition of the manuscripts of P. B. Shelley and others in the Carl H. Pforzheimer Collection at the New York Public Library], 8 vols., ed. K. N. Cameron (vols. i–iv) and D. Reiman (vols. v–viii), Cambridge, Mass., and London, 1961–86; also other Shelley materials in the Pforzheimer Collection.

Prothero	R. E. Prothero (ed.), *The Works of Lord Byron: Letters and Journals*, 6 vols., London, 1898–1904.
Rees	Joan Rees, *Shelley's Jane Williams*, London, 1985.
Rees, 'Notes'	Joan Rees's MS notes from Pforzheimer Collection in New York Public Library for *Shelley's Jane Williams*, 1985.
St Clair	William St Clair, *Trelawny: The Incurable Romancer*, London, 1977.
S. and M.	*Shelley and Mary*, ed. Jane Shelley and Richard Garnett, 4 vols., 1882.
SM	*Shelley Memorials: From Authentic Sources*, ed. Jane Shelley, London, 1859.
SN	Sylva Norman, *Flight of the Skylark: The Development of Shelley's Reputation*, London, 1954.
Tre.	*Adventures of a Younger Son*, ed. W. St Clair, London, 1974.
Tre. L.	*Letters of Edward John Trelawny*, ed. H. Buxton Forman, London, 1910.

CHAPTER 1

1. *J* 13.
2. *J* 32.
3. *Kegan Paul*, ii. 58.
4. Ibid. 129.
5. *Marshall*, 266.
6. *J* 426–8.
7. Ford K. Brown, 'Notes on 41 Skinner Street', *Modern Language Notes*, 54 (1939), 326–32.
8. *J* 18.
9. *Kegan Paul*, ii. 184–6.
10. Claire to Trelawny, Apr. 1871.
11. *Kegan Paul*, ii. 184.
12. Ibid. 188.
13. Aaron Burr, *Correspondence*, 18 Nov. 1811.
14. Ibid. 27 Jan. 1812.
15. *Kegan Paul*, ii. 191.
16. *Marshall*, 302.
17. *J* 19.
18. *Marshall*, 299.
19. *J* 19.
20. *NIW* i, p. xii, n. 5.
21. *Kegan Paul*, ii. 214.
22. *PBSL* i. 403.

23. *GG* 277.
24. *MSL* i. 438.
25. *MSJ* 18, n. 1.
26. *J* 31.
27. *J* 22.
28. *J* 24.
29. *J* 27.
30. *MSJ* 18
31. *J* 31.
32. *J* 33.
33. *J* 36.
34. *J* 40.

CHAPTER 2

1. Abinger, 4 July 1845.
2. *J* 43.
3. *J* 48–9.
4. *J* 51.
5. *J* 50.
6. *J* 51.
7. *J* 58. Shelley thought Rousseau 'the greatest man the world has produced since Milton', and encouraged Mary and Jane to read his works, including *La Nouvelle Héloïse*.
8. *KSMB* xxi. 24.
9. *MSJ* i. 45.
10. *MSJ* i. 47.
11. *MSJ* i. 45.
12. *MSJ* i. 60.
13. *MSJ* i. 65.
14. *MSJ* i. 68.
15. *MSJ* i. 70.
16. *MSJ* i. 29.
17. Quoted *GG* 51–2.
18. *J* 69.
19. *J* xiii.
20. *MSJ* i. 18.
21. *GG* 64–5.
22. L. A. Marchand, *Byron: A Biography*, ii. 627.
23. They usually called their cottage simply 'Montalègre'.
24. *NIW Shelley*, i. 444.
25. *MSL* i. 122 n. 1.
26. *Pforzheimer*, iv. 702–18.
27. Ibid. v. 103–17.

28. *KSMB* ix. 1–2.
29. *MSJ* 122 n. 1.

CHAPTER 3

1. *MSL* i. 22.
2. *MSJ* 140–1 and n.
3. *MSJ* 151 n.
4. *PBSL* i. 529.
5. L. A. Marchand, *Byron: A Portrait*, 262.
6. *J* 77 n. 40.
7. *MSJ* 168.
8. *MSL* i. 48–9.
9. T. L. Peacock, *Nightmare Abbey*, ch. 10.
10. *J* 143 n. 41.
11. *J* 80.
12. I. Origo, *Allegra*, 30.
13. *J* 86.
14. Marchand, *Byron: A Biography* i. 734.
15. *J* 88.
16. *J* 90.
17. *J* 89 n. 46.
18. *PBSL* ii. 9–13.
19. *Ibid.* 10.
20. *MSL* i. 66.
21. *NIW* ii. 14.
22. *J* 96 and App. C.
23. *MSL* i. 77.
24. *MSJ* 225.
25. *MSJ* 227 and n.
26. *NIW* ii. 41–7.
27. Mary Shelley's note on the poems of 1818.
28. *MSJ* 230.
29. *PBSL* ii. 62.
30. Ibid. 63.
31. Ibid. 69.
32. *PBSL* ii. 69.
33. *NIW* ii. 71.
34. *GG* 235.

CHAPTER 4

1. *J* 99.
2. *J* 100.

3. Above, ch. 3.
4. *MSJ* 262 n. 2.
5. *MSL* i. 93.
6. Ibid. 101.
7. Ibid. 100.
8. *J* 114.
9. *MSL* i. 103.
10. Ibid. 123–4.
11. *J* 117.
12. *J* 118.
13. *MSL* i. 124.
14. *J* 120.
15. *J* 119.
16. *J* 122.
17. *J* 130.
18. *J* 132–47.
19. *J* 143 n. 41.
20. *MSJ* 321, 579.
21. *MSL* i. 147.
22. *J* 153.
23. *J* 145, 148.
24. *J* app. C.
25. *J* 180 and app. C.
26. *J* 180.

CHAPTER 5

1. T. Medwin, *Life of Shelley*, 169–70.
2. Ibid. 279.
3. *J* 201.
4. *Epipsychidion*, 368–73.
5. *J* 216.
6. Ashley 4752; *Prothero*, v. 498–500.
7. *J* 145.
8. *Prothero*, iii. 437.
9. Byron to Moore, 4 Mar. 1822; *Pforzheimer*, ix. 118–19.
10. *J* 222.
11. *J* 228.
12. *J* 243.
13. *J* 274–9.
14. *J* 259.
15. *PBSL* ii. No. 656.

CHAPTER 6

1. *PBSL* ii. No. 653.
2. *J* 253.
3. Ashley 4752.
4. *MSL* i. 225–6.
5. *PBSL* ii. No. 692.
6. Ibid. No. 694.
7. Ibid.
8. *J* 276.
9. *PBSL* ii. No. 695.
10. *MSJ* 407.
11. Byron to John Murray, 26 May 1822; *Pforzheimer*, ix. 163–5.
12. The date should have been 19 Apr.
13. *PBSL* ii. No. 706.
14. Ibid. No. 715.

CHAPTER 7

1. *MSL* i. 253.
2. *PBSL* ii. No. 703.
3. *J* 436–7.
4. *J* 409.
5. *GG* 262–8.
6. St Claire, W., *Trelawny*, 49.
7. *Tre. L. 218–19.*
8. *SN* 21.
9. *J* 284 n. 18.
10. *J* 286 n. 21.
11. Abinger, n.d. Sept. 1822.
12. *MSJ* 517.
13. Jane's legal husband, Captain Johnson, lived until 1840.
14. *MSJ* 488.
15. *J* 437.
16. *J* 284.
17. *J* 356.
18. *S. and M.* 918.
19. *Tre. L.* xx–xxi.
20. Ashley 5119, n.d.
21. Ibid. 19 Sept. 1822, Pisa.
22. *J* 285.
23. *NIW* ii. 384 dates the departure 22 Sept.
24. *J* 285.
25. *J* 286.

26. Ashley 5119, 16 Dec. 1822, Trelawny to Claire.
27. Abinger, 24 Oct. 1822, to Jane Williams.
28. *J* 298n.
29. *GG* 165–6. Manuscript now lost.
30. Abinger, 24 Oct. 1822.
31. Mary was a stepsister and not a blood relation of the Clairmonts.
32. Vienna State Archives. *GG* 170–1 shows a photograph of this dossier, which was later damaged by fire.
33. Abinger, 22 Dec. 1822, Mrs Godwin to Jane Williams.
34. *GG* 168–170.
35. Abinger, 22 Feb. 1823, Charles Clairmont to Mary Shelley.
36. *J* 295–6.
37. Scrofula: tubercular infection of lymph nodes in the neck, known in Britain as 'the King's Evil' and reputedly curable by royal touch.
38. Abinger, 22 Aug. 1824, Mrs Mason to Mary Shelley.
39. *NIW* ii. 298 (not *literally* bankrupt).
40. Marshall, 351–5.
41. Origo, *Allegra*, 102–3.
42. *J* 294.
43. Ashley 5119, 10 Jan. 1823.
44. Ibid. 20 Apr. 1823.
45. *S. and M.* 922, to Mary Shelley.
46. *J* 297.
47. *Tre.L.* 44–5.
48. *J* 437.

CHAPTER 8

1. *MSJ* 474.
2. *MSL* i. 416.
3. Abinger, 14 Oct. 1844, to Mary Shelley, writing of 1824.
4. *J* 395.
5. Abinger 18 Mar. 1844, to Mary Shelley.
6. Her half-brother Charles showed the same tact with his Imperial pupils in Vienna. The Clairmonts certainly did not inherit it from their irritable, aggressive mother.
7. Abinger, 29 Apr. 1825, to Mary Shelley.
8. Ibid. 22 Jan. 1827.
9. Godwin, *Cloudesley*, 17–18.
10. Ibid. 63.
11. Ibid. 83–8.
12. *MSL* i. 426.
13. Belinsky, *Moscow and St Petersburg*.
14. *J* 312.

15. *J* 305.
16. *J* 306.
17. *J* 305.
18. Abinger, 29 Apr. 1825.
19. Ibid. 11 Sept. 1824, to Jane Williams.
20. *J* 311.
21. *MSL* ii. 448.
22. *J* 312.
23. Islavsky is now a sanatorium for tubercular children.
24. *J* 317–18.
25. *J* 334.
26. *J* 321.
27. *J* 324.
28. *J* 316.
29. *J* 316–17.
30. Many country houses had their own private theatres.
31. *J* 319.
32. *J* 325.
33. *J* 325–6.
34. *J* 332–3.
35. *J* 340.
36. *J* 327.
37. *J* 323.
38. *J* 309.
39. Abinger, postmarked 4 Dec. 1826.
40. *J* 351 prints the complete poem.
41. *J* 354.
42. *J* 501–17. Sir Timothy's death would bring Shelley's will into effect.
43. *J* 328.
44. Abinger, 29 Apr. 1825, to Mary Shelley, transcribed by John Gisborne.
45. Ibid., to Mary Shelley.
46. *J* 334.
47. Abinger, 2 May 1826, to Mary Shelley.
48. *J* 343.
49. *J* 314.
50. *J* 324.
51. Abinger, 27 Oct. 1825.
52. *J* 355.
53. *J* 357.
54. *J* 361.
55. *J* 364.
56. Ibid.
57. *J* 365.
58. Ibid.

CHAPTER 9

1. *J* 366–7.
2. *J* 392.
3. Abinger, 27 Oct. 1825.
4. *J* 369 and *passim.*
5. *J* 386.
6. *J* 387.
7. *J* 395.
8. H. Seton-Watson, *The Russian Empire.*
9. *J* 393.
10. L. Kelly, *Moscow,* 117. The writer, Charlotte Disbrowe, was the wife of the British plenipotentiary at St Petersburg.
11. *J* 393.
12. *J* 393–4.
13. Abinger, 2–14 May 1826, to Mary Shelley.
14. *J* 422.
15. *J* 408–9.
16. *J* 435.
17. Abinger, 27 Oct. 1825, to Jane Williams.
18. *J* 408.
19. *J* 394.
20. *J* 397.
21. Abinger, undated letter (Dec. 1826), to Jane Williams.
22. Ibid. 11 Dec. 1830, to Mary Shelley, from Nice.
23. *S. and M.* 1135.
24. Abinger, 27 Oct. 1825, to Jane Williams.
25. Ibid. 2 May 1826, to Mary Shelley.
26. Ibid. n.d. Dec. 1826, to Jane Williams. The monastery was demolished, but a number of Empire houses and the central gardens remain.
27. *J* 406.
28. Abinger, 27 Oct. 1825, to Jane Williams.
29. *S. and M.* 1058.
30. Kelly, *Moscow,* 265.
31. *GG* 199.
32. Abinger, 2–14 May 1826, to Mary Shelley.
33. *MSL* i. 572.
34. Abinger, 23 July 1827.
35. Ibid. 2–14 May 1826, to Mary Shelley.
36. Ibid. Dec. 1826, to Jane Williams, copied by Mr Gisborne.
37. Ibid. 5–16 May 1825, to Jane Williams.
38. Ibid. 29 Apr. 1825, to Jane Williams.
39. Ibid. n.d. Dec. 1826, to Jane Williams.
40. Ibid. n.d. Dec. 1826, to Jane Williams.

41. Ibid. n.d. Dec. 1826, to Jane Williams.
42. *KSMB* iv. 35–47.
43. *J* 404.
44. Abinger, 2 May 1826, to Mary Shelley.
45. *J* 403–6.
46. Abinger, 14 Mar. 1827, to Jane Williams Hogg.
47. *J* 405.
48. Abinger, 14 Mar. 1828, to Jane Williams Hogg.

CHAPTER 10

1. *J* 407.
2. *J* 411.
3. *J* 422–3.
4. Abinger, 11 Dec. 1830, to Mary Shelley.
5. Ibid. 22 July 1828.
6. Ibid. (reached London via Hamburg 8 Apr. 1827).
7. *J* 415–18.
8. *KSMB* viii. 12.
9. F. A. Marshall, *Life and Letters*, 362.
10. *S. and M.* 1079.
11. *Tre.* 110 (24 Oct. 1827).
12. *J* 416–17.
13. *Kegan Paul*, ii. 321.
14. *J* 431–2.
15. *MSL* i. 528.
16. Ibid. 301 n.; 569 n.
17. *NIW* ii. 384; ii. pp. 626–7, n. 16.
18. *J* 435.
19. *J* 432.
20. *MSL* i. 476.
21. *SN* 105.
22. Abinger, 14 Mar. 1830.
23. Ibid. 11 Dec. 1826.
24. *Rees*, 103–5.
25. Abinger, 14 Mar. 1828.
26. *St Clair*, 127.
27. *Tre.* 65 and 69.
28. Ibid. 112–13.
29. Ibid. 51.
30. Abinger, 27 Oct. 1826.
31. *J* 416.
32. *St Clair*, 151–2. This letter exists only in a copy by Trelawny.
33. Abinger, 22 Jan. 1827.

34. *St Clair*, 151–2.
35. *Tre.* 114–15.
36. *Tre.* 116.
37. *Tre.* 121.
38. *MSL* ii. 72.
39. Ashley 5119, 7 Apr. 1829.
40. Abinger, 22 July 1828.
41. *MSL* ii. 82; *MSJ* 509 n. 2.
42. *GG* 279; Mrs Godwin to Mrs Mason, copied by Claire.
43. *S. and M.* 1126.
44. *J* 418.

CHAPTER 11

1. *MSJ* 517.
2. Abinger, 22 July 1828.
3. Ibid. 11 Dec. 1830, to Mary Shelley.
4. Ibid. 28–30 Mar. 1830, to Mary Shelley.
5. Ibid. 28–30 Mar. 1830.
6. *J* 433–5.
7. *J* 436. Shortly after this point, 14 pages have been cut from the notebook.
8. Abinger, 3 Apr. 1830, to Jane Williams Hogg.
9. Ibid. 11 Dec. 1830, to Mary Shelley, describing long-term relationship of Kaisaroff mother and daughter.
10. Ibid. 28–30 Mar. 1830, to Mary Shelley.
11. *J* 406.
12. Abinger, 11 Dec. 1830.
13. *J* 429–30.
14. Abinger, 11 Dec. 1830.
15. Ibid.
16. *MSL* ii. 249.
17. Somerset Street ran through the area that is now covered by Selfridges department store.
18. *MSJ* 513.
19. Abinger, 5 Apr. 1830.
20. Ibid. 11 Dec. 1830.
21. *MSL* ii. 520.
22. Abinger, 16 Sept. 1834.
23. Abinger, (Feb.) 1830, to Jane Williams Hogg.
24. Abinger, 28–30 Mar. 1830.
25. *MSL* ii. 143. Her reply stated: 'My name will *never* be Trelawny.'
26. *St Clair*, 71.
27. *Tre.* 131–2.
28. *SN* 117.

29. *Tre.* 138.
30. Ibid.
31. Ibid. 166–7.
32. Ibid. 208–9.
33. Abinger, 13 Feb. 1836.
34. *Tre.* 131.
35. *St Clair*, 143.
36. *Tre.* 208–9.
37. *Tre.* 169.
38. *GG* 201.
39. *MSL* ii. 134 n. 12.
40. *MSJ* 610.
41. Abinger, 13 Apr. 1831, to Mary Shelley.
42. *Tre.* 166.
43. *J* 438.
44. *MSL* ii. 146.
45. Abinger, 5 Mar. 1832, to Mary Shelley.

CHAPTER 12

1. *Giornale agrario toscano*, 3 (1829), 339–60, 4 (1830), 1–32: 'Memorandum concerning a new variety of potato, with some experiences on the cultivation and use of potatoes in general'.
2. *NIW* ii. 109.
3. Ibid. 177, 362.
4. Abinger, 26 Oct. 1832.
5. Through their father from the Fourth Earl of Tankerville and through their mother from Lord William Russell.
6. *MSJ* 602–3n.
7. Abinger, 22 Feb. 1835.
8. Ibid. 3 Dec. 1832.
9. Ibid. 22 Feb. 1835, to Jane Williams.
10. Ibid. 3 Apr. 1830.
11. A. Gatherer, '*A Socio-Medical Study of the First Cholera Epidemic in Britain*' (MD thesis), Univ. of London.
12. Abinger, 24 Mar. 1832, Mary Shelley to Claire Clairmont.
13. Ibid.
14. *SN* 124.
15. Abinger, 26 Oct.–8 Nov. 1832, to Mary Shelley.
16. *Kegan Paul*, ii. 321.
17. *MSL* ii. 91n.
18. Abinger, 1 Feb. 1833.
19. Ibid. 1 Feb. 1833.
20. Ibid. 26 Oct.–8 Nov. 1832.

21. H. J. Torre, *Recollections of School Days at Harrow*, 1890.
22. Abinger, 15 Sept. 1833.
23. B. R. Haydon, *Diary*, 17 Oct. 1834.
24. Abinger, 15 Sept. 1833.
25. Ibid. 9 March 1834, to Mary Shelley.
26. *GG* 285–8, Pforzheimer Collection.
27. Abinger, 9 Mar. 1834.
28. *St Clair*, 152.
29. *Tre.* 182.
30. Abinger, 15 Sept. 1833, to Mary Shelley.
31. *Tre.* 192–3.
32. Abinger, 16 Sept. 1834.
33. *St Clair*, 154.
34. Abinger, ?16 Sept. 1864, to Mary Shelley.
35. Ibid. 16 Sept. 1835, to Mary Shelley.
36. Ibid.
37. *MSL* ii. 258.
38. Abinger, date obliterated by seal, to Mary Shelley.
39. Quoted F. A. Marshall, *Life and Letters*, 243–4.
40. Quoted *GG* 190.
41. *MSJ* 558.
42. Abinger, 9 Mar. 1834, to Mary Shelley.
43. Ibid. 13 Feb. 1836.
44. Ibid. 15 Mar. 1836.
45. *MSL* ii. 270.
46. Ibid. 271.

CHAPTER 13

1. *Marshall*, ii. 385.
2. *Tre.* 200–1.
3. *MSL* ii. 271–2 n. 1.
4. Ibid. n. 2.
5. Abinger, 19 Oct. 1836, Claire Clairmont to Mary Shelley.
6. *MSL* ii. 280–2. There is no evidence that she received the loan.
7. Ibid. 148.
8. Abinger, 24 Mar. 1832.
9. Ibid. 16 Sept. 1834.
10. *MSL* ii. 275.
11. *Poetical Works of Percy Bysshe Shelley*, ed. Mrs Shelley, 4 vols., London, 1839.
12. *MSL* ii. 303.
13. *MSJ* 560n. The passage is heavily cancelled in a different ink.
14. Ibid. 563.
15. *MSL* iii. app. i, p. 389.

16. *MSJ* 555.
17. *MSL* ii. 221 June 1835, Mary Shelley quoting a letter from Claire Clairmont.
18. J. S. Mill, *Autobiography*.
19. *Tre.* 205.
20. The mothers had also to be free from proven adultery.
21. *Tre.* 206.
22. *MSL* ii. 288.
23. Abinger, 30 Oct. 1840.
24. Ibid. 23 Aug. 1842.
25. *Alumni Cantabrigienses.*
26. H. Crabbe Robinson, *On Books and their Writers*, ed. E. J. Morley, ii. 669.
27. *GG* 206–7.
28. Abinger, 20 Apr. 1838.
29. Ibid. 5 Jan. 1838.
30. F. A. Marshall, *Life and Letters*, ii. 141.
31. Not as elsewhere stated Wingfield, which is in Suffolk.
32. *Alumni Oxonienses.*
33. Abinger, 20 Apr. 1838.
34. Ibid. 5 Jan. 1838.
35. Ibid. 5 Jan. 1838, to Percy Florence Shelley.
36. Ibid. 20 Apr. 1838, to Mary Shelley.
37. *MSL* ii. 297 n. 2.
38. Ibid. 278.
39. Ibid. 330.
40. Ibid. 341.
41. Ibid. 189.
42. Ibid. iii. 12.
43. Pforzheimer Collection, unpublished letters of Jane Williams Hogg, 9 May and 22 July 1842.
44. Note by Claire on Percy Bysshe Shelley's letter, 16 Dec. 1816.
45. Godwin's death ended Mary's self-imposed duty to help him with money. Also, Sir Timothy increased Percy's allowance to £400 a year from his 21st birthday.
46. *Rambles in Germany and Italy in 1840, 1842 and 1843*, 1844.
47. Abinger, 30 Oct. 1840.
48. *Alumni Cantabrigienses.*
49. H. D. Monro, *Remarks on Insanity*, 1850.
50. *Marshall*, ii. 356.

CHAPTER 14

1. Abinger, n.d., Dec. 1826, Claire Clairmont to Jane Williams Hogg.
2. Ibid. 19 Oct. 1836, to Mary Shelley.
3. Ibid. 23 Nov. 1841.

4. *MSL* iii. 89.
5. As actuarial tables show, this was a frequent arrangement. By 'post obit', bond repayment was promised on the death of a named person, in this case Sir Timothy Shelley. P. B. Shelley's will would then come into effect, and Claire would receive her legacy.
6. *MSL* ii. 151.
7. Abinger, n.d., May 1845, to Mary Shelley.
8. W. Graham, *Last Links with Byron, Shelley and Keats*. 1898.
9. Abinger, 2 June 1845.
10. Abinger (?22 Nov. 1842), quoted in *Pforzheimer*, viii. 990.
11. Rees 'Notes', 159.
12. Ibid. 24 Aug. 1842.
13. Since neither birth nor death of the child had been registered as the law required, an order was made for exhumation and a coroner's inquest. Jane successfully persuaded the coroner that this would be 'ruin'. See Rees, *Shelley's Jane Williams*, 159–60.
14. Abinger, 23 Aug. 1842.
15. *S. and M.* 1230.
16. Abinger, n.d., May 1845, to Mary Shelley.
17. *MSL* iii. 48 (29 Nov. 1842).
18. Ibid. 200 (12 Aug. 1845).
19. Abinger, n.d., May 1845, to Mary Shelley. The miniature is now in the Bodleian Library.
20. Ibid.
21. Ibid. 23 Aug. 1843, to Mary Shelley. Darkened by damp.
22. *MSL* iii. 58 (20 Feb. 1845).
23. Abinger, (?22 Nov. 1842).
24. Ibid., to Mary Shelley. (?26 May 1845).
25. Ibid. 18 Aug. 1844.
26. Ibid. 16 Sept. 1844.
27. *MSL* iii. 68 (15 Apr. 1843).
28. Abinger, 6 Aug. 1843, to Mary Shelley, after visit.
29. Ibid. 17 Aug. 1844.
30. He was overseas as postmaster-general of Jamaica.
31. Abinger, 7 Aug. 1844, to Mary Shelley.
32. *MSL* iii. 99 (9 Oct. 1843).
33. Ibid. 28 Dec. 1844, to Mary Shelley.
34. Ibid. 22 Aug. 1844.
35. Ibid. 9 Dec. 1844.
36. Ibid. 28 Dec. 1844, to Mary Shelley.
37. Ibid. 4 July 1845, to Mary Shelley.
38. *MSL* iii. 213 (18 Oct. 1845).
39. Ibid. 267 (25 Sept. 1845).
40. Ibid. 232–3. Claire's endorsement on a letter from Mary, 12 Oct. 1845.

41. Abinger, 20 Nov. 1845, to Mary Shelley.
42. *Alumni Catabrigienses.*
43. *MSL* iii. 361 (1 Dec. 1845).
44. Abinger, 13 July 1845, to Mary Shelley.

CHAPTER 15

1. Abinger, 23 Apr. 1844, to Mary Shelley.
2. 'Assignment of a Legacy of £6,000 and policy of Assurance with European Life Insurance Company, 10 Chatham Place, Blackfriars taken out on the life of P. F. Shelley for securing £500 and interest 8 April 1842 . . . during the life of Timothy Shelley Bart., £330 payable quarterly to Miss Mary Jane Clairmont.' 6 Feb. 1838.
3. *MSL* iii. 158 (27 Oct. 1844).
4. Ibid. 124 n. 2 (2 Apr. 1844).
5. *Pforzheimer*, iv. 712–13.
6. Abinger, 22 Aug. 1844, to Mary Shelley.
7. Ibid. 14 Oct. 1844.
8. Ibid. 22 Aug. 1844, to Mary Shelley.
9. Ibid.
10. Ibid. 7 May 1845, to Mary Shelley.
11. Ibid. 25 May 1845.
12. *MSL* ii. 194 (June–July 1845).
13. Abinger, 29 May 1845, Claire Clairmont to Mary Shelley.
14. Ibid. 30 Aug. 1845, Claire Clairmont to Mary Shelley.
15. Ibid. 18 Aug. 1844, Claire Clairmont to Mary Shelley.
16. Ibid. 12 May 1845.
17. Ibid. 4 July 1845.
18. F. A. Marshall, *Life and Letters*, 141.
19. Abinger, postmarked 29 Aug. 1845, Claire Clairmont to Mary Shelley.
20. Ibid. 17 Dec. 1845.
21. Ibid. 28 Dec. 1844.
22. Ibid. 7 May 1845.
23. Ibid. 19 Jan. 1846.
24. Ibid. 7 May 1845, to Mary Shelley.
25. Ibid. 19 Jan. 1846, to Mary Shelley.
26. *MSL* iii. 295.
27. Ibid. 296.
28. Ibid. 358.
29. Ibid. 295 n. 1.
30. Herbert Huscher, *KSMB* ix. 20. The terrace was demolished in the 1930s to build The White House apartment block. Nothing now survives of Nash's Osnaburgh Street but the name.
31. T. H. Shepherd, *Views in London*, ii. 85.

32. *Parliamentary Papers*, 1846 (719) xvii. 21.
33. Flyleaf of notebook.
34. Abinger, 11 Apr. 1849.
35. Ibid. 7 Aug. 1844.

CHAPTER 16

1. *KSMB* viii. 13–15.
2. *MSL* iii. 358.
3. *GG* 3 Apr. 1870.
4. F. A. Marshall, *Life and Letters*, 141–2.
5. Abinger, 9 Dec. 1844.
6. M. Rolleston, *Talks with Lady Shelley.*
7. General Registry.
8. *MSL* iii. 334 (18 Mar. 1848).
9. Ibid. 347 (30 Aug. 1848).
10. Ibid. iii. 354 1 Jan. (1849), Mary Shelley to Claire Clairmont, address on letter.
11. *MSL* iii. 350 (24 Nov. 1848).
12. *S. and M.*, 1234. The belief that Claire's legacy was 'a mistake' by a solicitor's clerk began in the Shelley family at this time and gave rise to the feeling that she had no 'moral right' to the full £12,000.
13. Abinger, 11 Apr. 1849.
14. Ibid.
15. Ibid. 1–23 Nov. 1845, Charles Clairmont to Claire Clairmont.
16. *KSMB* viii. 13–14.
17. Charles Clairmont's text-books—*Reine Grundlehrer der englischen Sprache* and *Völlstandige englische Sprachlehre*—sold well, reaching 6 editions and 12 editions respectively.
18. *KSMB* viii. 17.
19. *MSL* iii. 358 (11 Feb. 1849), to Mary Shelley.
20. Abinger, 11 Apr. 1849.
21. F. A. Marshall, *Life and Letters*, ii. 312–13.
22. *MSL* iii. 316 22 June 1847.
23. Abinger, (1 Apr. 1848), to Mary Shelley.
24. Ibid. 22 Apr. 1849, to Mary Shelley.
25. Ibid. 11 Apr. 1849.
26. Ibid.
27. Ibid. 22 Apr. 1849.
28. Ibid. 22 Apr. 1849.
29. *MSL* iii. 353 (15 Dec. 1848).
30. Ibid. 392 (3–5 Feb. 1851).
31. Ibid. 369 n. 1. (?3–5 Feb. 1851), Claire wildly wrote 'Mephistopheles' on the envelope of Mary's last letter to her.

32. Ibid. 392 (3–5 Feb. 1851).
33. Rolleston, *Conversations with Lady Shelley*, 41–2.
34. Ibid. 43–4.
35. F. A. Marshall, *Life and letters*, 312–13.
36. *MSL* iii. 391.
37. Among runaway couples married there were an innkeeper's daughter and her father's ostler, the parents of John Keats.
38. To omit a recorded event from the *Alumni* is most unusual. A. A. Knox's second marriage, in 1857, is fully recorded.
39. *KSMB* vi. 41 (10 Mar. 1850).
40. Ibid. (6 Sept. 1853).
41. Ibid. xi. 16.

CHAPTER 17

1. *MSL* iii. 325–6.
2. Jane Shelley believed that the box in the desk contained the ashes of Shelley's heart.
3. Grylls, *Mary Shelley*, 244.
4. *MSL* 3 Mar. 1851.
5. General Registry, Deaths 1851.
6. *Pforzheimer*, 4 Mar. 1851. We are grateful to Joan Rees for access to her notes from an unpublished MS in the Pforzheimer Collection, New York Public Library.
7. Claire foretold her own death with enthusiasm on a number of occasions. The journey into the unknown appealed to her love of adventure.
8. Abinger, (3–5 Feb. 1851). Printed in *MSL* iii. 391–2. There is no record of a reply to this letter.
9. *KSMB* viii. 9–10 (Diary of Archduchess Sophia, mother of Emperor Franz Joseph).
10. Ibid. vii. 41.
11. Personal information supplied by M. K. Stocking, gratefully acknowledged.
12. General Registry. Deaths 1855.
13. *KSMB* xi. 19.
14. Pforzheimer, 28 June 1852, q.v. n.6 above.
15. *Kegan Paul*, ii. 186.
16. Pforzheimer, Aug. 1852, q.v. n.6 above.
17. Ibid. 1 Jan. 1855.
18. Ibid. 19 Aug. 1857.
19. M. K. Stocking, '*Miss Tina and Miss Plin*', 376–7.
20. Shelley title deeds.
21. C. Mate and C. Riddle, *Bournemouth Illustrated*, 1910.
22. *SN* 196.
23. *Rees*, 174.

24. *Bournemouth Daily Echo*, 19 Sept. 1925.
25. *Rees*, 178.
26. *Tre.* 259 (6 May 1878).
27. This hardly accords with Mary's self-reproach for 'Harriet's sad fate' in her Journal 1839. In Lady Shelley's personal copy of *Shelley and Mary*, a reference to Harriet has been carefully cut out with scissors.
28. *SN* 211.
29. *SM* 68.
30. *SM* 70.
31. *SM* 78.
32. *SM* 91–5.
33. *SM* 135.
34. *NIW* ii. 355.
35. *SM* 192.
36. *SM* 198.
37. *J* 437.
38. *J* 81.
39. I. Jack, *English Literature*, x. 383.
40. Abinger, Oct. 1828.
41. Rees, 180 12 Dec. 1863.
42. HRC, to Dina Williams Hunt.
43. *KSMB* v. 20–6.
44. *J* 143 n. 41.
45. *J* 79.
46. Abinger, 27 Aug. 1824, 30 Aug. 1832, Lady Mount Cashell to Mary Shelley, quoted *J* 143 n. 41.
47. *Fraser's Magazine*, June 1856.
48. HRC, 31 Dec. 1862.
49. HRC.

CHAPTER 18

1. *KSMB* vi, facing page 36.
2. Ibid. 42. Florence became easily accessible when railway lines ran beside Via Valfonda into the Central Station.
3. This is the first mention of white hair; in the sketch the curls are still black, or possibly tinted.
4. *KSMB* vi. 43.
5. Ibid.
6. *Tre. L.* 218–19 (17 Sept. 1869).
7. Ibid. 220 (18 Oct. 1869).
8. *St Clair* 165–9.
9. *SN* 236–7.
10. *Tre. L.* 230 (13 June 1870).

11. Ibid. 235 (26 June 1871).
12. Ibid. 234 (26 Dec. 1870).
13. *GG* 271.
14. *GG* 265.
15. *GG* 267.
16. *GG* 266.
17. *KSMB* vi. 43.
18. *GG* 212–13.
19. M. K. Stocking, '*Miss Tina and Miss Plin*,' 378.
20. Ibid.
21. Ibid.
22. *KSMB* vi. 43–6.
23. *GG* 212.
24. Baedeker, *Eastern Alps*, 1879. Now in Yugoslavia: Maribor and Ptuj on the Drava.
25. *Tre. L.* 378–9 (26 Apr. 1872).
26. Ibid. 241 (7 Apr. and 1 May 1873).
27. *KSMB* vi. 45.
28. Stocking, '*Miss Tina and Miss Plin*', 378–9.
29. *Tre. L.* 242 (1 May 1873).
30. W. M. Rossetti, *Reminiscences*, ii. 352–3.
31. Ibid. 354.
32. *Pforzheimer*, iv. 787–8 (30 Aug.–21 Sept. 1875).
33. Ibid.
34. *Tre. L.* 248 (17 June 1875).
35. Ibid. 247 (31 May 1875).

CHAPTER 19

1. *KSMB* vi. 44–6.
2. W. M. Rossetti, *Reminiscences*, 511–13.
3. Stocking, '*Miss Tina and Miss Plin*', 373–82.
4. Rossetti, *Reminiscences*, 511–13.
5. The Shelley Notebook.
6. P. Clairmont, *Journal*, 31 July 1879, in Huscher, 'Claire Clairmont's Last Russian Journal'.
7. H. James. Preface to *The Aspern Papers* (New York 1908). The *KSMB* vi, 44 novella appeared first in *Atlantic Monthly*, 1888, while both Silsbee and Pauline (Paula) were living.
8. *Tre. L.* 246–7 (19 Mar. 1875).
9. Ibid. (17 June 1875).
10. *St Clair*, 189.
11. Grylls, *Mary Shelley*, 237.
12. The object of the sale was to raise money for Georgina's education.

13. Grylls, *Mary Shelley*, 236.
14. *GG* 213, 266 (Mar. 1870).
15. *GG* 214, 286–7 (11 Aug. 1876).
16. M. K. Stocking, '*Miss Tina and Miss Plin*', 2–3 Jan. 1879.
17. *J* 220 n.56.
18. *GG* 286.
19. *KSMB* vi. 46.
20. App. I.
21. Georgina inherited the Clairmont tendency to tuberculosis and died of the disease at 21. Six years later, Paula fell to her death mountain-climbing on the Sennenberg.
22. Personal information from M. K. Stocking, acknowledged with thanks.
23. Stocking, '*Miss Tina and Miss Plin*', 381.
24. *St Clair*, 180–1.
25. *Shelley and Mary* was compiled with the aid of Richard Garnett and privately printed.
26. F. A. Marshall, *Life and Letters*, 324.
27. *GG*, Holmes, *Shelley: The Pursuit.*
28. Graham, *Nineteenth Century* (Nov. 1893–Jan. 1894), repr. as *Last Links with Byron, Shelley and Keats*, Leonard Smithers, London 1898.
29. Ibid. 2.
30. The Curran portrait was at Boscombe, but copies were known to exist, also engravings of a portrait by Clint, sketches by Edward Williams, and a silhouette by Marianne Hunt.
31. *NIW* ii., App. v., 518–38; '*Portraits and Busts of Shelley*'.
32. Graham, *Last Links*, 4.
33. Ibid.
34. Ibid. 11.
35. Ibid. 24.
36. Ibid. 13–16.
37. *GG* 213.
38. *KSMB* vi. 45.
39. *Ibid.*
40. *GG* 287 (11 Aug. 1876).
41. *J* 437.
42. *GG* 215. The Camposanto della Misericordia di Santa Maria was at Antella, then a village three miles south-east of Florence.
43. *Notes and Queries*, 8 Oct. 1904.
44. *GG* 243–4. Information supplied by Signora Farina Cini.

APPENDIX

1. *KSMB* vi. 46–7.

Bibliography

Published Sources

Alumni Cantabrigienses

Alumni Oxonienses

Bennett, B. T. (ed.), *The Letters of Mary Wollstonecraft Shelley*, 3 vols., Baltimore, 1980–8.

Burr, Aaron, *Correspondence of Aaron Burr and his Daughter Theodosia*, ed. Mark Van Doren, New York, 1929.

—— *The Private Journal of Aaron Burr, reprinted from the Original MS. in the Library of W. K. Bixby, with Notes*, 2 vols., Rochester, NY, 1903.

Brown, Ford K., 'Notes on 41 Skinner Street', *Modern Language Notes*, 54 (1939), 326–32.

Cameron, Kenneth Neill (ed.), *Shelley and his Circle, 1773–1822* [an edition of the manuscripts of P. B. Shelley and others in the Carl H. Pforzheimer Library], vols. i–iv, Cambridge, Mass., and London, 1961–70. (See also D. Reiman.)

Feldman, P. R., and Scott-Kilvert, D. (eds.), *The Journals of Mary Shelley, 1814–1844*, 2 vols., Oxford, 1987.

Forman, H. Buxton (ed.), *Letters of Edward John Trelawney*, London, 1910.

Gatherer, A., 'A Socio-Medical Study of the First Cholera Epidemic in Britain' (MD thesis), University of London.

Godwin, William, *Cloudesley*, 3 vols., London, 1830.

Graham, W., *Last Links with Byron, Shelley, and Keats*, London, 1898 (repr. of articles originally published in *Nineteenth Century*, 1893–4.

Grylls, R. Glynn, *Claire Clairmont, Mother of Byron's Allegra*, London, 1939.

—— *Mary Shelley*, Oxford, 1938.

—— *William Godwin and his World*, London, 1953.

Haydon, B. R., *The Diary of Benjamin Robert Haydon*, ed. W. B. Pope, 5 vols., Cambridge, Mass., 1960–3.

Holmes, R., *Shelley: The Pursuit*, London, 1974.

Jack, I., *English Literature, 1815–1832*, Oxford History of English Literature, vol. x, Oxford, 1963.

James, Henry, Preface to *The Aspern Papers*, New York, 1908.

Kelly, Laurence (ed.), *Moscow: A Travellers' Companion*, London, 1983.

Lysons, Revd Daniel, *The Environs of London*, 4 vols., London, 1792–6; *Supplement to the First Edition of the Historical Account of the Environs of London*, London, 1811.

Marchand, L. A., *Byron: A Biography*, 3 vols., London, 1957.

—— *Byron: A Portrait*, London, 1971.

—— (ed.), *Byron's Letters and Journals*, 12 vols., London, 1973–82.

Marshall, Florence Ashton, *The Life and Letters of Mary Wollstonecraft Shelley*, 2 vols., London, 1889.

Marshall, Peter H., *William Godwin*, New Haven, 1984.

Mate, C., and Riddle, C., *Bournemouth Illustrated*, London, 1910.

Matthiessen, F. O., and Murdock, K. B. (eds.), *The Notebooks of Henry James*, New York, 1947.

Medwin, Thomas, *The Life of Percy Bysshe Shelley*, London, 1847.
——*Medwin's Conversations of Lord Byron*, ed. E. J. Lovell, Princeton, 1966.
Mellor, A. K., *Mary Shelley: Her Life, Her Fiction, Her Monsters*, New York and London, 1988.
Mill, J. S., *Autobiography*, London, 1873.
Monro, H. D., *Remarks on Insanity: Its Nature and Treatment*, London, 1850.
Norman, Sylva, *Flight of the Skylark: The Development of Shelley's Reputation*, London, 1954.
Murray, John (ed.), *Lord Byron's Correspondence*, London, 1922.
Origo, Iris, *Allegra*, London, 1935.
Paul, C. Kegan, *William Godwin, His Friends and Contemporaries*, 2 vols., London, 1876.
Peacock, T. L., *Nightmare Abbey*.
Prothero, R. E. (ed.), *The Works of Lord Byron: Letters and Journals*, 6 vols., London, 1898–1904.
Pugh, L. P., *From Farriery to Veterinary Medicine, 1785–1795*, Cambridge, 1962.
Rees, Joan, *Shelley's Jane Williams*, London, 1985.
Reiman, Donald H. (ed.), *Shelley and his Circle, 1773–1822* [an edition of the manuscripts of P. B. Shelley and others in the Carl H. Pforzheimer Library], vols. v–viii, Cambridge, Mass., 1973–86. (See also K. N. Cameron.)
Robinson, H. C., *Henry Crabb Robinson on Books and Their Writers*, ed. E. J. Morley, 3 vols., London, 1938.
Rolleston, M., *Talks with Lady Shelley*, London, 1925.
Rossetti, W. M., *Some Reminiscences of William Michael Rossetti*, 2 vols., London, 1906.
St Clair, William, *Trelawny: The Incurable Romancer*, London, 1977.
Seton-Watson, Hugh, *The Russian Empire, 1801–1917*, Oxford, 1967.
Shelley, Jane (ed.), *Shelley Memorials: From Authentic Sources*, London, 1859.
——and Garnett, Richard (eds.), *Shelley and Mary*, privately printed in twelve copies, 1882.
Shelley, Percy Bysshe, *Letters of Percy Bysshe Shelley*, ed. F. L. Jones, 2 vols., Oxford, 1964.
——*The Poetical Works of Percy Bysshe Shelley*, ed. Mrs Shelley, 4 vols., London, 1839.
Shepherd, T. H., and Elmes, James, *Metropolitan Improvements; or London in the Nineteenth Century; being a Series of Views*, 2 vols., London, 1829.
Sheppard, F. H. W., *London 1808–1870: The Infernal Wen*, London, 1971.
Stocking, M. K., 'Miss Tina and Miss Plin: The Papers behind *The Aspern Papers*', in Donald H. Reiman *et al.*, (eds.), *The Evidence of the Imagination: Studies of Interactions between Life and Art in English Romantic Literature*, New York, 1978, pp. 372–84.
——and D. M. (eds.), *Journals of Claire Clairmont*, Cambridge, Mass., 1968.
Thomson, D., *In Camden Town*, London, 1983.
Tighe, George William, 'Memoria intorno ad una nuova varietà di patata, con alcune esperienze riguardo alla coltura ed all'uso delle patate in generale', *Giornale agrario toscano* 3 (1829), 339–60; 4 (1830), 1–32.
Torre, H. J., *Recollections of School Days at Harrow more than Fifty Years Ago*, Manchester, 1890.

Trelawny, E. J., *Letters of Edward John Trelawny*, ed. H. Buxton Forman, London, 1910.

——*Adventures of a Younger Son*, ed. W. St Clair, London, 1974.

White, Newman Ivey, *Shelley*, 2 vols., London, 1947.

Manuscript Sources

Claire Clairmont's journals:
Ashley MSS, British Lib. 394 and 2819 (1–5)

Letters written by Claire Clairmont to:

Dina Hunt	Harry Ransom Humanities Research Center, University of Texas at Austin
Leigh Hunt	Abinger MSS, deposited at the Bodleian Library
Fanny Imlay	Abinger MSS, deposited at the Bodleian Library
Mrs Mason	Abinger MSS, deposited at the Bodleian Library
T. L. Peacock	Abinger MSS, deposited at the Bodleian Library
Mary Shelley	Abinger MSS, deposited at the Bodleian Library
Percy Shelley	Abinger MSS, deposited at the Bodleian Library
P. B. Shelley	Abinger MSS, deposited at the Bodleian Library
E. J. Trelawny	Abinger MSS, deposited at the Bodleian Library
Jane Williams (Hogg)	Abinger MSS, deposited at the Bodleian Library

Letters written to Claire Clairmont from:

Antonie Clairmont	Clairmont Letters (courtesy of M. Stocking)
Charles Clairmont	Clairmont Letters (courtesy of M. Stocking)
Paula Clairmont	Clairmont Letters (courtesy of M. Stocking)
Wilhelm Clairmont	Clairmont Letters (courtesy of M. Stocking)
E. J. Trelawny	Ashley MSS, British Lib. 5119
Jane Williams (Hogg)	Pforzheimer Library, New York Public Library
The Shelley Notebook	Harvard College Library
Shelley title deeds	Keats House, Hampstead

Index